PENGUIN BOOKS
Nudge

Richard H. Thaler is Ralph and Dorothy Keller Distinguished Service Professor of Behavioral Science and Economics, and Director of the Center for Decision Research, Graduate School of Business, University of Chicago. He is also research associate at the National Bureau of Economic Research.

Cass R. Sunstein is Karl N. Llewellyn Distinguished Service Professor of Jurisprudence, University of Chicago Law School and Department of Political Science.

Visit Cass Sunstein's (http://home.uchicago.edu/~csunstei/) and Richard Thaler's (http://faculty.chicagogsb.edu/richard.thaler/research/) homepages.

RICHARD H. THALER
and
CASS R. SUNSTEIN

Nudge
*Improving Decisions About health,
wealth and happiness*

PENGUIN BOOKS

PENGUIN BOOKS

Published by the Penguin Group
Penguin Books Ltd, 80 Strand, London WC2R ORL, England
Penguin Group (USA) Inc., 375 Hudson Street, New York, New York 10014, USA
Penguin Group (Canada), 90 Eglinton Avenue East, Suite 700, Toronto, Ontario, Canada M4P 2Y3
(a division of Pearson Penguin Canada Inc.)
Penguin Ireland, 25 St Stephen's Green, Dublin 2, Ireland (a division of Penguin Books Ltd)
Penguin Group (Australia), 250 Camberwell Road, Camberwell, Victoria 3124, Australia
(a division of Pearson Australia Group Pty Ltd)
Penguin Books India Pvt Ltd, 11 Community Centre, Panchsheel Park, New Delhi – 110 017, India
Penguin Group (NZ), 67 Apollo Drive, Rosedale, North Shore 0632, New Zealand
(a division of Pearson New Zealand Ltd)
Penguin Books (South Africa) (Pty) Ltd, 24 Sturdee Avenue,
Rosebank, Johannesburg 2196, South Africa

Penguin Books Ltd, Registered Offices: 80 Strand, London WC2R ORL, England

www.penguin.com

First published in Great Britain by Yale University Press 2008
First published in Great Britain in this revised edition in Penguin Books 2009

13

Copyright © Richard H. Thaler and Cass R. Sunstein, 2008, 2009
All rights reserved

The moral right of the authors has been asserted

Set in 9.25/12.5 pt Linotype Sabon
Typeset by Rowland Phototypesetting Ltd, Bury St Edmunds, Suffolk
Printed in England by Clays Ltd, St Ives plc

978-0-141-04001-1

*For France, who makes everything in
life better, even this book.*

RHT

*For Samantha, who makes
every day a joy.*

CRS

Contents

CONTENTS

PART III

Society

PART IV

Extensions and Objections

Acknowledgments

The research for this book has been made possible by funds from the University of Chicago Graduate School of Business and the Law and Economics Program at the University of Chicago Law School. We have also received generous support from the John Templeton Foundation through a grant to the Center for Decision Research.

Many people have helped us with this book. Sydelle Kramer, our agent, provided wonderful advice throughout. Michael O'Malley, our editor, made valuable suggestions on the manuscript. Special thanks to our fun and stellar team of research assistants, extending over two summers; they include Jonathan Balz (who gets double thanks for putting up with us for two summers), Rachael Dizard, Casey Fronk, Heidi Liu, Matthew Johnson, Brett Reynolds, Matthew Tokson, and Adam Wells. Kim Bartko was invaluable in helping us with the art work in the book. At the last stage, Dan Heaton did an excellent and meticulous copyedit.

Many colleagues made the book a lot better. For insights, hints, and even a few nudges beyond the call of both friendship and duty, we single out Shlomo Benartzi, Elizabeth Emens, Nick Epley, Dan Gilbert, Tom Gilovich, Jonathan Guryan, Justine Hastings, Eric Johnson, Christine Jolls, Daniel Kahneman, Emir Kamenica, Dean Karlan, David Leonhardt, Michael Lewis, Brigitte Madrian, Cade Massey, Phil Maymin, Sendhil Mullainathan, Don Norman, Eric Posner, Richard Posner, Raghu Rajan, Dennis Regan, Tom Russell, Eldar Shafir, Jesse Shapiro, Edna Ullmann-Margalit, Adrian Vermeule, Eric Wanner, Elke Weber, Roman Weil, Susan Woodward, and Marion Wrobel. Our toughest and wisest advice came from

France Leclerc and Martha Nussbaum; special thanks to both France and Martha for helping to produce countless improvements. Vicki Drozd helped out with everything, as she always does, and made sure that all the research assistants got paid, which they appreciated. Thanks too to Ellyn Ruddick-Sunstein, for helpful discussion, patience, both sense and amusement about behavioral economics, and good cheer.

We also owe a special thanks to all the staff at Noodles restaurant on 57th Street. They have fed us and listened to us planning and discussing this book, among other things, for several years now. We'll be back next week.

For the International Edition, we wish to thank once again the indispensable John Batz, who is our book architect. Thanks also to Chris Hsee, Dan Muldoon, Chiara Monticone, and Adair Turner.

Introduction

THE CAFETERIA

A friend of yours, Carolyn, is the director of food services for a large city school system. She is in charge of hundreds of schools, and hundreds of thousands of kids eat in her cafeterias every day. Carolyn has formal training in nutrition (a master's degree from the state university), and she is a creative type who likes to think about things in nontraditional ways.

One evening, over a good bottle of wine, she and her friend Adam, a statistically oriented management consultant who has worked with supermarket chains, hatched an interesting idea. Without changing any menus, they would run some experiments in her schools to determine whether the way the food is displayed and arranged might influence the choices kids make. Carolyn gave the directors of dozens of school cafeterias specific instructions on how to display the food choices. In some schools the desserts were placed first, in others last, in still others in a separate line. The location of various food items was varied from one school to another. In some schools the French fries, but in others the carrot sticks, were at eye level.

From his experience in designing supermarket floor plans, Adam suspected that the results would be dramatic. He was right. Simply by rearranging the cafeteria, Carolyn was able to increase or decrease the consumption of many food items by as much as 25 percent. Carolyn learned a big lesson: school children, like adults, can be greatly influenced by small changes in the context. The influence can be exercised for better or for worse. For example, Carolyn knows that she can increase consumption of healthy foods and decrease consumption of unhealthy ones.

With hundreds of schools to work with, and a team of graduate student volunteers recruited to collect and analyze the data, Carolyn believes that she now has considerable power to influence what kids eat. Carolyn is pondering what to do with her newfound power. Here are some suggestions she has received from her usually sincere but occasionally mischievous friends and coworkers:

1. Arrange the food to make the students best off, all things considered.
2. Choose the food order at random.
3. Try to arrange the food to get the kids to pick the same foods they would choose on their own.
4. Maximize the sales of the items from the suppliers that are willing to offer the largest bribes.
5. Maximize profits, period.

Option 1 has obvious appeal, yet it does seem a bit intrusive, even paternalistic. But the alternatives are worse! Option 2, arranging the food at random, could be considered fair-minded and principled, and it is in one sense neutral. But if the orders are randomized across schools, then the children at some schools will have less healthy diets than those at other schools. Is this desirable? Should Carolyn choose that kind of neutrality, if she can easily make most students better off, in part by improving their health?

Option 3 might seem to be an honorable attempt to avoid intrusion: try to mimic what the children would choose for themselves. Maybe that is really the neutral choice, and maybe Carolyn should neutrally follow people's wishes (at least where she is dealing with older students). But a little thought reveals that this is a difficult option to implement. Adam's experiment proves that what kids choose depends on the order in which the items are displayed. What, then, are the true preferences of the children? What does it mean to say that Carolyn should try to figure out what the students would choose 'on their own'? In a cafeteria, it is impossible to avoid some way of organizing food.

Option 4 might appeal to a corrupt person in Carolyn's job, and manipulating the order of the food items would put yet another weapon in the arsenal of available methods to exploit power. But Carolyn is honorable and honest, so she does not give this option any thought. Like Options 2 and 3, Option 5 has some appeal, especially if Carolyn thinks that the best cafeteria is the one that makes the most money. But should Carolyn really try to maximize profits if the result is to make children less healthy, especially since she works for the school district?

Carolyn is what we will be calling a *choice architect*. A choice architect has the responsibility for organizing the context in which people make decisions. Although Carolyn is a figment of our imagination, many real people turn out to be choice architects, most without realizing it. If you design the ballot voters use to choose candidates, you are a choice architect. If you are a doctor and must describe the alternative treatments available to a patient, you are a choice architect. If you design the form that new employees fill out to enroll in the company health care plan, you are a choice architect. If you are a parent, describing possible educational options to your son or daughter, you are a choice architect. If you are a salesperson, you are a choice architect (but you already knew that).

There are many parallels between choice architecture and more traditional forms of architecture. A crucial parallel is that there is no such thing as a 'neutral' design. Consider the job of designing a new academic building. The architect is given some requirements. There must be room for 120 offices, 8 classrooms, 12 student meeting rooms, and so forth. The building must sit on a specified site. Hundreds of other constraints will be imposed – some legal, some aesthetic, some practical. In the end, the architect must come up with an actual building with doors, stairs, windows, and hallways. As good architects know, seemingly arbitrary decisions, such as where to locate the bathrooms, will have subtle influences on how the people who use the building interact. Every trip to the bathroom creates an opportunity to run into colleagues (for better or for worse). A good building is not merely attractive; it also 'works.'

As we shall see, small and apparently insignificant details can have major impacts on people's behavior. A good rule of thumb is to assume that 'everything matters.' In many cases, the power of these small details comes from focusing the attention of users in a particular direction. A wonderful example of this principle comes from, of all places, the men's rooms at Schiphol Airport in Amsterdam. There the authorities have etched the image of a black housefly into each urinal. It seems that men usually do not pay much attention to where they aim, which can create a bit of a mess, but if they see a target, attention and therefore accuracy are much increased. According to the man who came up with the idea, it works wonders. 'It improves the aim,' says Aad Kieboom. 'If a man sees a fly, he aims at it.' Kieboom, an economist, directs Schiphol's building expansion. His staff conducted fly-in-urinal trials and found that etchings reduce spillage by 80 percent.[1]

The insight that 'everything matters' can be both paralyzing and empowering. Good architects realize that although they can't build the perfect building, they can make some design choices that will have beneficial effects. Open stairwells, for example, may produce more workplace interaction and more walking, and both of these are probably desirable. And just as a building architect must eventually build some particular building, a choice architect like Carolyn must choose a particular arrangement of the food options at lunch, and by so doing she can influence what people eat. She can nudge.*

---

* Please do not confuse *nudge* with *noodge*. As William Safire has explained in his 'On Language' column in the *New York Times Magazine* (October 8, 2000), the 'Yiddishism *noodge*' is 'a noun meaning "pest, annoying nag, persistent complainer." ... To *nudge* is "to push mildly or poke gently in the ribs, especially with the elbow." One who *nudges* in that manner – "to alert, remind, or mildly warn another" – is a far *geshrei* from a *noodge* with his incessant, bothersome whining.' *Nudge* rhymes with *judge*, while the *oo* sound in *noodge* is pronounced as in *book*.

While we are all down here, a small note about the reading architecture of this book when it comes to footnotes and references. Footnotes such as this one that we deem worth reading are keyed with a symbol and placed at the bottom of the page, so that they are easy to find. We have aimed to keep these to a minimum. Numbered endnotes contain information about source material. These can be skipped by all but the most scholarly of readers. When the authors of cited material are mentioned in the text, we sometimes add a date in parentheses – Smith (1982), for example – to enable readers to go directly to the bibliography without having first to find the endnote.

LIBERTARIAN PATERNALISM

If, all things considered, you think that Carolyn should take the opportunity to nudge the kids toward food that is better for them, Option 1, then we welcome you to our new movement: *libertarian paternalism*. We are keenly aware that this term is not one that readers will find immediately endearing. Both words are somewhat off-putting, weighted down by stereotypes from popular culture and politics that make them unappealing to many. Even worse, the concepts seem to be contradictory. Why combine two reviled and contradictory concepts? We argue that if the terms are properly understood, both concepts reflect common sense – and they are far more attractive together than alone. The problem with the terms is that they have been captured by dogmatists.

The libertarian aspect of our strategies lies in the straightforward insistence that, in general, people should be free to do what they like – and to opt out of undesirable arrangements if they want to do so. To borrow a phrase from the late Milton Friedman, libertarian paternalists urge that people should be 'free to choose.'[2] We strive to design policies that maintain or increase freedom of choice. When we use the term *libertarian* to modify the word *paternalism*, we simply mean liberty-preserving. And when we say liberty-preserving, we really mean it. Libertarian paternalists want to make it easy for people to go their own way; they do not want to burden those who want to exercise their freedom.

The paternalistic aspect lies in the claim that it is legitimate for choice architects to try to influence people's behavior in order to make their lives longer, healthier, and better. In other words, we argue for self-conscious efforts, by institutions in the private sector and also by government, to steer people's choices in directions that will improve their lives. In our understanding, a policy is 'paternalistic' if it tries to influence choices in a way that will make choosers better off, *as judged by themselves*.[3] Drawing on some well-established findings in social science, we show that in many cases, individuals make pretty bad decisions – decisions they would not have made if they had paid full attention and possessed complete information, unlimited cognitive abilities, and complete self-control.

Libertarian paternalism is a relatively weak, soft, and nonintrusive type of paternalism because choices are not blocked, fenced off, or significantly burdened. If people want to smoke cigarettes, to eat a lot of candy, to choose an unsuitable health care plan, or to fail to save for retirement, libertarian paternalists will not force them to do otherwise – or even make things hard for them. Still, the approach we recommend does count as paternalistic, because private and public choice architects are not merely trying to track or to implement people's anticipated choices. Rather, they are self-consciously attempting to move people in directions that will make their lives better. They nudge.

A nudge, as we will use the term, is any aspect of the choice architecture that alters people's behavior in a predictable way without forbidding any options or significantly changing their economic incentives. To count as a mere nudge, the intervention must be easy and cheap to avoid. Nudges are not mandates. Putting the fruit at eye level counts as a nudge. Banning junk food does not.

Many of the policies we recommend can and have been implemented by the private sector (with or without a nudge from the government). Employers, for example, are important choice architects in many of the examples we discuss in this book. In areas involving health care and retirement plans, we think that employers can give employees some helpful nudges. Private companies that want to make money, and to do good, can even benefit from environmental nudges, helping to reduce air pollution (and the emission of greenhouse gases). But as we shall show, the same points that justify libertarian paternalism on the part of private institutions apply to government as well.

HUMANS AND ECONS:
WHY NUDGES CAN HELP

Those who reject paternalism often claim that human beings do a terrific job of making choices, and if not terrific, certainly better than anyone else would do (especially if that someone else works for the government). Whether or not they have ever studied economics, many people seem at least implicitly committed to the idea of *homo economicus*, or economic man – the notion that each of us thinks and chooses unfailingly well, and thus fits within the textbook picture of human beings offered by economists.

If you look at economics textbooks, you will learn that homo economicus can think like Albert Einstein, store as much memory as IBM's Big Blue, and exercise the willpower of Mahatma Gandhi. Really. But the folks that we know are not like that. Real people have trouble with long division if they don't have a calculator, sometimes forget their spouse's birthday, and have a hangover on New Year's Day. They are not homo economicus; they are homo sapiens. To keep our Latin usage to a minimum we will hereafter refer to these imaginary and real species as Econs and Humans.

Consider the issue of obesity. Rates of obesity in the United States are now approaching 20 percent, and more than 60 percent of Americans are considered either obese or overweight. Worldwide, there are some 1 billion overweight adults, 300 million of whom are obese. Rates of obesity range from below 5 percent in Japan, China, and some African nations to more than 75 percent in urban areas of Samoa. Obesity rates have risen 3-fold since 1980 in some areas of North America, the United Kingdom, Eastern Europe, the Middle East, the Pacific Islands, Australia, and China, according to the World Health Organization. There is overwhelming evidence that obesity increases risks of heart disease and diabetes, frequently leading to premature death. It would be quite fantastic to suggest that everyone is choosing the right diet, or a diet that is preferable to what might be produced with a few nudges.

Of course, sensible people care about the taste of food, not simply about health, and eating is a source of pleasure in and of itself. We do not claim that everyone who is overweight is necessarily failing to act rationally, but we do reject the claim that all or almost all Americans are choosing their diet optimally. What is true for diets is true for other risk-related behavior, including smoking and drinking, which produce more than five hundred thousand premature deaths each year in the US. With respect to diet, smoking, and drinking, people's current choices cannot reasonably be claimed to be the best means of promoting their well-being. Indeed, many smokers, drinkers, and overeaters are willing to pay third parties to help them make better decisions.

But our basic source of information here is the emerging science of choice, consisting of careful research by social scientists over the past four decades. That research has raised serious questions about the rationality of many judgments and decisions that people make. To qualify as Econs, people are not required to make perfect forecasts (that would require omniscience), but they are required to make unbiased forecasts. That is, the forecasts can be wrong, but they can't be systematically wrong in a predictable direction. Unlike Econs, Humans predictably err. Take, for example, the 'planning fallacy' – the systematic tendency toward unrealistic optimism about the time it takes to complete projects. It will come as no surprise to anyone who has ever hired a contractor to learn that everything takes longer than you think, even if you know about the planning fallacy.

Hundreds of studies confirm that human forecasts are flawed and biased. Human decision making is not so great either. Again to take just one example, consider what is called the 'status quo bias,' a fancy name for inertia. For a host of reasons, which we shall explore, people have a strong tendency to go along with the status quo or default option.

When you get a new cell phone, for example, you have a series of choices to make. The fancier the phone, the more of these choices you face, from the background to the ring sound to the number of times the phone rings before the caller is sent to voice mail. The manufacturer has picked one option as the default for each of these choices. Research shows that whatever the default choices are, many people stick with them, even when the stakes are much higher than choosing the noise your phone makes when it rings.

Two important lessons can be drawn from this research. First, never underestimate the power of inertia. Second, that power can be harnessed. If private companies or public officials think that one policy produces better outcomes, they can greatly influence the outcome by choosing it as the default. As we will show, setting default options, and other similar seemingly trivial menu-changing strategies, can have huge effects on outcomes, from increasing savings to improving health care to providing organs for lifesaving transplant operations.

The effects of well-chosen default options provide just one illustration of the gentle power of nudges. In accordance with our definition, a nudge is any factor that significantly alters the behavior of Humans, even though it would be ignored by Econs. Econs respond primarily to incentives. If the government taxes candy, they will buy less candy, but they are not influenced by such 'irrelevant' factors as the order in which options are displayed. Humans respond to incentives too, but they are also influenced by nudges. By properly deploying both incentives and nudges, we can improve our ability to improve people's lives, and help solve many of society's major problems. And we can do so while still insisting on everyone's freedom to choose.

A FALSE ASSUMPTION AND TWO MISCONCEPTIONS

Many people who favor freedom of choice reject any kind of paternalism. They want the government to let citizens choose for themselves. The standard policy advice that stems from this way of thinking is to give people as many choices as possible, and then let them choose the one they like best (with as little government intervention or nudging as possible). The beauty of this way of thinking is that it offers a simple solution to many complex problems: Just Maximize (the number and variety) of Choices – full stop! The policy has been pushed in many domains, from education to prescription drug insurance plans. In some circles, Just Maximize Choices has become a policy mantra. Sometimes the only alternative to this mantra is thought to be a government mandate which is derided as 'One Size Fits All.' Those who favor Just Maximize Choices don't realize there is plenty of room between their policy and a single mandate. They oppose paternalism, or think they do, and they are skeptical about nudges. We believe that their skepticism is based on a false assumption and two misconceptions.

The false assumption is that almost all people, almost all of the time, make choices that are in their best interest or at the very least are better than the choices that would be made by someone else. We claim that this assumption is false – indeed, obviously false. In fact, we do not think that anyone believes it on reflection.

Suppose that a chess novice were to play against an experienced player. Predictably, the novice would lose precisely because he made inferior choices – choices that could easily be improved by some helpful hints. In many areas, ordinary consumers are novices, interacting in a world inhabited by experienced professionals trying to sell them things. More generally, how well people choose is an empirical question, one whose answer is likely to vary across domains. It seems reasonable to say that people make good choices in contexts in which they have experience, good information, and prompt feedback – say, choosing among ice cream flavors. People know whether they like chocolate, vanilla, coffee, licorice, or something else. They do less well in contexts in which they are inexperienced and poorly informed, and in which feedback is slow or infrequent – say, in choosing between fruit and ice cream (where the long-term effects are slow and feedback is poor) or in choosing among medical treatments or investment options. If you are given fifty prescription drug plans, with multiple and varying features, you might benefit from a little help. So long as people are not choosing perfectly, some changes in the choice architecture could make their lives go better (as judged by their own preferences, not those of some bureaucrat). As we will try to show, it is not only possible to design choice architecture to make people better off; in many cases it is easy to do so.

The first misconception is that it is possible to avoid influencing people's choices. In many situations, some organization or agent *must* make a choice that will affect the behavior of some other people. There is, in those situations, no way of avoiding nudging in some direction, and whether intended or not, these nudges will affect what people choose. As illustrated by the example of Carolyn's cafeterias, people's choices are pervasively influenced by the design elements selected by choice architects. It is true, of course, that some nudges are unintentional; employers may decide (say) whether to pay employees monthly or biweekly without intending to create any kind of nudge, but they might be surprised to discover that people save more if they get paid biweekly because twice a year they get three pay checks in one month. It is also true that private and public institutions can strive for one or another kind of neutrality – as, for example, by choosing randomly, or by trying to figure out what most people want. But unintentional nudges can have major effects, and in some contexts, these forms of neutrality are unattractive; we shall encounter many examples.

Some people will happily accept this point for private institutions but strenuously object to government efforts to influence choice with the goal of improving people's lives. They worry that governments cannot be trusted to be competent or benign. They fear that elected officials and bureaucrats will place their own interests first, or pay attention to the narrow goals of self-interested private groups. We share these concerns. In particular, we emphatically agree that for government, the risks of mistake, bias, and overreaching are real and sometimes serious. We favor nudges over commands, requirements, and prohibitions in part for that reason. But governments, no less than cafeterias (which governments frequently run), have to provide starting points of one or another kind. This is not avoidable. As we shall emphasize, they do so every day through the rules they set, in ways that inevitably affect some choices and outcomes. In this respect, the antinudge position is unhelpful – a literal nonstarter.

The second misconception is that paternalism always involves coercion. In the cafeteria example, the choice of the order in which to present food items does not force a particular diet on anyone, yet

Carolyn, and others in her position, might select some arrangement of food on grounds that are paternalistic in the sense that we use the term. Would anyone object to putting the fruit and salad before the desserts at an elementary school cafeteria if the result were to induce kids to eat more apples and fewer Twinkies? Is this question fundamentally different if the customers are teenagers, or even adults? Since no coercion is involved, we think that some types of paternalism should be acceptable even to those who most embrace freedom of choice.

In domains as varied as savings, organ donations, marriage, and health care, we will offer specific suggestions in keeping with our general approach. And by insisting that choices remain unrestricted, we think that the risks of inept or even corrupt designs are reduced. Freedom to choose is the best safeguard against bad choice architecture.

CHOICE ARCHITECTURE IN ACTION

Choice architects can make major improvements to the lives of others by designing user-friendly environments. Many of the most successful companies have helped people, or succeeded in the marketplace, for exactly that reason. Sometimes the choice architecture is highly visible, and consumers and employers are much pleased by it. (The iPod and the iPhone are good examples because not only are they elegantly styled, but it is also easy for the user to get the devices to do what they want.) Sometimes the architecture is taken for granted and could benefit from some careful attention.

Consider an illustration from our own employer, the University of Chicago. The university, like many large employers, has an 'open enrollment' period every November, when employees are allowed to revise the selections they have made about such benefits as health insurance and retirement savings. Employees are required to make their choices online. (Public computers are available for those who would otherwise not have Internet access.) Employees receive, by mail, a package of materials explaining the choices they have and instructions on how to log on to make these choices. Employees also receive both paper and email reminders.

Because employees are human, some neglect to log on, so it is crucial to decide what the default options are for these busy and absent-minded employees. To simplify, suppose there are two alternatives to consider: those who make no active choice can be given the same choice they made the previous year, or their choice can be set back to 'zero.' Suppose that last year an employee, Janet, contributed one thousand dollars to her retirement plan. If Janet makes no active choice for the new year, one alternative would be to default her to a one-thousand-dollar contribution; another would be to default her to zero contribution. Call these the 'status quo' and 'back to zero' options. How should the choice architect choose between these defaults?

Libertarian paternalists would like to set the default by asking what reflective employees in Janet's position would actually want. Although this principle may not always lead to a clear choice, it is certainly better than choosing the default at random, or making either 'status quo' or 'back to zero' the default for everything. For example, it is a good guess that most employees would not want to cancel their heavily subsidized health insurance. So for health insurance the status quo default (same plan as last year) seems strongly preferred to the back to zero default (which would mean going without health insurance).

Compare this to the employee's 'flexible spending account,' in which an employee sets aside money each month that can be used to pay for certain expenditures (such as uninsured medical or child care expenses). Money put into this account has to be spent each year or it is lost, and the predicted expenditures might vary greatly from one year to the next (for example, child care expenses go down when a child enters school). In this case, the zero default probably makes more sense than the status quo.

This problem is not merely hypothetical. We once had a meeting with three of the top administrative officers of the university to discuss similar issues, and the meeting happened to take place on the final day of the employees' open enrollment period. We mentioned this and asked whether the administrators had remembered to meet the deadline. One said that he was planning on doing it later that day and was glad for the reminder. Another admitted to having forgotten, and the third said that he was hoping that his wife had remembered to do it! The group then turned to the question of what the default should be for a supplementary salary reduction program (a tax-sheltered savings program). To that point, the default had been the 'back to zero' option. But since contributions to this program could be stopped at any time, the group unanimously agreed that it would be better to switch to the status quo 'same as last year' default. We are confident that many absent-minded professors will have more comfortable retirements as a result.

This example illustrates some basic principles of good choice architecture. Choosers are human, so designers should make life as easy as possible. Send reminders, and then try to minimize the costs imposed on those who, despite your (and their) best efforts, space out. As we will see, these principles (and many more) can be applied in both the private and public sectors, and there is much room for going beyond what is now being done.

A NEW PATH

We shall have a great deal to say about private nudges. But many of the most important applications of libertarian paternalism are for government, and we will offer a number of recommendations for public policy and law. Our hope is that those recommendations might appeal to both sides of the political divide. Indeed, we believe that the policies suggested by libertarian paternalism can be embraced by conservatives and liberals alike. Already some of these policies have been embraced by David Cameron, leader of the Conservative Party in Britain, and Barack Obama. A central reason is that many of those policies cost little or nothing; they impose no burden on taxpayers at all.

Many Republicans are now seeking to go beyond simple opposition to government action. As the experience with Hurricane Katrina showed, government is often required to act, for it is the only means by which the necessary resources can be mustered, organized, and deployed. Republicans want to make people's lives better; they are simply skeptical, and legitimately so, about eliminating people's options.

For their part, many Democrats are willing to abandon their enthusiasm for aggressive government planning. Sensible Democrats certainly hope that public institutions can improve people's lives. But in many domains, Democrats have come to agree that freedom of choice is a good and even indispensable foundation for public policy. There is a real basis here for crossing partisan divides.

Libertarian paternalism, we think, is a promising foundation for bipartisanship. In many domains, including environmental protection, family law, and school choice, we will be arguing that better governance requires less in the way of government coercion and constraint, and more in the way of freedom to choose. If incentives and nudges replace requirements and bans, government will be both smaller and more modest. So, to be clear: *we are not for bigger government, just for better governance.*

Actually we have evidence that our optimism (which we admit may be a bias) is more than just rosy thinking. Libertarian paternalism with respect to savings, discussed in Chapter 6, has received enthusiastic and widespread bipartisan support in Congress, including from current and former conservative Republican senators such as Robert Bennett (Utah) and Rick Santorum (Pa.) and liberal Democrats such as Rahm Emanuel of Illinois. In 2006 some of the key ideas were quietly enacted into law. The new law will help many Americans have more comfortable retirements but costs essentially nothing in taxpayer dollars.

In short, libertarian paternalism is neither left nor right, neither Democratic nor Republican. In many areas, the most thoughtful Democrats are going beyond their enthusiasm for choice-eliminating programs. In many areas, the most thoughtful Republicans are abandoning their knee-jerk opposition to constructive governmental initiatives. For all their differences, we hope that both sides might be willing to converge in support of some gentle nudges.

PART I

Humans and Econs

I

Biases and Blunders

Have a look, if you will, at these two tables:

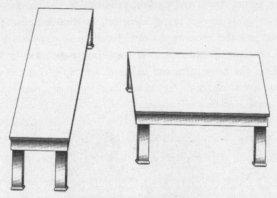

Figure 1.1. *Two tables (Adapted from Shepard [1990])*

Suppose that you are thinking about which one would work better as a coffee table in your living room. What would you say are the dimensions of the two tables? Take a guess at the ratio of the length to the width of each. Just eyeball it.

If you are like most people, you think that the table on the left is much longer and narrower than the one on the right. Typical guesses are that the ratio of the length to the width is 3:1 for the left table and 1.5:1 for the right table. Now take out a ruler and measure each table. You will find that the two table tops are identical. Measure them until you are convinced, because this is a case where seeing is not believing. (When Thaler showed this example to Sunstein at

19

their usual lunch haunt, Sunstein grabbed his chopstick to check.)

What should we conclude from this example? If you see the left table as longer and thinner than the right one, you are certifiably human. There is nothing wrong with you (well, at least not that we can detect from this test). Still, your judgment in this task was biased, and predictably so. No one thinks that the right table is thinner! Not only were you wrong; you were probably confident that you were right. If you like, you can put this visual to good use when you encounter others who are equally human and who are disposed to gamble away their money, say, at a bar.

Now consider Figure 1.2. Do these two shapes look the same or different? Again, if you are human, and have decent vision, you probably see these shapes as being identical, as they are. But these two shapes are just the table tops from Figure 1.1, removed from their legs and reoriented. Both the legs and the orientation facilitate the illusion that the table tops are different in Figure 1.1, so removing these distracters restores the visual system to its usual amazingly accurate state.*

Figure 1.2. *Tabletops (Adapted from Shepard [1990])*

These two figures capture the key insight that behavioral economists have borrowed from psychologists. Normally the human mind works remarkably well. We can recognize people we have not seen in years, understand the complexities of our native language, and run

* One of the tricks used in drawing these tables is that vertical lines look longer than horizontal lines.

down a flight of stairs without falling. Some of us can speak twelve languages, improve the fanciest computers, and/or create the theory of relativity. However, even Einstein would probably be fooled by those tables. That does not mean something is wrong with us as humans, but it does mean that our understanding of human behavior can be improved by appreciating how people systematically go wrong.

To obtain that understanding, we need to explore some aspects of human thinking. Knowing something about the visual system allowed Roger Shepard (1990), a psychologist and artist, to draw those deceptive tables. He knew what to draw to lead our mind astray. Knowing something about the cognitive system has allowed others to discover systematic biases in the way we think.

HOW WE THINK: TWO SYSTEMS

The workings of the human brain are more than a bit befuddling. How can we be so ingenious at some tasks and so clueless at others? Beethoven wrote his incredible ninth symphony while he was deaf, but we would not be at all surprised if we learned that he often misplaced his house keys. How can people be simultaneously so smart and so dumb? Many psychologists and neuroscientists have been converging on a description of the brain's functioning that helps us make sense of these seeming contradictions. The approach involves a distinction between two kinds of thinking, one that is intuitive and automatic, and another that is reflective and rational.[1] We will call the first the Automatic System and the second the Reflective System. (In the psychology literature, these two systems are sometimes referred to as System 1 and System 2, respectively.) The key features of each system are shown in Table 1.1.

The Automatic System is rapid and is or feels instinctive, and it does not involve what we usually associate with the word *thinking*. When you duck because a ball is thrown at you unexpectedly, or get nervous when your airplane hits turbulence, or smile when you see a cute puppy, you are using your Automatic System. Brain scientists are

Table 1.1 *Two cognitive systems*

Automatic System	Reflective System
Uncontrolled	Controlled
Effortless	Effortful
Associative	Deductive
Fast	Slow
Unconscious	Self-aware
Skilled	Rule-following

able to say that the activities of the Automatic System are associated with the oldest parts of the brain, the parts we share with lizards (as well as puppies).[2]

The Reflective System is more deliberate and self-conscious. We use the Reflective System when we are asked, 'How much is 411 times 37?' Most people are also likely to use the Reflective System when deciding which route to take for a trip and whether to go to law school or business school. When we are writing this book we are (mostly) using our Reflective Systems, but sometimes ideas pop into our heads when we are in the shower or taking a walk and not thinking at all about the book, and these probably are coming from our Automatic Systems. (Voters, by the way, seem to rely primarily on their Automatic System.[3] A candidate who makes a bad first impression, or who tries to win votes by complex arguments and statistical demonstrations, may well run into trouble.)*

Most of the world has an Automatic System reaction to a temperature given in Celsius but has to use their Reflective System to process a temperature given in Fahrenheit; for Americans, the opposite is true. People speak their native languages using their Automatic Systems and tend to struggle to speak another language using their

* It is possible to predict the outcome of congressional elections with frightening accuracy simply by asking people to look quickly at pictures of the candidates and say which one looks more competent. These judgments, by students who did not know the candidates, forecast the winner of the election two-thirds of the time! (Toderov et al. [2005]; Benjamin and Shapiro [2007])

Reflective Systems. Being truly bilingual means that you speak two languages using the Automatic System. Accomplished chess players and professional athletes have pretty fancy intuitions; their Automatic Systems allow them to size up complex situations rapidly and to respond with both amazing accuracy and exceptional speed.

One way to think about all this is that the Automatic System is your gut reaction and the Reflective System is your conscious thought. Gut feelings can be quite accurate, but we often make mistakes because we rely too much on our Automatic System. The Automatic System says, 'The airplane is shaking, I'm going to die,' while the Reflective System responds, 'Planes are very safe!' The Automatic System says, 'That big dog is going to hurt me,' and the Reflective System replies, 'Most pets are quite sweet.' (In both cases, the Automatic System is squawking all the time.) The Automatic System starts out with no idea how to play golf or tennis. Note, however, that countless hours of practice enable an accomplished golfer to avoid reflection and to rely on her Automatic System – so much so that good golfers, like other good athletes, know the hazards of 'thinking too much' and might well do better to 'trust the gut,' or 'just do it.' The Automatic System can be trained with lots of repetition – but such training takes a lot of time and effort. One reason why teenagers are such risky drivers is that their Automatic Systems have not had much practice, and using the Reflective System is much slower.

To see how intuitive thinking works, try the following little test. For each of the three questions, begin by writing down the first answer that comes to your mind. Then pause to reflect.

1. A bat and ball cost $1.10 in total. The bat costs $1.00 more than the ball. How much does the ball cost? ____ cents
2. If it takes 5 machines 5 minutes to make 5 widgets, how long would it take 100 machines to make 100 widgets? ____ minutes
3. In a lake, there is a patch of lily pads. Every day, the patch doubles in size. If it takes 48 days for the patch to cover the entire lake, how long would it take for the patch to cover half of the lake? ____ days

What were your initial answers? Most people say 10 cents, 100 minutes, and 24 days. But all these answers are wrong. If you think for a minute, you will see why. If the ball costs 10 cents and the bat costs one dollar more than the ball, meaning $1.10, then together they cost $1.20, not $1.10. No one who bothers to check whether his initial answer of 10 cents could possibly be right would give that as an answer, but research by Shane Frederick (2005) (who calls this series of questions the cognitive reflection test) finds that these are the most popular answers even among bright college students.

The correct answers are 5 cents, 5 minutes, and 47 days, but you knew that, or at least your Reflective System did if you bothered to consult it. Econs never make an important decision without checking with their Reflective Systems (if they have time). But Humans sometimes go with the answer the lizard inside is giving without pausing to think. If you are a television fan, think of Mr Spock of *Star Trek* fame as someone whose Reflective System is always in control. (Captain Kirk: 'You'd make a splendid computer, Mr Spock.' Mr Spock: 'That is very kind of you, Captain!') In contrast, Homer Simpson seems to have forgotten where he put his Reflective System. (In a commentary on gun control, Homer once replied to a gun store clerk who informed him of a mandatory five-day waiting period before buying a weapon, 'Five days? But I'm mad now!')

One of our major goals in this book is to see how the world might be made easier, or safer, for the Homers among us (and the Homer lurking somewhere in each of us). If people can rely on their Automatic Systems without getting into terrible trouble, their lives should be easier, better, and longer.

RULES OF THUMB

Most of us are busy, our lives are complicated, and we can't spend all our time thinking and analyzing everything. When we have to make judgments, such as guessing Angelina Jolie's age or the distance between Cleveland and Philadelphia, we use simple rules of thumb to help us. We use rules of thumb because most of the time they are quick and useful.

In fact, there is a great collection edited by Tom Parker titled *Rules of Thumb*. Parker wrote the book by asking friends to send him good rules of thumb. For example, 'One ostrich egg will serve 24 people for brunch.' 'Ten people will raise the temperature of an average size room by one degree per hour.' And one to which we will return: 'No more than 25 percent of the guests at a university dinner party can come from the economics department without spoiling the conversation.'

Although rules of thumb can be very helpful, their use can also lead to systematic biases. This insight, first developed decades ago by two Israeli psychologists, Amos Tversky and Daniel Kahneman (1974), has changed the way psychologists (and eventually economists) think about thinking. Their original work identified three heuristics, or rules of thumb – anchoring, availability, and representativeness – and the biases that are associated with each. Their research program has come to be known as the 'heuristics and biases' approach to the study of human judgment. More recently, psychologists have come to understand that these heuristics and biases emerge from the interplay between the Automatic System and the Reflective System. Let's see how.

Anchoring

Suppose we are asked to guess the population of Milwaukee, a city about two hours north of Chicago, where we live. Neither of us knows much about Milwaukee, but we think that it is the biggest city in Wisconsin. How should we go about guessing? Well, one thing we could do is start with something we do know, which is the population of Chicago, roughly three million. So we might think, Milwaukee is a major city, but clearly not as big as Chicago, so, hmmm, maybe it is one-third the size, say one million. Now consider someone from Green Bay, Wisconsin, who is asked the same question. She also doesn't know the answer, but she does know that Green Bay has about one hundred thousand people and knows that Milwaukee is larger, so guesses, say, three times larger – three hundred thousand.

This process is called 'anchoring and adjustment.' You start with some anchor, the number you know, and adjust in the direction you think is appropriate. So far, so good. The bias occurs because the adjustments are typically insufficient. Experiments repeatedly show that, in problems similar to our example, people from Chicago are likely to make a high guess (based on their high anchor) while those from Green Bay guess low (based on their low anchor). As it happens, Milwaukee has about 580,000 people.[4]

Even obviously irrelevant anchors creep into the decision-making process. Try this one yourself. Take the last three digits of your phone number and add two hundred. Write the number down. Now, when do you think Attila the Hun sacked Europe? Was it before or after that year? What is your best guess? (We will give you one hint: It was after the birth of Jesus.) Even if you do not know much about European history, you do know enough to know that whenever Attila did whatever he did, the date has nothing to do with your phone number. Still, when we conduct this experiment with our students, we get answers that are more than three hundred years later from students who start with high anchors rather than low ones. (The right answer is 411.)

Anchors can even influence how you think your life is going. In one experiment, college students were asked two questions: (a) How happy are you? (b) How often are you dating? When the two questions were asked in this order the correlation between the two questions was quite low (.11). But when the question order was reversed, so that the dating question was asked first, the correlation jumped to .62. Apparently, when prompted by the dating question, the students use what might be called the 'dating heuristic' to answer the question about how happy they are. 'Gee, I can't remember when I last had a date! I must be miserable.' Similar results can be obtained from married couples if the dating question is replaced by a love-making question.[5]

In the language of this book, anchors serve as nudges. We can influence the figure you will choose in a particular situation by ever-so-subtly suggesting a starting point for your thought process. When charities ask you for a donation, they typically offer you a range of options such as $100, $250, $1,000, $5,000, or 'other.' If the charity's fund-raisers have an idea of what they are doing, these values are not picked at random, because the options influence the amount of money people decide to donate. People will give more if the options are $100, $250, $1,000, and $5,000, than if the options are $50, $75, $100, and $150.

In many domains, the evidence shows that, within reason, the more you ask for, the more you tend to get. Lawyers who sue cigarette companies often win astronomical amounts, in part because they have successfully induced juries to anchor on multimillion-dollar figures. Clever negotiators often get amazing deals for their clients by producing an opening offer that makes their adversary thrilled to pay half that very high amount.

Availability

How much should you worry about hurricanes, nuclear power, terrorism, mad cow disease, alligator attacks, or avian flu? And how much care should you take in avoiding risks associated with each? What, exactly, should you do to prevent the kinds of dangers that you face in ordinary life?

In answering questions of this kind, most people use what is called the availability heuristic. They assess the likelihood of risks by asking how readily examples come to mind. If people can easily think of relevant examples, they are far more likely to be frightened and concerned than if they cannot. A risk that is familiar, like that associated with terrorism in the aftermath of 9/11, will be seen as more serious than a risk that is less familiar, like that associated with sunbathing or hotter summers. Homicides are more available than suicides, and so people tend to believe, wrongly, that more people die from homicide.

Accessibility and salience are closely related to availability, and they are important as well. If you have personally experienced a serious earthquake, you're more likely to believe that an earthquake is likely than if you read about it in a weekly magazine. Thus vivid and easily imagined causes of death (for example, tornadoes) often receive inflated estimates of probability, and less-vivid causes (for example, asthma attacks) receive low estimates, even if they occur with a far greater frequency (here a factor of twenty). So, too, recent events have a greater impact on our behavior, and on our fears, than earlier ones. In all these highly available examples, the Automatic System is keenly aware of the risk (perhaps too keenly), without having to resort to any tables of boring statistics.

The availability heuristic helps to explain much risk-related behavior, including both public and private decisions to take precautions. Whether people buy insurance for natural disasters is greatly affected by recent experience.[6] In the aftermath of an earthquake, purchases of new earthquake insurance policies rise sharply – but purchases decline steadily from that point, as vivid memories recede. If floods have not occurred in the immediate past, people who live on floodplains are far less likely to purchase insurance. And people who know someone who has experienced a flood are more likely to buy flood insurance for themselves, regardless of the flood risk they actually face.

Biased assessments of risk can perversely influence how we prepare for and respond to crises, business choices, and the political process. When Internet stocks have done very well, people might well buy Internet stocks, even if by that point they've become a bad investment. Or suppose that people falsely think that some risks (a nuclear power accident) are high, whereas others (a stroke) are relatively low. Such misperceptions can affect policy, because governments are likely to allocate their resources in a way that fits with people's fears rather than in response to the most likely danger.

When 'availability bias' is at work, both private and public decisions may be improved if judgments can be nudged back in the direction of true probabilities. A good way to increase people's fear of a bad outcome is to remind them of a related incident in which things went wrong; a good way to increase people's confidence is to remind them of a similar situation in which everything worked out for the best. The pervasive problems are that easily remembered events may inflate people's probability judgments, and that if no such events come to mind, their judgments of likelihoods might be distorted downward.

Representativeness

The third of the original three heuristics bears an unwieldy name: representativeness. Think of it as the similarity heuristic. The idea is that when asked to judge how likely it is that A belongs to category B, people (and especially their Automatic Systems) answer by asking themselves how similar A is to their image or stereotype of B (that is, how 'representative' A is of B). Like the other two heuristics we have discussed, this one is used because it often works. We think a 6-foot-8-inch African-American man is more likely to be a professional basketball player than a 5-foot-6-inch Jewish guy because there are lots of tall black basketball players and not many short Jewish ones (at least not these days). Stereotypes are sometimes right!

Again, biases can creep in when similarity and frequency diverge. The most famous demonstration of such biases involves the case of a hypothetical woman named Linda. In this experiment, subjects were told the following: 'Linda is thirty-one years old, single, outspoken, and very bright. She majored in philosophy. As a student, she was deeply concerned with issues of discrimination and social justice and also participated in antinuclear demonstrations.' Then people were asked to rank, in order of the probability of their occurrence, eight possible futures for Linda. The two crucial answers were 'bank teller' and 'bank teller and active in the feminist movement.' Most people said that Linda was less likely to be a bank teller than to be a bank teller and active in the feminist movement.

This is an obvious logical mistake. It is, of course, not logically possible for any two events to be more likely than one of them alone. It just has to be the case that Linda is more likely to be a bank teller than a feminist bank teller, because all feminist bank tellers are bank tellers. The error stems from the use of the representativeness heuristic: Linda's description seems to match 'bank teller and active in the feminist movement' far better than 'bank teller.' As Stephen Jay Gould (1991) once observed, 'I know [the right answer], yet a little homunculus in my head continues to jump up and down, shouting at me – "But she can't just be a bank teller; read the description!"' Gould's homunculus is the Automatic System in action.

Use of the representativeness heuristic can cause serious misperceptions of patterns in everyday life. When events are determined by chance, such as a sequence of coin tosses, people expect the resulting string of heads and tails to be representative of what they think of as random. Unfortunately, people do not have accurate perceptions of what random sequences look like. When they see the outcomes of random processes, they often detect patterns that they think have great meaning but in fact are just due to chance. You might flip a coin three times, see it come up heads every time, and conclude that there is something funny about the coin. But the fact is that if you flip any coin a lot, it won't be so unusual to see three heads in a row. (Try it and you'll see. As a little test, Sunstein, having just finished this paragraph, flipped a regular penny three times – and got heads every time. He was amazed. He shouldn't have been.)

A less trivial example, from the Cornell psychologist Tom Gilovich (1991), comes from the experience of London residents during the German bombing campaigns of World War II. London newspapers published maps, such as the one shown in Figure 1.3, displaying the location of the strikes from German V-1 and V-2 missiles that landed in central London. As you can see, the pattern does not seem at all random. Bombs appear to be clustered around the River Thames and also in the northwest sector of the map. People in London expressed concern at the time because the pattern seemed to suggest that the Germans could aim their bombs with great precision. Some Londoners even speculated that the blank spaces were probably the neighborhoods where German spies lived. They were wrong. In fact the Germans could do no better than aim their bombs at central London and hope for the best. A detailed statistical analysis of the dispersion of the location of the bomb strikes determined that within London the distribution of bomb strikes was indeed random.

Still, the location of the bomb strikes does not *look* random. What is going on here? We often see patterns because we construct our informal tests only after looking at the evidence. The World War II example is an excellent illustration of this problem. Suppose we divide the map into quadrants, as in Figure 1.4a. If we then do a formal statistical test – or, for the less statistically inclined, just count the

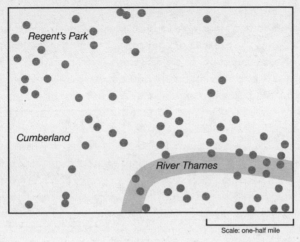

Scale: one-half mile

Figure 1.3. *Map of London showing V-1 rocket strikes (Adapted from Gilovich [1991])*

number of hits in each quadrant – we do find evidence of a non-random pattern. However, nothing in nature suggests that this is the right way to test for randomness. Suppose instead we form the quadrants diagonally as in Figure 1.4b. We are now unable to reject the hypothesis that the bombs land at random. Unfortunately, we do not subject our own perceptions to such rigorous alternative testing.

Gilovich (with colleagues Vallone and Tversky [1985]) is also responsible for perhaps the most famous (or infamous) example of misperception of randomness, namely the widely held view among basketball fans that there is a strong pattern of 'streak shooting.' We will not go into this in detail, because our experience tells us that the cognitive illusion here is so powerful that most people (influenced by their Automatic System) are unwilling even to consider the possibility that their strongly held beliefs might be wrong. But here is the short version. Most basketball fans think that a player is more likely to make his next shot if he has made his last shot, or even better, his last few shots. Players who have hit a few shots in a row, or even most of their recent shots, are said to have a 'hot hand,' which is taken by all sports announcers to be a good signal about the future. Passing the

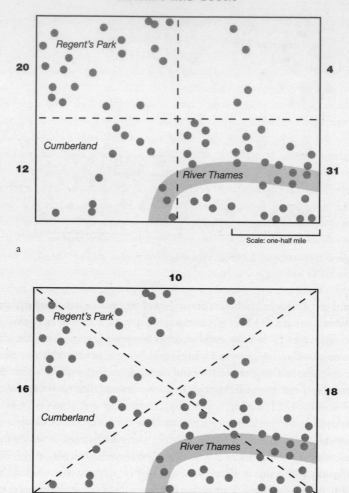

Figure 1.4. *Map of London showing V-1 rocket strikes, with vertical-horizontal grid (a) and diagonal grid (b). The figures outside the grid refer to the number of dots in the quadrant. (Adapted from Gilovich [1991])*

ball to the player who is hot is taken to be an obvious bit of good strategy.

It turns out that the 'hot hand' is just a myth. Players who have made their last few shots are no more likely to make their next shot (actually a bit less likely). Really.

Once people are told these facts, they quickly start forming alternative versions of the hot-hand theory. Maybe the defense adjusts and guards the 'hot' player more closely. Maybe the hot player adjusts and starts taking harder shots. These are fine observations that need to be investigated. But notice that, before seeing the data, when fans were asked about actual shooting percentages after a series of made shots, they routinely subscribed to the hot-hand theory – no qualifiers were thought necessary. Many researchers have been so sure that the original Gilovich results were wrong that they set out to find the hot hand. To date, no one has found it.[7]

Jay Koehler and Caryn Conley (2003) performed a particularly clean test using the annual three-point shooting contest held at the National Basketball Association All-Star Game. In this contest, the players (among the best three-point shooters in the league) take a series of shots from behind the three-point shooting arc. Their goal is to make as many shots as possible in sixty seconds. Without any defense or alternative shots, this would seem to be an ideal situation in which to observe the hot hand. However, as in the original study, there was no evidence of any streakiness. This absence of streak shooting did not stop the announcers from detecting sudden temperature variations in the players. ('Johnson is hot!' 'Smith is on fire!') But these outbursts by the announcers had no predictive power. Before the announcers spoke of hotness, the players had made 80.5 percent of their three previous shots. After the hotness pronouncements, players made only 55.2 percent – not significantly better than their overall shooting percentage in the contest, 53.9 percent.

Of course, it is no great problem if basketball fans are confused about what they see when they are watching games on television. But the same cognitive biases occur in other, more weighty domains. Consider the phenomenon of 'cancer clusters.' These can cause a great deal of private and public consternation, and they often attract sustained investigations, designed to see what on earth (or elsewhere) could possibly have caused a sudden and otherwise inexplicable outbreak of cancer cases. Suppose that in a particular neighborhood we find an apparently elevated cancer rate – maybe ten people, in a group of five hundred, have been diagnosed with cancer within the same six-month period. Maybe all ten people live within three blocks of one another. And in fact, American officials receive reports of more than one thousand suspected cancer clusters every year, with many of these suspected clusters investigated further for a possible 'epidemic.'[8]

The problem is that in a population of three hundred million, it is inevitable that certain neighborhoods will see unusually high cancer rates within any one-year period. The resulting 'cancer clusters' may be products of random fluctuations. Nonetheless, people insist that they could not possibly occur by chance. They get scared, and sometimes government wrongly intervenes on their behalf. Mostly, though, there is thankfully nothing to worry about, except for the fact that the use of the representativeness heuristic can cause people to confuse random fluctuations with causal patterns.

OPTIMISM AND OVERCONFIDENCE

Before the start of Thaler's class in Managerial Decision Making, students fill out an anonymous survey on the course Web site. One of the questions is 'In which decile do you expect to fall in the distribution of grades in this class?' Students can check the top 10 percent, the second 10 percent, and so forth. Since these are MBA students, they are presumably well aware that in any distribution, half the population will be in the top 50 percent and half in the bottom. And only 10 percent of the class can, in fact, end up in the top decile.

Nevertheless, the results of this survey reveal a high degree of unrealistic optimism about performance in the class. Typically less than 5 percent of the class expects their performance to be below the median (the 50th percentile) and more than half the class expects to perform in one of the top two deciles. Invariably, the largest group of students put themselves in the second decile. We think this is most likely explained by modesty. They really think they will end up in the top decile, but are too modest to say so.

MBA students are not the only ones overconfident about their abilities. The 'above average' effect is pervasive. Ninety percent of all drivers think they are above average behind the wheel, even if they don't live in Lake Wobegon. And nearly everyone (including some who are rarely seen smiling) thinks he has an above-average sense of humor. (That is because they know what is funny!) This applies to professors, too. About 94 percent of professors at a large university were found to believe that they are better than the average professor, and there is every reason to think that such overconfidence applies to professors in general.[9] (Yes, we admit to this particular failing.)

People are unrealistically optimistic even when the stakes are high. About 50 percent of marriages end in divorce, and this is a statistic most people have heard. But around the time of the ceremony, almost all couples believe that there is approximately a zero percent chance that their marriage will end in divorce – even those who have already been divorced![10] (Second marriage, Samuel Johnson once quipped, 'is the triumph of hope over experience.') A similar point applies to entrepreneurs starting new businesses, where the failure rate is at least 50 percent. In one survey of people starting new businesses (typically small businesses, such as contracting firms, restaurants, and salons), respondents were asked two questions: (a) What do you think is the chance of success for a typical business like yours? (b) What is your chance of success? The most common answers to these questions were 50 percent and 90 percent, respectively, and many said 100 percent to the second question.[11]

Unrealistic optimism can explain a lot of individual risk taking, especially in the domain of risks to life and health. Asked to envision their future, students typically say that they are far less likely than their classmates to be fired from a job, to have a heart attack or get cancer, to be divorced after a few years of marriage, or to have a drinking problem. Gay men systematically underestimate the chance that they will contract AIDS, even though they know about AIDS risks in general. Older people underestimate the likelihood that they will be in a car accident or suffer major diseases. Smokers are aware of the statistical risks, and often even exaggerate them, but most believe that they are less likely to be diagnosed with lung cancer and heart disease than most nonsmokers. Lotteries are successful partly because of unrealistic optimism.[12]

Unrealistic optimism is a pervasive feature of human life; it characterizes most people in most social categories. When they overestimate their personal immunity from harm, people may fail to take sensible preventive steps. If people are running risks because of unrealistic optimism, they might be able to benefit from a nudge. In fact, we have already mentioned one possibility: if people are reminded of a bad event, they may not continue to be so optimistic.

GAINS AND LOSSES

People hate losses (and their Automatic Systems can get pretty emotional about them). Roughly speaking, losing something makes you twice as miserable as gaining the same thing makes you happy. In more technical language, people are 'loss averse.' How do we know this?

Consider a simple experiment.[13] Half the students in a class are given coffee mugs with the insignia of their home university embossed on it. The students who do not get a mug are asked to examine their neighbor's mugs. Then mug owners are invited to sell their mugs and nonowners are invited to buy them. They do so by answering the question 'At each of the following prices, indicate whether you would be willing to (give up your mug/buy a mug).' The results show that those with mugs demand roughly twice as much to give up their mugs as others are willing to pay to get one. Thousands of mugs have been used in dozens of replications of this experiment, but the results are nearly always the same. Once I have a mug, I don't want to give it up. But if I don't have one, I don't feel an urgent need to buy one. What this means is that people do not assign specific values to objects. When they have to give something up, they are hurt more than they are pleased if they acquire the very same thing.

It is also possible to measure loss aversion with gambles. Suppose I ask you whether you want to make a bet. Heads you win $X, tails you lose $100. How much does X have to be for you to take the bet? For most people, the answer to this question is somewhere around $200. This implies that the prospect of winning $200 just offsets the prospect of losing $100.

Loss aversion helps produce inertia, meaning a strong desire to stick with your current holdings. If you are reluctant to give up what you have because you do not want to incur losses, then you will turn down trades you might have otherwise made. In another experiment, half the students in a class received coffee mugs (of course) and half got large chocolate bars. The mugs and the chocolate cost about the same, and in pretests students were as likely to choose one as the other. Yet when offered the opportunity to switch from a mug to a candy bar or vice versa, only one in ten switched.

As we will see, loss aversion operates as a kind of cognitive nudge, pressing us not to make changes, even when changes are very much in our interests.

STATUS QUO BIAS

Loss aversion is not the only reason for inertia. For lots of reasons, people have a more general tendency to stick with their current situation. This phenomenon, which William Samuelson and Richard Zeckhauser (1988) have dubbed the 'status quo bias,' has been demonstrated in numerous situations. Most teachers know that students tend to sit in the same seats in class, even without a seating chart. But status quo bias can occur even when the stakes are much larger, and it can get us into a lot of trouble.

For example, in retirement savings plans most participants pick an asset allocation and then forget about it. In one study conducted in the late 1980s among participants in the pension plan of many college professors in the United States, the median number of changes in the asset allocation over a lifetime was, believe it or not, zero. In other words, over the course of their careers, more than half of the participants made exactly no changes to the way their contributions were being allocated. Perhaps even more telling, many married participants who were single when they joined the plan still have their mothers listed as their beneficiaries!

Status quo bias is easily exploited. Many years ago American Express wrote Sunstein a cheerful letter telling him that he could receive, for free, three-month subscriptions to five magazines of his choice. Free subscriptions seem like a bargain, even if the magazines rarely get read, so Sunstein happily made his choices. What he didn't realize was that unless he took some action to cancel his subscription, he would continue to receive the magazines, paying for them at the normal rate. For about a decade, he has continued to subscribe to magazines that he hardly ever reads. (He keeps intending to cancel those subscriptions, but somehow never gets around to it. We hope to get around to discussing procrastination in the next chapter.)

One of the causes of status quo bias is a lack of attention. Many people adopt what we will call the 'yeah, whatever' heuristic. A good illustration is the carryover effect in television viewing. Network executives spend a lot of time working on scheduling because they know that a viewer who starts the evening on NBC tends to stay there. Since remote controls have been pervasive in this country for decades, the actual 'switching' costs in this context are literally one thumb press. But when one show ends and the next one comes on, a surprisingly high number of viewers (implicitly) say, 'yeah, whatever' and keep watching. Nor is Sunstein the only victim of automatic renewal of magazine subscriptions. Those who are in charge of circulation know that when renewal is automatic, and when people have to make a phone call to cancel, the likelihood of renewal is much higher than it is when people have to indicate that they actually want to continue to receive the magazine.

The combination of loss aversion with mindless choosing implies that if an option is designated as the 'default,' it will attract a large market share. Default options thus act as powerful nudges. In many contexts defaults have some extra nudging power because consumers may feel, rightly or wrongly, that default options come with an implicit endorsement from the default setter, be it the employer, government, or TV scheduler. For this and other reasons, setting the best possible defaults will be a theme we explore often in the course of this book.

FRAMING

Suppose that you are suffering from serious heart disease and that your doctor proposes a grueling operation. You're understandably curious about the odds. The doctor says, 'Of one hundred patients who have this operation, ninety are alive after five years.' What will you do? If we fill in the facts in a certain way, the doctor's statement will be pretty comforting, and you'll probably have the operation.

But suppose the doctor frames his answer in a somewhat different way. Suppose that he says, 'Of one hundred patients who have this operation, ten are dead after five years.' If you're like most people, the doctor's statement will sound pretty alarming, and you might not have the operation. The Automatic System thinks: 'A significant number of people are dead, and I might be one of them!' In numerous experiments, people react very differently to the information that 'ninety of one hundred are alive' than to the information that 'ten of one hundred are dead' – even though the content of the two statements is exactly the same. Even experts are subject to framing effects. When doctors are told that 'ninety of one hundred are alive,' they are more likely to recommend the operation than if told that 'ten of one hundred are dead.'[14]

Framing matters in many domains. When credit cards started to become popular forms of payment in the 1970s, some retail merchants wanted to charge different prices to their cash and credit card customers. (Credit card companies typically charge retailers 1 percent of each sale.) To prevent this, credit card companies adopted rules that forbade their retailers from charging different prices to cash and credit customers. However, when a bill was introduced in Congress to outlaw such rules, the credit card lobby turned its attention to language. Its preference was that if a company charged different prices to cash and credit customers, the credit price should be considered the 'normal' (default) price and the cash price a discount – rather than the alternative of making the cash price the usual price and charging a surcharge to credit card customers.

The credit card companies had a good intuitive understanding of what psychologists would come to call 'framing.' The idea is that choices depend, in part, on the way in which problems are stated. The point matters a great deal for public policy. Energy conservation is now receiving a lot of attention, so consider the following information campaigns: (a) If you use energy conservation methods, you will save $350 per year; (b) If you do not use energy conservation methods, you will lose $350 per year. It turns out that information campaign (b), framed in terms of losses, is far more effective than information campaign (a). If the government wants to encourage energy conservation, option (b) is a stronger nudge.

Framing works because people tend to be somewhat mindless, passive decision makers. Their Reflective System does not do the work that would be required to check and see whether reframing the questions would produce a different answer. One reason they don't do this is that they wouldn't know what to make of the contradiction. This implies that frames are powerful nudges, and must be selected with caution.

SO WHAT?

Our goal in this chapter has been to offer a brief glimpse at human fallibility. The picture that emerges is one of busy people trying to cope in a complex world in which they cannot afford to think deeply about every choice they have to make. People adopt sensible rules of thumb that sometimes lead them astray. Because they are busy and have limited attention, they accept questions as posed rather than trying to determine whether their answers would vary under alternative formulations. The bottom line, from our point of view, is that people are, shall we say, nudge-able. Their choices, even in life's most important decisions, are influenced in ways that would not be anticipated in a standard economic framework. Here is one final example to illustrate.

One of the most scenic urban thoroughfares in the world is Chicago's Lake Shore Drive, which hugs the Lake Michigan coastline that is the city's eastern boundary. The drive offers stunning views of Chicago's magnificent skyline. There is one stretch of this road that puts drivers through a series of S curves. These curves are dangerous. Many drivers fail to take heed of the reduced speed limit (25 mph) and wipe out. Recently, the city has employed a new way of encouraging drivers to slow down.

At the beginning of the dangerous curve, drivers encounter a sign painted on the road warning of the lower speed limit, and then a series of white stripes painted onto the road. The stripes do not provide much if any tactile information (they are not speed bumps) but rather just send a visual signal to drivers. When the stripes first appear, they are evenly spaced, but as drivers reach the most dangerous portion of the curve, the stripes get closer together, giving the sensation that driving speed is increasing (see Figure 1.5). One's natural instinct is to slow down. When we drive on this familiar stretch of road, we find that those lines are speaking to us, gently urging us to touch the brake before the apex of the curve. We have been nudged.

Figure 1.5. *Lake Shore Drive, Chicago (Courtesy of the city of Chicago)*

2

Resisting Temptation

TEMPTATION

Many years ago, Thaler was hosting dinner for some guests (other then-young economists) and put out a large bowl of cashew nuts to nibble on with the first bottle of wine. Within a few minutes it became clear that the bowl of nuts was going to be consumed in its entirety, and that the guests might lack sufficient appetite to enjoy all the food that was to follow. Leaping into action, Thaler grabbed the bowl of nuts, and (while sneaking a few more nuts for himself) removed the bowl to the kitchen, where it was put out of sight.

When he returned, the guests thanked him for removing the nuts. The conversation immediately turned to the theoretical question of how they could possibly be happy about the fact that there was no longer a bowl of nuts in front of them. (You can now see the wisdom of the rule of thumb mentioned in Chapter 1 about a cap on the proportion of economists among attendees at a dinner party.) In economics (and in ordinary life), a basic principle is that you can never be made worse off by having more options, because you can always turn them down. Before Thaler removed the nuts the group had the choice of whether to eat the nuts or not – now they didn't. In the land of Econs, it is against the law to be happy about this!

To help us understand this example, consider how the preferences of the group seemed to evolve over time. At 7:15, just before Thaler removed the nuts, the dinner guests had three options: eat a few nuts; eat all the nuts; and eat no more nuts. Their first choice would be to eat just a few more nuts, followed by eating no more nuts. The worst option was finishing the bowl, since that would ruin dinner. But by 7:30, had the nuts remained on the table, the group would have finished the bowl, thereby reaching their least favorite option. Why would the group change its mind in the space of just fifteen minutes? Or do we really want to say that the group has changed its mind?

In the language of economics, the group is said to display behavior that is *dynamically inconsistent*. Initially people prefer A to B, but they later choose B over A. We can see dynamic inconsistency in many places. On Saturday morning people might say that they prefer exercising to watching television, but once the afternoon comes, they are on the couch at home watching the football game. How can such behavior be understood?

Two factors must be introduced in order to understand the cashew phenomenon: temptation and mindlessness. Human beings have been aware of the concept of temptation at least since the time of Adam and Eve, but for purposes of understanding the value of nudges, that concept needs elaboration. What does it mean for something to be 'tempting'?

The American Supreme Court Justice Potter Stewart famously said that although he could not define pornography, 'I know it when I see it.' Similarly, temptation is easier to recognize than to define. Our preferred definition requires recognizing that people's state of arousal varies over time. To simplify things we will consider just the two end points: hot and cold. When Sally is very hungry and appetizing aromas are emanating from the kitchen, we can say she is in a hot state. When Sally is thinking abstractly on Tuesday about the right number of cashews she should consume before dinner on Saturday, she is in a cold state. We will call something 'tempting' if we consume more of it when hot than when cold. None of this means that decisions made in a cold state are always better. For example, sometimes we have to be in a hot state to overcome our fears about trying new things. Sometimes dessert really is delicious, and we do best to go for it. Sometimes it is best to fall in love. But it is clear that when we are in a hot state, we can often get into a lot of trouble.

Most people realize that temptation exists, and they take steps to overcome it. The classic example is that of Ulysses, who faced the peril of the Sirens and their irresistible songs. While in a cold state, Ulysses instructed his crew to fill their ears with wax so that they would not be tempted by the music. He also asked the crew to tie him to the mast so that he could listen for himself but be restrained from submitting to the temptation to steer the ship closer when the music put him into a hot state.

Ulysses successfully solved his problem. For most of us, however, self-control issues arise because we underestimate the effect of arousal. This is something the behavioral economist George Loewenstein (1996) calls the 'hot–cold empathy gap.' When in a cold state, we do not appreciate how much our desires and our behavior will be altered when we are 'under the influence' of arousal. As a result, our behavior reflects a certain naïveté about the effects that context can have on choice. Tom is on a diet and agrees to go out on a business dinner, thinking that he will be able to limit himself to one glass of wine and no dessert. But the host orders a second bottle of wine and the waiter brings by the dessert cart, and all bets are off. Marilyn thinks that she can go into a department store when they are having a big sale and just see whether they have something on sale that she really needs. She ends up with shoes that hurt (but were 70 percent off). Robert thinks he will engage only in safe sex, but then must make all the crucial decisions while aroused. Similar problems affect those who have problems with smoking, alcohol, a failure to exercise, excessive borrowing, and insufficient savings.

Self-control problems can be illuminated by thinking about an individual as containing two semiautonomous selves, a far-sighted 'Planner' and a myopic 'Doer.' You can think of the Planner as speaking for your Reflective System, or the Mr Spock lurking within you, and the Doer as heavily influenced by the Automatic System, or everyone's Homer Simpson. The Planner is trying to promote your long-term welfare but must cope with the feelings, mischief, and strong will of the Doer, who is exposed to the temptations that come with arousal. Recent research in neuroeconomics (yes, there really is such a field) has found evidence consistent with this two-system conception of self-control. Some parts of the brain get tempted, and other parts are prepared to enable us to resist temptation by assessing how we should react to the temptation.[1] Sometimes the two parts of the brain can be in severe conflict – a kind of battle that one or the other is bound to lose.

MINDLESS CHOOSING

The cashew problem is not only one of temptation. It also involves the type of mindless behavior we discussed in the context of inertia. In many situations, people put themselves into an 'automatic pilot' mode, in which they are not actively paying attention to the task at hand. (The Automatic System is very comfortable that way.) On a Saturday morning when we set out to run an errand, we can easily find ourselves driving our usual route to work – until we realize we are headed in the opposite direction from our intended destination, the grocery store. On a Sunday morning, we follow our ordinary routine with coffee and the newspaper – until we realize that we had arranged to meet a friend for brunch an hour earlier. Eating turns out to be one of the most mindless activities we do. Many of us simply eat whatever is put in front of us. That is why even massive bowls of cashews are likely to be consumed completely, regardless of the quality of the food that is soon to be arriving.

The same is true of popcorn – even stale popcorn. A few years ago, Brian Wansink and his colleagues ran an experiment in a Chicago movie theater in which moviegoers found themselves with a free bucket of stale popcorn.[2] (It had been popped five days earlier and stored so as to ensure that it would actually squeak when eaten.) People were not specifically informed of its staleness, but they didn't like the popcorn. As one moviegoer said, 'It was like eating Styrofoam packing peanuts.' In the experiment, half of the moviegoers received a big bucket of popcorn and half received a medium-sized bucket. On average, recipients of the big bucket ate about 53 percent more popcorn – even though they didn't really like it. After the movie, Wansink asked the recipients of the big bucket whether they might have eaten more because of the size of their bucket. Most denied the possibility, saying, 'Things like that don't trick me.' But they were wrong.

The same is true of soup. In another Wansink (2006) masterpiece, people sat down to a large bowl of Campbell's tomato soup and were told to eat as much as they wanted. Unbeknownst to them, the soup bowls were designed to refill themselves (with empty bottoms connected to machinery beneath the table). No matter how much soup subjects ate, the bowl never emptied. Many people just kept eating, not paying attention to the fact that they were really eating a great deal of soup, until the experiment was (mercifully) ended. Large plates and large packages mean more eating; they are a form of choice architecture, and they work as major nudges. (Hint: if you would like to lose weight, get smaller plates, buy little packages of what you like, and don't keep tempting food in the refrigerator.)

When self-control problems and mindless choosing are combined, the result is a series of bad outcomes for real people. Millions of Americans still smoke in spite of the evidence that smoking has terrible health consequences, and, significantly, the overwhelming majority of smokers say that they would like to quit. Nearly two-thirds of Americans are overweight or obese. Many people never get around to joining their company's retirement savings plan, even when it is heavily subsidized. Together, these facts suggest that significant numbers of people could benefit from a nudge.

SELF-CONTROL STRATEGIES

Since people are at least partly aware of their weaknesses, they take steps to engage outside help. We make lists to help us remember what to buy at the grocery store. We buy an alarm clock to help us get up in the morning. We ask friends to stop us from having dessert or to fortify our efforts to quit smoking. In these cases, our Planners are taking steps to control the actions of our Doers, often by trying to change the incentives that Doers face.

Unfortunately, Doers are often difficult to rein in (think of controlling Homer), and they can foil the best efforts of Planners. Consider the mundane but revealing example of the alarm clock. The optimistic Planner sets the alarm for 6:15 a.m., hoping for a full day of work, but the sleepy Doer turns off the alarm and goes back to sleep until 9:00. This can lead to fierce battles between the Planner and the Doer. Some Planners put the alarm clock on the other side of the room, so the Doer at least has to get up to turn it off, but if the Doer crawls back into bed, all is lost. Fortunately, enterprising firms sometimes offer to help the Planner out.

Consider the alarm clock 'Clocky,' pictured in Figure 2.1. Clocky is the 'alarm clock that runs away and hides if you don't get out of bed.' With Clocky, the Planner sets the number of snooze minutes

PRODUCT

Clocky® (patent pending) is an alarm clock that runs away and hides if you don't get out of bed on time. The alarm sounds, you press the snooze, and Clocky will roll off of the bedside table, jump to the floor, and wheel away, bumping mindlessly into objects until he finds a spot to rest. When the alarm sounds again, you must awaken to search for him. Clocky will find new spots everyday, kind of like a hide-and-seek game.

Clocky alarm clocks were designed to reinterpret the common alarm clock into something that is not stressful and obnoxious but amusing and a better fit between humans and technology.

Figure 2.1. *Clocky advertisement (Used by permission of nanda llc.)*

the Doer will be permitted in the morning. When that number runs out, the clock jumps off the night stand and moves around the room making annoying sounds. The only way to turn the damn thing off is to get out of bed and find it. By that time, even a groggy Doer is awake.

Planners have a number of available strategies, such as Clocky, to control recalcitrant Doers, but they can sometimes use some help from outsiders. We will be exploring how private and public institutions can provide that help. In daily life, one strategy involves informal bets. Thaler once helped a young colleague by using this strategy. The colleague (let's call him David) had been hired as a new faculty member with the expectation that he would complete the requirements for his Ph.D. before he arrived, or at worst within his first year as a faculty member. David had lots of incentives to finish his thesis, including a strong financial incentive: until he graduated the university treated him as an 'instructor' rather than an assistant professor and did not make its normal contributions to his retirement plan, which amounted to 10 percent of his salary (thousands of dollars a year). David's inner Planner knew that he needed to stop procrastinating and get his thesis done, but his Doer was involved in many other more exciting projects and always put off the drudgery of writing up the thesis. (Thinking about new ideas is usually more fun than writing up old ones.)

That is when Thaler intervened by offering David the following deal. David would write Thaler a series of checks for $100, payable on the first day of each of the next few months. Thaler would cash each check if David did not put a copy of a new chapter of the thesis under his door by midnight of the corresponding month. Furthermore, Thaler promised to use the money to have a party to which David would not be invited. David completed his thesis on schedule four months later, never having missed a deadline (though most chapters were completed within mere minutes of being due). It is instructive that this incentive scheme worked even though David's monetary incentive from the university was greater than $100 a month, just from the retirement contribution alone.

The scheme worked because the pain of having Thaler cash the

49

check and consume some good wine without him was more salient than the rather abstract and pallid forgone contribution to his retirement savings plan. Many of Thaler's friends have threatened to go into business competing with him on this incentive plan, though Thaler points out that in order to go into this business, you have to be known as a big enough jerk actually to cash the check.

Sometimes friends can adopt such betting strategies together. John Romalis and Dean Karlan, two economists, adopted an ingenious arrangement for weight loss. When John and Dean were in graduate school in economics, they noticed that they were putting on weight, especially during the period when they were on the job market and being wined and dined by potential employers. They made a pact. Each agreed to lose thirty pounds over a period of nine months. If either failed, he had to pay the other $10,000. The bet was a big success; both met their target. They then turned to the more difficult problem of keeping the weight off. The rules they adopted were that on one day's notice, either one could call for a weigh-in. If either was found to be over the target weight, he would have to pay the other an agreed sum. In four years, there were several weigh-ins, and only once was either one over target (the resulting fine was paid in full immediately). Notice that as in the case of David's thesis bet, Dean and John were acknowledging that without the bet to encourage them, they would have eaten too much, even though they still would have wanted to lose the weight.

More formal versions of these strategies are easy to imagine. In Chapter 14 we will encounter the Web site Stickk.com (of which Karlan is a cofounder), which gives people a method by which their Planners can constrain their Doers. In some situations, people may even want the government to help them deal with their self-control problems. In extreme cases, governments might ban some items (such as heroin use, prostitution, and drunken driving). Such bans can be seen as pure rather than libertarian paternalism, though third-party interests are also at stake. In other cases, individuals may prefer a less intrusive role for the government. For example, smokers might benefit from cigarette taxes, which discourage consumption without forbidding it.[3] Also, some states have attempted to help gamblers by creating a mechanism by which they can put themselves on a list of people who are banned from casinos (again see Chapter 14 for details). Since no one is required to sign up, and since a refusal to do so is close to costless, this approach really can be counted as libertarian as we understand the term.

One interesting example of a government-imposed self-control strategy is daylight saving time (or summer time, as it is called in many parts of the world). Surveys reveal that most people think that daylight saving time is a great idea, primarily because they enjoy the 'extra' hour of daylight during the evening. Of course, the number of daylight hours on a given day is fixed, and setting the clocks ahead one hour does nothing to increase the amount of daylight. The simple change of the labels on the hours of the day, calling 'six o'clock' by the name 'seven o'clock,' nudges us all into waking up an hour earlier. Along with having more time to enjoy an evening softball game, we end up saving energy too. Historical note: the idea was first suggested by Benjamin Franklin during his tenure as an American delegate in Paris. A well-known skinflint, Franklin calculated that thousands of pounds of candle wax could be saved with his idea. However, the idea did not catch on until World War I.

In many cases, markets provide self-control services, and government is not needed at all. Companies can make a lot of money by strengthening Planners in their battle with Doers, often doing well by doing good. An interesting example is a distinctive financial services institution that used to be quite popular: the Christmas savings club. Here is how a Christmas club typically works. In November (around Thanksgiving) a customer opens an account at her local bank and commits herself to depositing a given amount (say $10) each week for the next year. Funds cannot be withdrawn until a year later, when the total amount is redeemed, just in time for the Christmas shopping season. The usual interest rate on these accounts is close to zero.

Think about the Christmas club in economic terms. This is an account with no liquidity (you can't take your money out for a year), high transaction costs (you have to make deposits every week), and a near-zero rate of return. It is an easy homework exercise in an economics class to prove that such an institution cannot exist. Yet for many years Christmas clubs were widely used, with billions of dollars in investments. If we realize that we are dealing with Humans rather than Econs, it is not hard to explain why the clubs flourished. Households lacking enough money for Christmas giving would resolve to solve the problem next year by joining a Christmas club. The inconvenience of making the deposits and the loss of money paid in interest would be small prices to pay in return for the assurance of having enough money to buy gifts. And think back to Ulysses, tying himself to the mast – the fact that money could not be withdrawn was a plus, not a minus. The absence of liquidity was precisely the point. Christmas clubs are in many ways an adult version of a child's piggy bank, designed to make it easier to put money in than to take money out. The fact that it is hard to withdraw money is entirely the point of the device.

While Christmas clubs still exist, they have been made unnecessary for most households by the advent of credit cards.* Since Christmas shopping can now be financed, households no longer find it necessary to save up in advance. This is not to say, of course, that the new regime is in all respects better. Saving at a zero percent interest rate with no opportunity to withdraw the funds may seem dumb, and it is clearly worse than just depositing the money into an interest-bearing account, but earning a zero interest rate may well be preferable to paying 18 percent or more on credit card debt.

The market battle between credit cards and Christmas clubs is a good illustration of a more general point, one to which we will return. Markets provide strong incentives for firms to cater to the demands of consumers, and firms will compete to meet those demands, whether or not those demands represent the wisest choices. One firm might

* Although Christmas clubs have become unpopular, most Americans still make use of a non-interest bearing savings vehicle that might be called the Easter account. Three-quarters of Americans get refunds when they file their tax return, with the average refund being more than two thousand dollars. If these refunds were described as interest-free loans to the government they would probably not be so popular. Although taxpayers could adjust their withholding rates to reduce the size of their refund, and in principle could earn interest on these funds throughout the year, many prefer to get the refund as a way of being forced to save. When the refund comes, it feels like a windfall.

devise a clever self-control device such as a Christmas club, but that firm cannot prevent another firm from offering to lend people money in anticipation of the receipts of those funds. Credit cards and Christmas clubs compete, and indeed both are offered by the same institutions – banks. While competition does drive down prices, it does not always lead to an outcome that is best for consumers.

Even when we're on our way to making good choices, competitive markets find ways to get us to overcome our last shred of resistance to bad ones. At O'Hare Airport in Chicago, two food vendors compete across the aisle from each other. One sells fruit, yogurt, and other healthy foods. The other sells Cinnabons, sinful cinnamon buns that have a whopping 730 calories and 24 grams of fat. Your Planner may have set the course for the yogurt and fruit stand, but the Cinnabon outlet blasts the aromas from their ovens directly into the walkway in front of the store. Care to guess which of the two stores always has the longer line?

MENTAL ACCOUNTING

Alarm clocks and Christmas clubs are external devices people use to solve their self-control problems. Another way to approach these problems is to adopt internal control systems, otherwise known as *mental accounting*. Mental accounting is the system (sometimes implicit) that households use to evaluate, regulate, and process their home budget. Almost all of us use mental accounts, even if we're not aware that we're doing so.

The concept is beautifully illustrated by an exchange between the actors Gene Hackman and Dustin Hoffman in one of those extra features offered on DVDs. Hackman and Hoffman were friends back in their starving artist days, and Hackman tells the story of visiting Hoffman's apartment and having his host ask him for a loan. Hackman agreed to the loan, but then they went into Hoffman's kitchen, where several mason jars were lined up on the counter, each containing money. One jar was labeled 'rent,' another 'utilities,' and so forth. Hackman asked why, if Hoffman had so much money in jars, he could possibly need a loan, whereupon Hoffman pointed to the food jar, which was empty.*

According to economic theory (and simple logic), money is 'fungible,' meaning that it doesn't come with labels. Twenty dollars in the rent jar can buy just as much food as the same amount in the food jar. But households adopt mental accounting schemes that violate fungibility for the same reasons that organizations do: to control spending. Most organizations have budgets for various activities, and anyone who has ever worked in such an organization has experienced the frustration of not being able to make an important purchase because the relevant account is already depleted. The fact that there is unspent money in another account is considered no more relevant than the money sitting in the rent jar on Dustin Hoffman's kitchen counter.

At the household level, violations of fungibility are everywhere. One of the most creative examples of mental accounting was invented by a finance professor we know. At the beginning of each year, he designates a certain amount of money (say $2,000) as his intended gift to the United Way charity. Then if anything bad happens to him during the year – a parking ticket, for example – he mentally deducts the fine against the United Way gift. This provides him 'insurance' against minor financial mishaps.†

You can also see mental accounting in action at the casino. Watch a gambler who is lucky enough to win some money early in the evening. You might see him take the money he has won and put it into one pocket and put the money he brought with him to gamble that evening (yet another mental account) into a different pocket. Gamblers even have a term for this. The money that has recently been won is called 'house money' because in gambling parlance the casino is referred to as the house. Betting some of the money that you have just won is referred to as 'gambling with the house's money,' as if it were, somehow, different from some other kind of money.

---

* We have posted this Hackman-Hoffman clip on the Nudge blog at nudges.word press.com.
† You might think that this deprives the United Way of money, but not so. The professor has to make sure his intended gift is large enough to cover all his mishaps.

Experimental evidence reveals that people are more willing to gamble with money that they consider house money.[4]

This same mentality affects people who never gamble. When investments pay off, people are willing to take big chances with their 'winnings.' For example, mental accounting contributed to the large increase in stock prices in the 1990s, as many people took on more and more risk with the justification that they were playing only with their gains from the past few years. Similarly, people are far more likely to splurge impulsively on a big luxury purchase when they receive an unexpected windfall than with savings that they have accumulated over time, even if those savings are fully available to be spent.

Mental accounting matters precisely because the accounts are treated as nonfungible. True, the mason jars used by Dustin Hoffman (and his parents' generation) have largely disappeared. But many households continue to designate accounts for various uses: children's education, vacations, retirement, and so forth. In many cases these are literally different accounts, as opposed to entries in a ledger. The sanctity of these accounts can lead to seemingly bizarre behavior, such as simultaneously borrowing and lending at very different rates. David Gross and Nick Souleles (2002) found that the typical household in their sample of Americans had more than $5,000 in liquid assets (typically in savings accounts earning less than 5 percent a year) and nearly $3,000 in credit card balances, carrying a typical interest rate of 18 percent or more. Using the money from the savings account to pay off the credit card debt amounts to what economists call an arbitrage opportunity – buying low and selling high – but the vast majority of households fail to take advantage.

Just as with Christmas clubs, though, this behavior might not be as stupid as it looks. Many of these households have borrowed up to the limits that their credit cards set. They may realize that if they paid off the credit card debt from the savings account, they would soon run up the cards to their limits once again. (And credit card companies, fully aware of this, are often more than willing to extend more credit to those who have reached the limit, as long as they aren't yet falling behind on interest payments.) Keeping the money in the separate accounts is thus another costly self-control strategy, just like the Christmas club.

Of course, many people do not suffer from an inability to save. Some people actually have trouble spending. If their problem is extreme, we call such people misers, but even regular folks can find that they don't give themselves enough treats. We have a friend named Dennis who has adopted a clever mental accounting strategy to deal with this problem. When Dennis turned sixty-five, he started collecting Social Security payments, although both he and his wife continue to work full-time. Since he has been a good saver over the years (in part because his employer has a mandatory and generous retirement plan), Dennis wanted to be sure he would do the things he enjoys (especially trips to Paris with lots of eating) now while he is still healthy, and not be put off by the expense. So he opened a special savings account for his Social Security checks and has designated the money in this account as a 'fun account.' A fancy new bike or a case of good wine would be acceptable purchases from this account, but a repair to the roof would certainly not.

For each of us, using mental accounts can be extremely valuable. They make life both more fun and more secure. Many of us could benefit from a near-sacrosanct 'rainy day' account *and* from a freely available 'entertainment and fun' account. Understanding mental accounts would also improve public policy. As we will see, if we want to encourage savings, it will be important to direct the increased savings into a mental (or real) account where spending it will not be too big a temptation.

3

Following the Herd

The Reverend Jim Jones was the founder and leader of the People's Temple. In 1978 Jones, facing charges of tax evasion, moved most of his one thousand followers from San Francisco to a small settlement in Guyana, which he named Jonestown. Facing a federal investigation for reported acts of child abuse and torture, Jones decided that his followers should poison their children and then themselves. They prepared vats of poison. A few people resisted; a few others shouted out their protest, but they were silenced. Following Jones's orders, and the social pressures imposed by one another, mothers and fathers duly poisoned their children. Then they poisoned themselves. Their bodies were found arm in arm, lying together.[1]

Econs (and some economists we know) are pretty unsociable creatures. They communicate with others if they can gain something from the encounter, they care about their reputations, and they will learn from others if actual information can be obtained, but Econs are not followers of fashion. Their hemlines will not go up and down except for practical reasons, and ties, if they exist at all in a world of Econs, will not grow narrower and wider simply as a matter of style. (By the way, ties were originally used as napkins; they actually had a function.) Humans, on the other hand, are frequently nudged by other Humans. Sometimes massive social changes, in markets and politics alike, start with a small social nudge.

Humans are not exactly lemmings, but they are easily influenced by the statements and deeds of others. (Again by the way, lemmings do not really commit mass suicide by following one another into the ocean. Our widely shared and somewhat defamatory beliefs about lemmings are based on an all-too-human urban legend – that is, people believe this because they are following other people. By contrast, the tale of mass suicide at Jonestown is no legend.) If you see a movie scene in which people are smiling, you are more likely to smile yourself (whether or not the movie is funny); yawns are contagious, too. Conventional wisdom has it that if two people live together for a long time, they start to look like each other. This bit of folk wisdom turns out to be true. (For the curious: they grow to look alike partly because of nutrition – shared diets and eating habits – but much of the effect is simple imitation of facial expressions.) In fact couples who end up looking alike also tend to be happier!

In this chapter, we try to understand how and why social influences work. An understanding of those influences is important in our context for two reasons. First, most people learn from others. This is usually good, of course. Learning from others is how individuals and societies develop. But many of our biggest misconceptions also come from others. When social influences have caused people to have false or biased beliefs, then some nudging may help. The second reason why this topic is important for our purposes is that one of the most effective ways to nudge (for good or evil) is via social influence. In Jonestown, that influence was so strong that an entire population committed suicide. But social influences have also created miracles, large and small. In many cities, including ours, dog owners now carry plastic bags when they walk their dogs, and strolling through the park has become much more pleasant as a result. This has happened even though the risk of being fined for unclean dog walking is essentially zero. Choice architects need to know how to encourage other socially beneficial behavior, and also how to discourage events like the one that occurred in Jonestown.

Social influences come in two basic categories. The first involves information. If many people do something or think something, their actions and their thoughts convey information about what might be best for you to do or think. The second involves peer pressure. If you care about what other people think about you (perhaps in the mistaken belief that they are paying some attention to what you are doing – see below), then you might go along with the crowd to avoid their wrath or curry their favor.

For a quick glance at the power of social nudges, consider just a few research findings:

1. Teenage girls who see that other teenagers are having children are more likely to become pregnant themselves.*
2. Obesity is contagious. If your best friends get fat, your risk of gaining weight goes up.
3. Broadcasters mimic one another, producing otherwise inexplicable fads in programming. (Think reality television, *American Idol* and its siblings, game shows that come and go, the rise and fall and rise of science fiction, and so forth.)
4. The academic effort of college students is influenced by their peers, so much so that the random assignments of first-year students to dormitories or roommates can have big consequences for their grades and hence on their future prospects. (Maybe parents should worry less about which college their kids go to and more about which roommate they get.)
5. In the American judicial system, federal judges on three-judge panels are affected by the votes of their colleagues. The typical Republican appointee shows pretty liberal voting patterns when sitting with two Democratic appointees, and the typical Democratic appointee shows pretty conservative voting patterns when sitting with two Republican appointees. Both sets of appointees show far more moderate voting patterns when they are sitting with at least one judge appointed by a president of the opposing political party.[2]

The bottom line is that Humans are easily nudged by other Humans. Why? One reason is that we like to conform.

---

* For this and all the other examples, we leave out the implied phrase 'holding everything else constant.' So what we mean here is that controlling for other risk factors that predict teenage pregnancy, girls are more likely to get pregnant if they see other girls doing so.

DOING WHAT OTHERS DO

Imagine that you find yourself in a group of six people, engaged in a test of visual perception. You are given a ridiculously simple task. You are supposed to match a particular line, shown on a large white card, to the one of three comparison lines, projected onto a screen, that is identical to it in length.

In the first three rounds of this test, everything proceeds smoothly and easily. People make their matches aloud, in sequence, and everyone agrees with everyone else. But on the fourth round, something odd happens. The five other people in the group announce their matches before you – and every one makes an obvious error. It is now time for you to make your announcement. What will you do?

If you are like most people, you think it is easy to predict your behavior in this task: You will say exactly what you think. You'll call it as you see it. You are independent-minded and so you will tell the truth. But if you are a Human, and you really participated in the experiment, you might well follow those who preceded you, and say what they say, thus defying the evidence of your own senses.

In the 1950s Solomon Asch (1995), a brilliant social psychologist, conducted a series of experiments in just this vein. When asked to decide on their own, without seeing judgments from others, people almost never erred, since the test was easy. But when everyone else gave an incorrect answer, people erred more than one-third of the time. Indeed, in a series of twelve questions, nearly three-quarters of people went along with the group at least once, defying the evidence of their own senses. Notice that in Asch's experiment, people were responding to the decisions of strangers, whom they would probably never see again. They had no particular reason to want those strangers to like them.

Asch's findings seem to capture something universal about humanity. Conformity experiments have been replicated and extended in more than 130 experiments from seventeen countries, including Zaire, Germany, France, Japan, Norway, Lebanon, and Kuwait (Sunstein, 2003). The overall pattern of errors – with people conforming between 20 and 40 percent of the time – does not show huge differences across nations. And though 20 to 40 percent of the time might not seem large, remember that this task was very simple. It is almost as if people can be nudged into identifying a picture of a dog as a cat as long as other people before them have done so.

Why, exactly, do people sometimes ignore the evidence of their own senses? We have already sketched the two answers. The first involves the information conveyed by people's answers; the second involves peer pressure and the desire not to face the disapproval of the group. In Asch's own studies, several of the conformists said, in private interviews, that their initial perceptions must have been wrong. If everyone in the room accepts a certain proposition, or sees things in a certain way, you might conclude that they are probably right. Remarkably, recent brain-imaging work has suggested that when people conform in Asch-like settings, they actually see the situation as everyone else does.[3]

On the other hand, social scientists generally find less conformity, in the same basic circumstances as Asch's experiments, when people are asked to give anonymous answers. People become more likely to conform when they know that other people will see what they have to say. Sometimes people will go along with the group even when they think, or know, that everyone else has blundered. Unanimous groups are able to provide the strongest nudges – even when the question is an easy one, and people ought to know that everyone else is wrong.

Asch's experiments involved evaluations with pretty obvious answers. Most of the time, it isn't hard to assess the length of lines. What if the task is made a bit more difficult? The question is especially important for our purposes, because we are particularly interested in how people are influenced, or can be influenced, in dealing with problems that are both hard and unfamiliar. Some key studies were undertaken in the 1930s by the psychologist Muzafer Sherif (1937). In Sherif's experiment, people were placed in a dark room, and a small pinpoint of light was positioned at some distance in front of them. The light was actually stationary, but because of a perceptual illusion called the autokinetic effect, it appeared to move.

On each of several trials, Sherif asked people to estimate the distance that the light had moved. When polled individually, subjects did not agree with one another, and their answers varied significantly from one trial to another. This is not surprising; because the light did not move, any judgment about distance was a stab in the literal dark.

But Sherif found big conformity effects when people were asked to act in small groups and to make their estimates in public. Here the individual judgments converged and a group norm, establishing the consensus distance, quickly developed. Over time, the norm remained stable within particular groups, thus leading to a situation in which different groups made, and were strongly committed to, quite different judgments. There is an important clue here about how seemingly similar groups, cities, and even nations can converge on very different beliefs and actions simply because of modest and even arbitrary variations in starting points.

Sherif also tried a nudge. In some experiments, he added a confederate – his own ally, unbeknownst to the people in the study. When he did that, something else happened. If the confederate spoke confidently and firmly, his judgment had a strong influence on the group's assessment. If the confederate's estimate was much higher than those initially made by others, the group's judgment would be inflated; if the confederate's estimate was very low, the group's estimate would fall. A little nudge, if it was expressed confidently, could have major consequences for the group's conclusion. The clear lesson here is that consistent and unwavering people, in the private or public sector, can move groups and practices in their preferred direction.

More remarkable still, the group's judgments became thoroughly internalized, so that people would adhere to them even when reporting on their own – indeed even a year later, and even when participating in new groups whose members offered different judgments. Significantly, the initial judgments were also found to have effects across 'generations.' Even when enough fresh subjects were introduced and others retired so that all the participants were new to the situation, the original group judgment tended to stick, although the person who was originally responsible for it had been long gone.[4] In a series of experiments, people using Sherif's basic method have shown that an arbitrary 'tradition,' in the form of some judgment about the distance, can become entrenched over time, so that many people follow it notwithstanding its original arbitrariness.[5]

We can see here why many groups fall prey to what is known as 'collective conservatism': the tendency of groups to stick to established patterns even as new needs arise. Once a practice (like wearing ties) has become established, it is likely to be perpetuated, even if there is no particular basis for it. Sometimes a tradition can last for a long time, and receive support or at least acquiescence from large numbers of people, even though it was originally the product of a small nudge from a few people or perhaps even one. Of course, a group will shift if it can be shown that the practice is causing serious problems. But if there is uncertainty on that question, people might well continue doing what they have always done.

An important problem here is 'pluralistic ignorance' – that is, ignorance, on the part of all or most, about what other people think. We may follow a practice or a tradition not because we like it, or even think it defensible, but merely because we think that most other people like it. Many social practices persist for this reason, and a small shock, or nudge, can dislodge them.[6] A dramatic example is communism in the former Soviet bloc, which lasted in part because people were unaware how many people despised the regime. Dramatic but less world-historical changes, rejecting long-standing practices, can often be produced by a nudge that starts a kind of bandwagon effect.

Additional experiments, growing out of Asch's basic method, find large conformity effects for judgments of many different kinds.[7] Consider the following finding. People were asked, 'Which one of the following do you feel is the most important problem facing our country today?' Five alternatives were offered: economic recession, educational facilities, subversive activities, mental health, and crime and corruption. Asked privately, a mere 12 percent chose subversive activities. But when exposed to an apparent group consensus unanimously selecting that option, 48 percent of people made the same choice!

In a similar finding, people were asked to consider this statement: 'Free speech being a privilege rather than a right, it is proper for a society to suspend free speech when it feels threatened.' Asked this question individually, only 19 percent of the control group agreed, but confronted with the shared opinion of only four others, 58 percent of people agreed. These results are closely connected with one of Asch's underlying interests, which was to understand how Nazism had been possible. Asch believed that conformity could produce a very persistent nudge, ultimately generating behavior (such as the events in Jonestown) that might seem unthinkable.

Whether or not Asch's work provides an adequate account of the rise of fascism, or the events in Jonestown, there is no question that social pressures nudge people to accept some pretty odd conclusions – and those conclusions might well affect their behavior. An obvious question is whether choice architects can exploit this fact to move people in better directions. Suppose, for example, that a city is trying to encourage people to exercise more, so as to improve their health. If many people are exercising, the city might be able to produce significant changes simply by mentioning that fact. A few influential people, offering strong signals about appropriate behavior, can have a similar effect.

Consider Texas's imaginative and stunningly successful effort to reduce littering on its highways.[8] Texas officials were enormously frustrated by the failure of their well-funded and highly publicized advertising campaigns, which attempted to convince people that it was their civic duty to stop littering. Many of the litterers were men between the ages of eighteen and twenty-four, who were not exactly impressed by the idea that a bureaucratic elite wanted them to change their behavior. Public officials decided that they needed 'a tough-talking slogan that would also address the unique spirit of Texas pride.' Explicitly targeting the unresponsive audience, the state enlisted popular Dallas Cowboys football players to participate in television ads in which they collected litter, smashed beer cans in their bare hands, and growled, 'Don't mess with Texas!' Other spots included popular singers, such as Willie Nelson.

People can now get all kinds of 'Don't Mess with Texas' products,

Figure 3.1. *Don't Mess with Texas logo (Used with permission of Don't Mess with Texas, Texas Department of Transportation)*

from decals to shirts to coffee mugs. One popular decal offers patriotic colors, reflecting both the U.S. flag, and – perhaps more important – the Texas flag (Figure 3.1)!

About 95 percent of Texans now know this slogan, and in 2006 'Don't Mess with Texas' was voted America's favorite slogan by a landslide and was honored with a parade down New York City's Madison Avenue. (We are not making this up. Only in America, to be sure.) More to the point: Within the first year of the campaign, litter in the state had been reduced by a remarkable 29 percent. In its first six years, there was a 72 percent reduction in visible roadside litter. All this happened not through mandates, threats, or coercion but through a creative nudge.

THE SPOTLIGHT EFFECT

One reason why people expend so much effort conforming to social norms and fashions is that they think that others are closely paying attention to what they are doing. If you wear a suit to a social event where everyone else has gone casual, you feel like everyone is looking at you funny and wondering why you are such a geek. If you are subject to such fears, here is a possibly comforting thought: they aren't really paying as much attention to you as you think.

Tom Gilovich and his colleagues have demonstrated that people fall prey to what he calls the 'spotlight effect.'[9] In a typical experiment, Gilovich's team started by doing some research about which entertainer would be most unhip to display on the front of a T-shirt. This research was conducted in the late 1990s, and the winner of this dubious honor was the singer Barry Manilow. When a student arrived for the experiment, he was told to put on a T-shirt with Barry Manilow's picture prominently displayed on the front. The student was then asked to join another group of students who were busy filling out questionnaires. After a minute or so, the experimenter returned, and told the student wearing the T-shirt that he now realized he wanted him to participate in a different study. The student and the experimenter then left the room. At this point the student was asked to guess how many of the other students in the room would be able to identify who was on his T-shirt. The average guess was a bit less than half, 46 percent. In fact, only 21 percent of the group could say who was pictured on his T-shirt.

The moral is that people are paying less attention to you than you believe. If you have a stain on your shirt, don't worry, they probably won't notice. But in part because people do think that everyone has their eyes fixed on them, they conform to what they think people expect.

CULTURAL CHANGE, POLITICAL CHANGE, AND UNPREDICTABILITY

Might culture and politics be affected by conformity? Might companies be able to make money by enlisting conformity? Consider some evidence involving music downloads. Matthew Salganik and his coauthors (2006) created an artificial music market, with 14,341 participants who were visitors to a Web site popular with young people. The participants were given a list of previously unknown songs from unknown bands. They were asked to listen to a brief selection of any songs that interested them, to decide which songs (if any) to download, and to assign a rating to the songs they chose. About half of the participants were asked to make their decisions independently, based on the names of the bands and the songs and their own judgment about the quality of the music. The other half could see how many times each song had been downloaded by other participants. Each participant in this second group was also randomly assigned to one or another of eight possible 'worlds,' each of which evolved on its own; those in any particular world could see only the downloads in their own world. A key question was whether people would be affected by the choices of others – and whether different music would become popular in the different 'worlds.'

Were people nudged by what other people did? There is not the slightest doubt. In all eight worlds, individuals were far more likely to download songs that had been previously downloaded in significant numbers, and far less likely to download songs that had not been as popular. Most strikingly, the success of songs was quite unpredictable, and the songs that did well or poorly in the control group, where people did not see other people's judgments, could perform very differently in the 'social influence worlds.' In those worlds, most songs could become popular or unpopular, with much depending on the choices of the first downloaders. The identical song could be a hit or a failure simply because other people, at the start, were seen to have chosen to download it or not.

In many domains people are tempted to think, after the fact, that an outcome was entirely predictable, and that the success of a musician, an actor, an author, or a politician was inevitable in light of his or her skills and characteristics. Beware of that temptation. Small interventions and even coincidences, at a key stage, can produce large variations in the outcome. Today's hot singer is probably indistinguishable from dozens and even hundreds of equally talented performers whose names you've never heard. We can go further. Most of today's governors are hard to distinguish from dozens or even hundreds of politicians whose candidacies badly fizzled.

The effects of social influences may or may not be deliberately planned by particular people. For a vivid and somewhat hilarious example of how social influences can affect beliefs even if no one plans anything, consider the Seattle Windshield Pitting Epidemic.[10] In late March 1954, a group of people in Bellingham, Washington, noticed some tiny holes, or pits, on their windshields. Local police speculated that the pits had resulted from the actions of vandals, using BBs or buckshot. Soon thereafter, a few people in cities south of Bellingham reported similar damage to their windshields. Within two weeks, the apparent work of vandals had gone even farther south, to the point where two thousand cars were reported as damaged – these evidently not the work of vandals. The threat approached Seattle. The Seattle newspapers duly reported the risk in mid-April, and soon thereafter, several reports of windshield pits came to the attention of local police.

Before long those reports reached epidemic proportions, leading to intense speculation about what on earth, or elsewhere, could possibly be the cause. Geiger counters found no radioactivity. Some people thought that some odd atmospheric event must have been responsible; others invoked sound waves and a possible shift in the earth's magnetic field; still others pointed to cosmic rays from the sun. By April 16 no fewer than three thousand windshields in the Seattle area were reported to have been 'pitted,' and Seattle's mayor promptly wrote the governor and President Eisenhower: 'What appeared to be a localized outbreak of vandalism in damaged auto windshields and windows in the northern part of Washington State has now spread throughout the Puget Sound area . . . Urge appropriate federal (and state) agencies be instructed to cooperate with local authorities on emergency basis.' In response, the governor created a committee of scientists to investigate this ominous and startling phenomenon.

Their conclusion? The damage, such as it was, was probably 'the result of normal driving conditions in which small objects strike the windshields of cars.' A later investigation, supporting the scientists' conclusion, found that brand new cars lacked pits. The eventual judgment was that the pits 'had been there all along, but no one had noticed them until now.' (You might have a look at your car right now; if you've had it for a while, there's probably a pit, or two, or more.)

The Seattle Windshield Pitting Epidemic was an extreme example of unintentional social nudging, but every day we are influenced by people who are not trying to influence us. Most of us are affected by the eating habits of our eating companions, whatever their intentions. As we have said, obesity is contagious; you're more likely to be overweight if you have a lot of overweight friends. An especially good way to gain weight is to have dinner with other people.[11] On average, those who eat with one other person eat about 35 percent more than they do when they are alone; members of a group of four eat about 75 percent more; those in groups of seven or more eat 96 percent more.*

We are also greatly influenced by consumption norms within the relevant group. A light eater eats much more in a group of heavy eaters. A heavy eater will show more restraint in a light-eating group. The group average thus exerts a significant influence. But there are gender differences as well. Women often eat less on dates; men tend to eat a lot more, apparently with the belief that women are impressed by a lot of manly eating. (Note to men: they aren't.) So if you want to lose some weight, look for a thin colleague to go to lunch with (and don't finish the food on her plate).

If you find yourself nudged by your friends' eating choices, it is unlikely to be because one or another friend decided to nudge you. At the same time, social influences are often used strategically. In particular, advertisers are entirely aware of the power of social influences. Frequently they emphasize that 'most people prefer' their own product, or that 'growing numbers of people' are switching from another brand, which was yesterday's news, to their own, which represents the future. They try to nudge you by telling you what most people are now doing.

In many nations, candidates for public office, or political parties, do the same thing; they emphasize that 'most people are turning to' their preferred candidates, hoping that the very statement can make itself true. Nothing is worse than a perception that voters are leaving

---

* A colleague who raises chickens tells us that they behave the same way. A chicken who has already eaten enough to feel sated will start eating again if a hungry chicken is brought into the next cage.

a candidate in droves. In the United States, a perception of that kind helped to account for the Democratic nomination of John Kerry in 2004 and for the nominations of Barack Obama and John McCain in 2008. When, for example, Democrats shifted from Howard Dean to John Kerry, it was not because each Democratic voter made an independent judgment on Kerry's behalf. It was in large part because of a widespread perception that other people were flocking to Kerry. Duncan Watts's amusing account (2004) is worth quoting at length:

A few weeks before the Iowa caucuses, Kerry's campaign seemed dead, but then he unexpectedly won Iowa, then New Hampshire, and then primary after primary. How did this happen? ... When *everyone* is looking to someone else for an opinion – trying, for example, to pick the Democratic candidate they think everyone else will pick – it's possible that whatever information other people might have gets lost, and instead we get a cascade of imitation that, like a stampeding herd, can start for no apparent reason and subsequently go in any direction with equal likelihood ... We think of ourselves as autonomous individuals, each driven by our internal abilities and desires and therefore solely responsible for our own behavior, particularly when it comes to voting. No voter ever admits – even to herself – that she chose Kerry because he won New Hampshire.

Do social influences matter to the economy? There is no question. As for eating and political choices, so too for money: people's investment decisions are often influenced by the investment decisions of their friends and neighbors. Sometimes it is rational to follow what others have done, but not always, and when investors travel in herds, they can get into serious trouble. Consider the case of investment clubs, which perform especially poorly when members are conformists. In such clubs, too little information gets out; people follow those who speak first, and as a result, the club makes poor investment decisions, and everyone loses a lot of money (Harrington, 2008). Social influences can also have significant effects on the entire market. In fact, they played a key role in producing the recent speculative boom and resulting financial crisis of 2008.

The best account has been given by Robert Shiller, who emphasizes the role of psychological factors and herd behavior in volatile markets (Shiller, 2008). Shiller contends that 'the most important single element to be reckoned with in understanding this or any other speculative boom is the *social contagion* of boom thinking, mediated by the common observation of rapidly rising prices.' He urges that in the process of social contagion, public knowledge is subject to a kind of escalation or spiral, in which most people come to think that optimistic view is correct, simply because everyone else seems to accept it. As the media endorses that view, people end up believing that we are in a 'new era,' and feedback loops help to bring about ever-increasing prices. In his words, the 'price-story-price loop repeats again and again during a speculative bubble.' Eventually the bubble is bound to pop, because it depends on social judgments that cannot be sustained over the long-term.

Of course it is always possible to offer such keen analysis in hindsight, but Shiller predicted it well in advance, and with explicit reference to the effects of social interactions in producing the real estate bubble. His account offers important lessons for future bubbles. There is a warning here for private investors, who should be wary of herd behavior. When your neighbor tells you that you can't lose money buying (fill in the blank here), that is probably a good sign that it is time to get out of that type of investment. There are also lessons for policymakers, who should understand that when people are influencing one another, dramatic upward movements in markets may produce serious risks for investors and for the economy itself.

SOCIAL NUDGES AS CHOICE ARCHITECTURE

The general lesson is clear. If choice architects want to shift behavior and to do so with a nudge, they might simply inform people about what other people are doing. Sometimes the practices of others are surprising, and hence people are much affected by learning what they are. Consider four examples.

Conformity and Tax Compliance

In the context of tax compliance, a real-world experiment conducted by officials in Minnesota produced big changes in behavior.[12] Groups of taxpayers were given four kinds of information. Some were told that their taxes went to various good works, including education, police protection, and fire protection. Others were threatened with information about the risks of punishment for noncompliance. Others were given information about how they might get help if they were confused or uncertain about how to fill out their tax forms. Still others were just told that more than 90 percent of Minnesotans already complied, in full, with their obligations under the tax law.

Only one of these interventions had a significant effect on tax compliance, and it was the last. Apparently some taxpayers are more likely to violate the law because of a misperception – plausibly based on the availability of media or other accounts of cheaters – that the level of compliance is pretty low. When informed that the actual compliance level is high, they become less likely to cheat. It follows that either desirable or undesirable behavior can be increased, at least to some extent, by drawing public attention to what others are doing. (Note to political parties: If you would like to increase turnout, please do *not* lament the large numbers of people who fail to vote.)*

Preserving Petrified Wood

In many contexts, of course, the incidence of undesirable behavior is high. This unhappy fact seems to be a real obstacle to change: if people follow one another, we might end up with a vicious cycle or even a spiral. Is it nonetheless possible to nudge people in better directions?

* In the same category is the finding that people are more likely to recycle if they learn that lots of people are recycling. If a hotel wants people to reuse their towels, for environmental or economic reasons, it would do well to emphasize that most other guests are reusing their towels. The hotel would do even better to provide guests with information about how responsible the previous guests in their room have been!

An ingenious study suggests an affirmative answer, and it reinforces the view that the specific framing of the problem can have a powerful effect. The study was conducted in the Petrified Forest National Park in Arizona, where some visitors like to take souvenir samples home with them, a practice that threatens the very existence of the park. Signs at the park implore people not to take samples away. The question at issue is what the signs should say. The investigators, led by Robert Cialdini, the great guru of social influence who is a professor down the road in Tempe, were pretty sure that the signs currently being used in the park could be improved.[13] So he arranged an experiment.

In all the conditions of the experiment, pieces of petrified wood were scattered along a trail, tempting visitors to take something with them. At two-hour intervals, the language on the signs along the trail was varied. Some signs, similar to those currently used in the park, stressed how bad the problem was: 'Many past visitors have removed the petrified wood from the park, changing the natural state of the Petrified Forest.' Other signs emphasized an injunctive norm: 'Please don't remove the petrified wood from the park, in order to preserve the natural state of the Petrified Forest.' Cialdini's theory predicted that the positive, injunctive norm would be more effective than the negative, informational one. This prediction was confirmed.[14]

Socializing Nondrinking

A related example is the 'social norms' approach, which tries to reduce drinking and other undesirable activities.[15] Consider, for instance, the problem of alcohol abuse by (mostly underage) college students. A survey by the Harvard School of Public Health found that about 44 percent of college students engaged in binge drinking in the two-week period preceding the survey.[16] This is, of course, a problem, but a clue to how to correct it lies in the fact that most students believe that alcohol abuse is far more pervasive than it actually is.[17]

Misperceptions of this kind result in part from the availability heuristic. Incidents of alcohol abuse are easily recalled, and the consequence is to inflate perceptions. College students are influenced by their beliefs about what other college students do, and hence alcohol abuse will inevitably increase if students have an exaggerated sense of how much other students are drinking.

Alert to the possibility of changing behavior by emphasizing the statistical reality, many public officials have tried to nudge people in better directions. Montana, for example, has adopted a large-scale educational campaign, one that has stressed the fact that strong majorities of citizens of Montana do not drink.[18] One advertisement attempts to correct misperceived norms on college campuses by asserting, 'Most (81 percent) of Montana college students have four or fewer alcoholic drinks each week.' Montana applies the same approach to cigarette smoking with an advertisement suggesting that 'Most (70 percent) of Montana teens are tobacco free.' The strategy has produced big improvements in the accuracy of social perceptions and also statistically significant decreases in smoking.[19]

Smiles, Frowns, and Saving Energy

Social nudges can also be used to decrease energy use. To see how, consider a study of the power of social norms, involving nearly three hundred households in San Marcos, California.[20] All of the households were informed about how much energy they had used in previous weeks; they were also given (accurate) information about the average consumption of energy by households in their neighborhood. The effects on behavior were both clear and striking. In the following weeks, the above-average energy users significantly decreased their energy use; the below-average energy users significantly increased their energy use. The latter finding is called a boomerang effect, and it offers an important warning. If you want to nudge people into socially desirable behavior, do not, by any means, let them know that their current actions are better than the social norm.

But here is an even more interesting finding. About half of the households were given not merely descriptive information but also a small, nonverbal signal that their energy consumption was socially approved or socially disapproved. More specifically those households that consumed more than the norm received an unhappy 'emoticon,'

Figure 3.2. *Visual feedback given to power customers in San Marcos, California*

like Figure 3.2a, whereas those that consumed less than the norm received a happy emoticon, like Figure 3.2b.

Unsurprisingly, but significantly, the big energy users showed an even larger decrease when they received the unhappy emoticon. The more important finding was that when below-average energy users received the happy emoticon, the boomerang effect completely disappeared! When they were merely told that their energy use was below average, they felt that they had some 'room' to increase consumption, but when the informational message was combined with an emotional nudge, they didn't adjust their use upward.

Many people, including Republicans and Democrats alike, are arguing for energy conservation on grounds of national security, economic growth, and environmental protection. To promote energy conservation, a great deal can be done with well-chosen social nudges. We will have more to say about how choice architecture can be used to help the environment later.

PRIMING

Thus far we have been focusing on people's attention to the thoughts and behavior of other people. Closely related work shows the power of 'priming.' Priming refers to the somewhat mysterious workings of the Automatic System of the brain. Research shows that subtle influences can increase the ease with which certain information comes to mind. Imagine playing a word-association game with Homer Simpson and you will get the idea. Sometimes the merest hint of an idea or concept will trigger an association that can stimulate action. These 'primes' occur in social situations, and their effects can be surprisingly powerful.

In surveys, people are often asked whether they are likely to engage in certain behavior – to vote, to lose weight, to purchase particular products. Those who engage in surveys want to catalogue behavior, not to influence it. But social scientists have discovered an odd fact: when they measure people's intentions, they affect people's conduct. The 'mere-measurement effect' refers to the finding that when people are asked what they intend to do, they become more likely to act in accordance with their answers. This finding can be found in many contexts. If people are asked whether they intend to eat certain foods, to diet, or to exercise, their answers to the questions will affect their behavior.[21] In our parlance, the mere-measurement effect is a nudge, and it can be used by private or public nudgers.

Campaign officials want to encourage their supporters to vote. How can they do that? One obvious method is to emphasize the stakes; another is to decrease the cost and burdens, by making it easier for people to get to the polls. But there is another way. It turns out that if you ask people, the day before the election, whether they intend to vote, you can increase the probability of their voting by as much as 25 percent![22] Or suppose that the goal is to increase new purchases of a certain product, such as cell phones or automobiles. A study of a nationally representative sample of more than forty thousand people asked a simple question: Do you intend to buy a new car in the next six months?[23] The very question increased purchase rates by 35 percent. Or suppose that an official wants to encourage people to take steps to improve their own health. With respect to health-related behavior, significant changes have been produced by measuring people's intentions.[24] If people are asked how often they expect to floss their teeth in the next week, they floss more. If people are asked whether they intend to consume fatty foods in the next week, they consume less in the way of fatty foods.

The nudge provided by asking people what they intend to do can be accentuated by asking them when and how they plan to do it. This insight falls into the category of what the great psychologist Kurt Lewin called 'channel factors,' a term he used for small influences that could either facilitate or inhibit certain behaviors. Think about the 'channel' as similar to the path a river takes after the spring snow melt. The path can be determined by seemingly tiny changes in the landscape. For people, Lewin argued that similarly tiny factors can create surprisingly strong inhibitors to behavior that people 'want' to take. Often we can do more to facilitate good behavior by removing some small obstacle than by trying to shove people in a certain direction. An early illustration of Lewin's idea was produced by Leventhal, Singer, and Jones (1965) on the campus of Yale University. The subjects were Yale seniors who were given some persuasive education about the risks of tetanus and the importance of going to the health center to receive an inoculation. Most of the students were convinced by the lecture and said that they planned to go get the shot, but these good intentions did not lead to much action. Only 3 percent actually went and got the shot.

Other subjects were given the same lecture but were also given a copy of a campus map with the location of the health center circled. They were then asked to look at their weekly schedules, make a plan for when they would go and get the shot, and look at the map and decide what route they would take. With these nudges, 28 percent of the students managed to show up and get their tetanus shot. Notice that this manipulation was very subtle. The students were all seniors and surely knew where the health center was located (Yale is not a huge campus), and they were not given an actual appointment. Still, nine times as many students got shots, illustrating the potential power of channel factors.

Slightly broadening these findings, social scientists have found that they can 'prime' people into certain forms of behavior by offering simple and apparently irrelevant cues. It turns out that if certain objects are made visible and salient, people's behavior can be affected. Objects characteristic of business environments, such as briefcases and boardroom tables, make people more competitive, less cooperative, and less generous.[25] Smells matter too: mere exposure to the scent of an all-purpose cleaner makes people keep their environment cleaner while they eat.[26] In both cases, people were not consciously aware of the effect of the cue on their behavior. Or consider this one: people's judgments about strangers are affected by whether they are drinking iced coffee or hot coffee! Those given iced coffee are more likely to see other people as more selfish, less sociable, and, well, colder than those who are given hot coffee.[27] This, too, happens quite unconsciously.

The three social influences that we have emphasized – information, peer pressure, and priming – can easily be enlisted by private and public nudgers. As we will see, both business and governments can use the power of social influence to promote many good (and bad) causes.

4

When Do We Need a Nudge?

We have seen that people perform amazing feats but also commit ditzy blunders. What's the best response? Choice architecture and its effects cannot be avoided, and so the short answer is an obvious one, call it the golden rule of libertarian paternalism: offer nudges that are most likely to help and least likely to inflict harm.* A slightly longer answer is that people will need nudges for decisions that are difficult and rare, for which they do not get prompt feedback, and when they have trouble translating aspects of the situation into terms that they can easily understand.

In this chapter we try to put some flesh on these points. We begin by specifying the kinds of situations in which people are least likely to make good choices. We then turn to questions about the potential magic of markets and ask whether and when free markets and open competition will tend to exacerbate rather than mitigate the effects of human frailty. The key point here is that for all their virtues, markets often give companies a strong incentive to cater to (and profit from) human frailties, rather than to try to eradicate them or to minimize their effects.

---

* Camerer et al. (2003) call for 'asymmetric paternalism,' which they define as taking steps to help the least sophisticated people while imposing minimal harm on everyone else. Our golden rule is in the spirit of their formulation.

FRAUGHT CHOICES

Suppose you are told that a group of people will have to make some choice in the near future. You are the choice architect. You are trying to decide how to design the choice environment, what kinds of nudges to offer, and how subtle the nudges should be. What do you need to know to design the best possible choice environment?

Benefits Now – Costs Later

We have seen that predictable problems arise when people must make decisions that test their capacity for self-control. Many choices in life, such as whether to wear a blue shirt or a white one, lack important self-control elements. Self-control issues are most likely to arise when choices and their consequences are separated in time. At one extreme are what might be called investment goods, such as exercise, flossing, and dieting. For these goods the costs are borne immediately, but the benefits are delayed. For investment goods, most people err on the side of doing too little. Although there are some exercise nuts and flossing freaks, it seems safe to say that not many people are resolving on New Year's Eve to floss less next year and to stop using the exercise bike so much.

At the other extreme are what might be called sinful goods: smoking, alcohol, and jumbo chocolate doughnuts are in this category. We get the pleasure now and suffer the consequences later. Again we can use the New Year's resolution test: how many people vow to smoke more cigarettes, drink more martinis, or have more chocolate doughnuts in the morning next year? Both investment goods and sinful goods are prime candidates for nudges. Most (nonanorexic) people do not need any special encouragement to eat another brownie, but they could use some help exercising more.

Degree of Difficulty

Nearly everyone over the age of six can tie shoelaces, play a respectable game of tic-tac-toe, and spell the word *cat*. But only a few of us can tie a decent bow tie, play a masterly game of chess, or spell (much less pronounce) the name of the psychologist Mihály Csíkszentmihályi. Of course, we learn to cope with the harder problems. We can buy a pretied bow tie, read a book about chess, and look up the spelling of Csíkszentmihályi on the Web (then copy and paste every time we have to use the name). We use spell checkers and spreadsheets to help with harder problems. But many problems in life are quite difficult, and often there is no technology as easy as a spell checker available to help. We are more likely to need more help picking the right mortgage than choosing the right loaf of bread.

Frequency

Even hard problems become easier with practice. Both of us have managed to learn how to serve a tennis ball into the service court with reasonable regularity (and in Sunstein's case, even velocity), but it took some time. The first time people try to execute this motion, they are lucky if the ball goes over the net, much less into the service box. Practice makes perfect (or at least better).

Unfortunately, some of life's most important decisions do not come with many opportunities to practice. Most students choose a college only once. Outside of Hollywood, most of us choose a spouse, well, not more than two or three times. Few of us get to try many different careers. And outside of science fiction, we get one chance to save for retirement (though we can make some adjustments along the way). Generally, the higher the stakes, the less often we are able to practice. Most of us buy houses and cars not more than once or twice a decade, but we are really practiced at grocery shopping. Most families have mastered the art of milk inventory control, not by solving the relevant mathematical equation but through trial and error.*

---

* There is a deep irony here. Many economists have dismissed psychology experiments on the grounds that the experiments are only for 'low stakes' and that people

None of this is to say that the government should be telling people whom to marry or what to study. This is a book about *libertarian* paternalism. At this stage we just want to stress that rare, difficult choices are good candidates for nudges.

Feedback

Even practice does not make perfect if people lack good opportunities for learning. Learning is most likely if people get immediate, clear feedback after each try. Suppose you are practicing your putting skills on the practice green. If you hit ten balls toward the same hole, it is easy to get a sense of how hard you have to hit the ball. Even the least talented golfers will soon learn to gauge distance under these circumstances. Suppose instead you were putting the golf balls but not getting to see where they were going. In that environment, you could putt all day and never get any better.

Alas, many of life's choices are like practicing putting without being able to see where the balls end up, and for one simple reason: the situation is not structured to provide good feedback. For example, we usually get feedback only on the options we select, not the ones we reject. Unless people go out of their way to experiment, they may never learn about alternatives to the familiar ones. If you take the long route home every night, you may never learn there is a shorter one. Long-term processes rarely provide good feedback.

---

are often not given sufficient opportunities to learn. These economists argue that if the stakes were raised, and subjects were given practice trials, then people would 'get it right.' There are at least two problems with this argument. First, there is little evidence that performance improves when the stakes go up. To a first approximation, the stakes just don't seem to matter much (see Camerer and Hogarth, 1999). Second, and more important, economics is supposed to help explain life's big decisions, and these are the decisions that come without many practice trials. There might be a lower divorce rate if people had several 'practice marriages' in their twenties and thirties before settling down to the real thing (though we are not confident about that prediction), but the fact is that in real life choosing a life partner is hard and people often fail. Similarly, there might be fewer philosophy Ph.D.s driving cabs if choices about graduate school came with practice trials, but at age thirty-five it is hard to ask for a 'do-over.'

Someone can eat a high-fat diet for years without having any warning signs until the heart attack. When feedback does not work, we may benefit from a nudge.

Knowing What You Like

Most of us have a good sense of whether we prefer coffee ice cream to vanilla, Frank Sinatra to Bob Dylan, and mysteries to science fiction. These are examples for which we have had the time to sample the alternatives and learn about our tastes. But suppose that you have to forecast your preferences for the unfamiliar, such as when dining for the first time in a country with an exotic cuisine. Smart tourists often rely on others (waiters, for example) for help: 'Most foreigners like x and hate y.' Even in less exotic locales, it can be smart to let someone else choose for you. Two of the best restaurants in Chicago (Alinea and Charlie Trotter's) give their diners the fewest choices. At Alinea diners just decide whether they want fifteen very small plates or twenty-five tiny ones. At Charlie Trotter's, the diner is asked only whether to limit the dining to vegetables or not. (In both, one is asked about dietary restrictions and allergies.) The benefit of having so little choice is that the chef is authorized to cook you things you would never have thought to order.

It is particularly hard for people to make good decisions when they have trouble translating the choices they face into the experiences they will have. A simple example is ordering a dish from a menu in a language you do not understand. But even when you do know the meaning of the words being used, you may not be able to translate the alternatives you are considering into terms that make the slightest sense to you.

Take the problem of choosing a mutual fund for your retirement portfolio. Most investors (including us) would have trouble knowing how to compare a 'capital appreciation' fund with a 'dynamic dividend' fund, and even if the use of those words were made comprehensible, the problem would not be solved. What an investor needs to know is how a choice between those funds affects her spending power during retirement under various scenarios – something even an expert armed with a good software package and complete knowledge of the portfolios held by each fund can have trouble analyzing. The same problem arises for the choice among health plans; we may have little understanding of the effects of our selection. If your daughter gets a rare disease, will she be able to see a good specialist? How long will she have to wait in line? When people have a hard time predicting how their choices will end up affecting their lives, they have less to gain by numerous options and perhaps even by choosing for themselves. A nudge might be welcomed.

MARKETS: A MIXED VERDICT

The discussion thus far suggests that people may most need a good nudge for choices that have delayed effects; those that are difficult, infrequent, and offer poor feedback; and those for which the relation between choice and experience is ambiguous. A natural question is whether free markets can solve people's problems, even under such circumstances. Often market competition will do a lot of good. But in some cases, companies have a strong incentive to cater to people's frailties and to exploit them.

Notice first that many insurance products have all of the fraught features that we have sketched. The benefits from holding the insurance are delayed, the probability of having a claim is hard to analyze, consumers do not get useful feedback on whether they are getting a good return on their insurance purchases, and the mapping from what they are buying to what they are getting can be ambiguous. But the insurance market is competitive, so a natural question to ask is whether market forces can be relied upon to 'solve' the problem of fraught choices.

Let's imagine two different worlds. In one world, Econworld, all the consumers are Econs and they have no problem with difficult choices. All quantitative decisions, including insurance purchases, are a piece of cake for them. (Econs are part actuary.) The other world is called Humanworld, and in this world some of the consumers are Humans, who have all the features that generally characterize the tribe, while the rest are Econs. In both worlds, there are well-functioning markets and at least some perfectly rational firms that have hired Econs as managers. The key question is whether the insurance purchases in Humanworld will be the same as the ones in Econworld. In other words, do well-functioning markets render the humanness of the Humans irrelevant?

To analyze this question, let's start with a simple example inspired by a wonderful poem by Shel Silverstein (1974) entitled 'Smart.' The poem is fun as well as brilliant, so if you have a computer nearby, we suggest that you type 'Smart' and 'Shel Silverstein' into Google and read the poem now.* We will wait for you to get back before continuing.

For those of you reading this on a plane (or too lazy to get up out of bed), the poem's tale is simple. The child narrator explains that his father gave him a dollar bill, which he wisely traded for two quarters because he (unlike his dumb trading partners) knows that two is more than one. He continues trading – the two quarters for three dimes; three dimes for four nickels; and finally four nickels for five pennies. Eventually the son comes back to his father to report on his series of brilliant trades. When he does so, he reports that his father was 'too proud of [him] to speak.'

Suppose that some Humans in a well-functioning market economy prefer two quarters to one dollar because two is more than one. What happens to these quarter lovers? Are they harmed? And do they influence market prices? The answers to these questions depend a bit on how dumb the quarter lovers are, but let's suppose that while they prefer two quarters to one dollar, they still prefer more quarters to fewer quarters (since they love quarters). That means that while they would, in principle, be willing to trade two quarters for a dollar, they won't have to do that, because banks (among others) will compete

* Silverstein had personally given Thaler permission to use the poem in an academic paper published in 1985 – he said he was tickled to see his work appear in the *American Economic Review* – but the poem is now controlled by his estate, which, after several nudges (otherwise known as desperate pleas), has denied us permission to reprint the poem here. Since we would have been happy to pay royalties, unlike the Web sites you will find via Google, we can only guess that the managers of the estate (to paraphrase the poem) don't know that some is more than none.

for their business, and will be happy to give them four quarters for each dollar. Of course the quarter lovers will think they are getting a great deal on this trade, but as long as there is competition in the provision of quarters, quarters will still sell for twenty-five cents and the irrational love of quarters will be essentially harmless to those who have this affliction.

The example is obviously an extreme one, but many markets are not so different from this situation. Most of the time, competition ensures that price serves as a good signal of quality. Usually (but not always) the fifty-dollar bottles of wine are better than the twenty-dollar bottles. And irrational consumers will not alter the market as long as they do not predominate. So if some people choose wine by how much they like the label, they will not be harmed, but if many people start to do that, then wine with attractive labels will be overpriced.

For irrational consumers to be protected there has to be competition. Sometimes that competition does not exist. Consider the case of extended warranties on small appliances, typically a bad deal for consumers. To take a specific hypothetical example, suppose that a cell phone costs two hundred dollars. The cell phone has a free warranty for the first year, but the cell phone company offers, for twenty dollars, an extended warranty for the second year of the phone's life. After that the consumer plans to buy a new phone. Suppose that the chance that the phone will break during the second year is 1 percent, so on average consumers will get two dollars' worth of benefits from having this policy – but the price of the extended warranty is twenty dollars in order to include a normal profit to the insurer and a kickback (er, commission) to the salesperson at the cell phone store.

Of course, Econs understand all this and thus do not purchase extended warranties. But Humans want extended warranties, perhaps because the salesman offers the 'friendly' advice that the extended warranty is a good idea, or perhaps because they mistakenly think that cell phones break 15 percent of the time rather than 1 percent, or perhaps because they just think that it's 'better to be safe than sorry.'

What happens? Do market forces drive these unduly expensive

extended warranties from the market? Or does competition drive the price of the extended warranties down to two dollars, the expected value of the claims? The answers to these questions are no and no. (Before we explain, notice that extended warranties are plentiful in the real world and that many people buy them. Hint: Don't.)*

On our assumptions, the extended warranty is a product that simply should not exist. If Humans realized that they were paying twenty dollars for two dollars' worth of insurance, they would not buy the insurance. But if they do not realize this, markets cannot and will not unravel the situation. Competition will not drive the price down, in part because it takes the salesperson a while to persuade someone to pay twenty dollars for two dollars' worth of insurance, and in part because it is difficult for third parties to enter this market efficiently. You might think that firms could educate people not to buy the warranty, and indeed they might. But why should firms do that? If you are buying something that you shouldn't, how do I make any money persuading you not to buy it?

There is a general point here. If consumers have a less than fully rational belief, firms often have more incentive to cater to that belief than to eradicate it. When many people were still afraid of flying, it was common to see airline flight insurance sold at airports at exorbitant prices. There were no booths in airports selling people advice not to buy such insurance.

In many markets, firms will be competing for the same consumers but will be offering products that are not merely different but that directly oppose each other. Some firms sell cigarettes; others sell products that help you quit smoking. Some firms sell fast food; others sell diet advice. If all consumers are Econs, then there is no reason to worry about which of these competing interests wins. But if some of the consumers are Humans who sometimes make bad choices (as judged by themselves, of course), then all of us may have an interest

---

* Consider the Simpsons episode in which Homer has a crayon hammered into his nose to lower his IQ. (Don't ask.) The writers illustrate the lowering of Homer's IQ by having Homer make ever-stupider statements. The surgeon knows the operation is complete when Homer finally exclaims: 'Extended warranty! How can I lose?' (Thanks to Matthew Rabin for this tidbit.)

in which set of firms wins the battle. Government can, of course, outlaw some kinds of activities, but as libertarian paternalists we prefer to nudge – and we are keenly aware that governments are populated by Humans.

What can be done to help? In the next chapter we describe our primary tool: choice architecture.

5

Choice Architecture

Early in Thaler's career, he was teaching a class on managerial decision making to business school students. Students would sometimes leave class early to go for job interviews (or a golf game) and would try to sneak out of the room as surreptitiously as possible. Unfortunately for them, the only way out of the room was through a large double door in the front, in full view of the entire class (though not directly in Thaler's line of sight). The doors were equipped with large, handsome wood handles, vertically mounted cylindrical pulls about two feet in length. When the students came to these doors, they were faced with two competing instincts. One instinct says that to leave a room you push the door. The other instinct says, when faced with large wooden handles that are obviously designed to be grabbed, you pull. It turns out that the latter instinct trumps the former, and every student leaving the room began by pulling on the handle. Alas, the door opened outward.

At one point in the semester, Thaler pointed this out to the class, as one embarrassed student was pulling on the door handle while trying to escape the classroom. Thereafter, as a student got up to leave, the rest of the class would eagerly wait to see whether the student would push or pull. Amazingly, most still pulled! Their Automatic Systems triumphed; the signal emitted by that big wooden handle simply could not be screened out. (And when Thaler would leave that room on other occasions, he sheepishly found himself pulling too.)

Those doors are bad architecture because they violate a simple psychological principle with a fancy name: stimulus response compatibility. The idea is that you want the signal you receive (the

89

stimulus) to be consistent with the desired action. When there are inconsistencies, performance suffers and people blunder.

Consider, for example, the effect of a large, red, octagonal sign that said GO. The difficulties induced by such incompatibilities are easy to show experimentally. One of the most famous such demonstrations is the Stroop (1935) test. In the modern version of this experiment people see words flashed on a computer screen and they have a very simple task. They press the right button if they see a word that is displayed in red, and press the left button if they see a word displayed in green. People find the task easy and can learn to do it very quickly with great accuracy. That is, until they are thrown a curve ball, in the form of the word GREEN displayed in red, or the word RED displayed in green. For these incompatible signals, response time slows and error rates increase. A key reason is that the Automatic System reads the word faster than the color naming system can decide the color of the text. See the word GREEN in red text and the nonthinking Automatic System rushes to press the left button, which is, of course, the wrong one. You can try this for yourself. Just get a bunch of colored crayons and write a list of color names, making sure that most of the names are not the same as the color they are written in. (Better yet, get a nearby kid to do this for you.) Then name the color names as fast as you can (that is, read the words and ignore the color): easy, isn't it? Now say the color that the words are written in as fast as you can and ignore the word itself: hard, isn't it? In tasks like this, Automatic Systems always win over Reflective ones.

Although we have never seen a green stop sign, doors such as the ones described above are commonplace, and they violate the same principle. Flat plates say 'push me' and big handles say 'pull me,' so don't expect people to push big handles! This is a failure of architecture to accommodate basic principles of human psychology. Life is full of products that suffer from such defects. Isn't it obvious that the largest buttons on a television remote control should be the power, channel, and volume controls? Yet how many remotes do we see that have the volume control the same size as the 'input' control button (which if pressed accidentally can cause the picture to disappear)?

It is possible, however, to incorporate human factors into design, as Don Norman's wonderful book *The Design of Everyday Things* (1990) illustrates. One of his best examples is the design of a basic four-burner stove (Figure 5.1). Most such stoves have the burners in a symmetric arrangement, as in the stove pictured at the top, with the controls arranged in a linear fashion below. In this set-up, it is easy to get confused about which knob controls the front burner and which controls the back, and many pots and pans have been burned as a result. The other two designs we have illustrated are only two of many better possibilities.

No piece of choice architecture has received as much attention as the now famous fly in the Amsterdam airport urinals. As you may recall, putting the fake fly in the urinals reduced spillage by 80 per-cent, an extraordinary nudging success. Entrepreneur and engineer Doug Kempel turned the fly experiment into a small business selling fly stickers online. 'My goal is nothing less than to save the world, one urinal at a time,' he told us. 'I truly believe that this simple product can keep restrooms cleaner and safer. Less cleaning means less harmful cleaners being used. It doesn't hurt that it makes people laugh.' Kempel said his flies have sold particularly well in the United Kingdom, and he has shipped them to bars, restaurants, schools, churches, and yes, airports.

Friends and others have reported seeing these flies all around the world, including Terminal 4 of New York's John F. Kennedy airport, Moscow, Munich, Singapore, Seattle, and Detroit airports, Purdue University, the University of Colorado, Broward Community College, and throughout Holland. One of our intrepid reporters, Steffen Altmann, spotted a urinal inspired by the 'beautiful game' (soccer, for our American readers) with a small plastic goal in the bowl's center in Bonn, Germany. Not all urinals are fun and games, though. Take the 'Piss Screen' (yes, that's the name), also from Germany.

It is a game, but one with a serious message: Don't drink and drive. Billed as 'an interactive experience – not to be mistaken for the Wii', the Piss Screen is actually a pressure-sensitive inlay set in urinals that simulates what it's like to hit the road after a few drinks. A group of

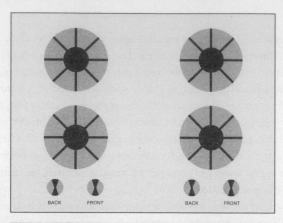

BACK   FRONT   BACK   FRONT

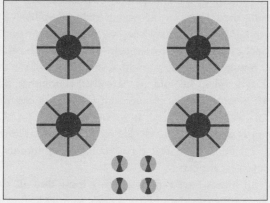

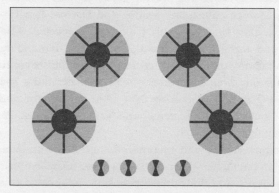

Figure 5.1. *Three designs of four-burner stovetops*

video game developers teamed up with Frankfurt Taxi Services to create a sophisticated driving simulator game that begins when you, well, begin, and turns the car when you, well, turn. It requires quick reactions, which drunks lack, and ends with a shocking crash experience that leaves no doubt about the consequences of mixing alcohol and fast rides. 'Too pissed to drive? Take a taxi instead,' the final screen reads, followed by the Frankfurt Taxi Services phone number.

The lesson of the urinal fly is that designers need to keep in mind that the users of their objects are Humans who are confronted every day with myriad choices and cues. The goal of this chapter is to develop the same idea for choice architects. If you indirectly influence the choices other people make, you are a choice architect. And since the choices you are influencing are going to be made by Humans, you will want your architecture to reflect a good understanding of how humans behave. In particular, you will want to ensure that the Automatic System doesn't get all confused. In this chapter, we offer some basic principles of good (and bad) choice architecture.

DEFAULTS: PADDING THE PATH OF LEAST RESISTANCE

For reasons we have discussed, many people will take whatever option requires the least effort, or the path of least resistance. Recall the discussion of inertia, status quo bias, and the 'yeah, whatever' heuristic. All these forces imply that if, for a given choice, there is a default option – an option that will obtain if the chooser does nothing – then we can expect a large number of people to end up with that option, whether or not it is good for them. And as we have also stressed, these behavioral tendencies toward doing nothing will be reinforced if the default option comes with some implicit or explicit suggestion that it represents the normal or even the recommended course of action.

Defaults are ubiquitous and powerful. They are also unavoidable in the sense that for any node of a choice architecture system, there must be an associated rule that determines what happens to the decision maker if she does nothing. Of course, usually the answer is that if I do nothing, nothing changes; whatever is happening continues to happen. But not always. Some dangerous machines, such as chain saws and lawn mowers, are designed with 'dead man switches,' so that once you are no longer gripping the machine, it stops. When you leave your computer alone for a while to answer a phone call, nothing is likely to happen until you have talked for a long time, at which point the screen saver comes on, and if you neglect the computer long enough, it may lock itself.

Of course, you can choose how long it takes before your screen saver comes on, but implementing that choice takes some action. Your computer probably came with a default time lag and a default screen saver. Chances are, those are the settings you still have.

Many organizations in both the public and the private sector have discovered the immense power of default options. Successful businesses certainly have. Remember the idea of automatic renewal for magazine subscriptions? If renewal is automatic, many people will subscribe, for a long time, to magazines they don't read. Business offices at most magazines are aware of that fact. When you download a new piece of software, you will often have numerous choices to make. Do you want the 'regular' or 'custom' installation? Normally, one of the boxes is already checked, indicating it is the default. Which boxes do the software suppliers check? Two different motives are readily apparent: helpful and self-serving. In the helpful category would be making the regular installation the default if most users will have trouble with the custom installation. In the self-serving category would be making the default a willingness to receive emails with information about new products. In our experience, most software comes with helpful defaults regarding the type of installation, but many come with self-serving defaults on other choices. We will have more to say about motives later. For now, note that not all defaults are selected to make the chooser's life easier or better.

We have emphasized that default rules are inevitable – that private institutions and the legal system cannot avoid choosing them. In some cases, though not all, there is an important qualification to this claim. The choice architect can force the choosers to make their own choice. We call this approach 'required choice' or 'mandated choice.' In the software example, required choice would be implemented by leaving all the boxes unchecked, and by requiring that at every opportunity one of the boxes be checked in order for people to proceed. In the case of the provision of contact information to the military recruiters, one could imagine a system in which all students (or their parents) are required to fill out a form indicating whether they want to make their contact information available. For emotionally charged issues like this one, such a policy has considerable appeal, because people might not want to be defaulted into an option that they might hate (but fail to reject because of inertia, or real or apparent social pressure).

We believe that required choice, favored by many who like freedom, is sometimes the best way to go. But consider two points about that approach. First, Humans will often consider required choice to be a nuisance or worse, and would much prefer to have a good default. Most downloaded software comes with two installation choices, regular and custom. The regular setting is a long list of functions. It would be helpful if companies highlighted the most common or popular of these. In the software example, it is really helpful to know what the recommended settings are. Most users do not want to have to read an incomprehensible manual in order to determine which arcane setting to select. When choice is complicated and difficult, people might greatly appreciate a sensible default. It is hardly clear that they should be forced to choose.

Second, required choosing is generally more appropriate for simple yes-or-no decisions than for more complex choices. At a restaurant, the default option is to take the dish as the chef usually prepares it, with the option to ask that certain ingredients be added or removed. In the extreme, required choosing would imply that the diner has to give the chef the recipe for every dish she orders! When choices are highly complex, required choosing may not be a good idea; it might not even be feasible.

EXPECT ERROR

Humans make mistakes. A well-designed system expects its users to err and is as forgiving as possible. Some examples from the world of real design illustrate this point:

- In the Paris subway system, Le Métro, users insert a paper card the size of a movie ticket into a machine that reads the card, leaves a record on the card that renders it 'used,' and then spits it out from the top of the machine. The cards have a magnetic strip on one side but are otherwise symmetric. On Thaler's first visit to Paris, he was not sure how to use the system, so he tried putting the card in with the magnetic strip face up and was pleased to discover that it worked. He was careful thereafter to insert the card with the strip face up. Many years and trips to Paris later, he was proudly demonstrating to a visiting friend the correct way to use the Métro system when his wife started laughing. It turns out that it doesn't matter which way you put the card into the machine!

  In stark contrast to Le Métro is the system used in most Chicago parking garages. When entering the garage, you put your credit card into a machine that reads it and remembers you. Then when leaving, you must insert the card again into another machine at the exit. This involves reaching out of the car window and inserting the card into a slot. Because credit cards are not symmetric, there are four possible ways to put the card into the slot (face up or down, strip on the right or left). Exactly one of those ways is the right way. And in spite of a diagram above the slot, it is very easy to put the card in the wrong way, and when the card is spit back out, it is not immediately obvious what caused the card to be rejected or to recall which way it was inserted the first time. Both of us have been stuck for several painful minutes behind some idiot who was having trouble with this machine, and have to admit to having occasionally been the idiot that is making all the people behind him start honking.

- Over the years, automobiles have become much friendlier to their Human operators. If you do not buckle your seat belt, you are buzzed. If you are about to run out of gas, a warning sign appears and you might be beeped. If you need an oil change, your car might tell you. Many cars come with an automatic switch for the headlights that turns them on when you are operating the car and off when you are not, eliminating the possibility of leaving your lights on overnight and draining the battery.

But some error-forgiving innovations are surprisingly slow to be adopted. Take the case of the gas tank cap. On any sensible car the gas cap is attached by a piece of plastic, so that when you remove the cap you cannot possibly drive off without it. Our guess is that this bit of plastic cannot cost more than ten cents. Once some firm had the good idea to include this feature, what excuse can there ever have been for building a car without one?

Leaving the gas cap behind is a special kind of predictable error psychologists call a 'postcompletion' error.[1] The idea is that when you have finished your main task, you tend to forget things relating to previous steps. Other examples include leaving your ATM card in the machine after getting your cash, or leaving the original in the copying machine after getting your copies. Most ATMs (but not all) no longer allow this error because you get your card back immediately. Another strategy, suggested by Norman, is to use what he calls a 'forcing function,' meaning that in order to get what you want, you have to do something else first. So if in order to get your cash, you have to remove the card, you will not forget to do so.

- Another automobile-related bit of good design involves the nozzles for different varieties of gasoline. The nozzles that deliver diesel fuel are too large to fit into the opening on cars that use gasoline, so it is not possible to make the mistake of putting diesel fuel in your gasoline-powered car (though it is still possible to make the opposite mistake). The same principle has been used to reduce the number of errors involving anesthesia. One study found that human error (rather than equipment failure) caused 82 percent of the 'critical incidents.' A common error was that the hose for one drug was hooked up to the wrong delivery port, so the patient received the wrong drug. This problem was solved by designing the equipment so that the gas nozzles and connectors were different for each drug. It became physically impossible to make this previously frequent mistake.[2]

- A major problem in health care is called 'drug compliance.' Many patients, especially the elderly, are on medicines they must take regularly, and in the correct dosage. So here is a choice architecture question. If you are designing a drug, and you have complete flexibility, how often would you want your patients to have to take their medicine?

If we rule out a one-time dose administered immediately by the doctor (which would be best on all dimensions but is often technically infeasible), then the next-best solution is a medicine taken once a day, preferably in the morning. It is clear why once a day is better than twice (or more) a day, because the more often you have to take the drug, the more opportunities you have to forget. But frequency is not the only concern; regularity is also important. Once a day is much better than once every other day, because the Automatic System can be educated to think: 'My pill(s) every morning, when I wake up.' Taking the pill becomes a habit, and habits are controlled by the Automatic System. By contrast, remembering to take your medicine every other day is beyond most of us. (Similarly, meetings that occur every week are easier to remember than those that occur every other week.) Some medicines are taken once a week, and most patients take this medicine on Sundays (because that day is different from other days for most people and thus easy to associate with taking one's medicine).

Birth control pills present a special problem along these lines, because they are taken every day for three weeks and then skipped for one week. To solve this problem and to make the process automatic, the pills are typically sold in a special container that contains twenty-eight pills, each in a numbered compartment. Patients are instructed to take a pill every day, in order. The pills for days twenty-two through twenty-eight are placebos whose only role is to facilitate compliance for Human users.

• While working on this book, Thaler sent an email to his economist friend Hal Varian, who is affiliated with Google. Thaler intended to attach a draft of the introduction to give Hal a sense of what the book was about, but forgot the attachment. When Hal wrote back to ask for the missing attachment, he noted with pride that Google was experimenting with a new feature on its email program 'gmail' that would solve this problem. A user who mentions the word *attachment* but does not include one would be prompted, 'Did you forget your attachment?' Thaler sent the attachment along and told Hal that this was exactly what the book was about.

- Visitors to London who come from the United States or Europe have a problem being safe pedestrians. They have spent their entire lives expecting cars to come at them from the left, and their Automatic System knows to look that way. But in the United Kingdom automobiles drive on the left-hand side of the road, and so the danger often comes from the right. Many pedestrian accidents occur as a result. The city of London tries to help with good design. On many corners, especially in neighborhoods frequented by tourists, the pavement has signs that say, 'Look right!'

GIVE FEEDBACK

The best way to help Humans improve their performance is to provide feedback. Well-designed systems tell people when they are doing well and when they are making mistakes. Some examples:

- Digital cameras generally provide better feedback to their users than film cameras. After each shot, the photographer can see a (small) version of the image just captured. This eliminates all kinds of errors that were common in the film era, from failing to load the film properly (or at all), to forgetting to remove the lens cap, to cutting off the head of the central figure of the picture. However, early digital cameras failed on one crucial feedback dimension. When a picture was taken, there was no audible cue to indicate that the image had been captured. Modern models now include a very satisfying but completely fake 'shutter click' sound when a picture has been taken. (Some cell phones, aimed at the elderly, include a fake dial tone, for similar reasons.)

- An important type of feedback is a warning that things are going wrong, or, even more helpful, are about to go wrong. Our laptops warn us to plug in or shut down when the battery is dangerously low. But warning systems have to avoid the problem of offering so many warnings that they are ignored. If our computer constantly nags us about whether we are sure we want to open that attachment, we begin to click 'yes' without thinking about it. These warnings are thus rendered useless.

- Feedback can be improved in many activities. Consider the simple task of painting a ceiling. This task is more difficult than it might seem because ceilings are nearly always painted white, and it can be hard to see exactly where you have painted. Later, when the paint dries, the patches of old paint will be annoyingly visible. How to solve this problem? Some helpful person invented a type of ceiling paint that goes on pink when wet but turns white when dry. Unless the painter is so colorblind that he can't tell the difference between pink and white, this solves the problem.

UNDERSTANDING 'MAPPINGS': FROM CHOICE TO WELFARE

Some tasks are easy, like choosing a flavor of ice cream; other tasks are hard, like choosing a medical treatment. Consider, for example, an ice cream shop where the varieties differ only in flavor, not calories or other nutritional content. Selecting which ice cream to eat is merely a matter of choosing the one that tastes best. If the flavors are all familiar, such as vanilla, chocolate, and strawberry, most people will be able to predict with considerable accuracy the relation between their choice and their ultimate consumption experience. Call this relation between choice and welfare a mapping. Even if there are some exotic flavors, the ice cream store can solve the mapping problem by offering a free taste.

Choosing among treatments for some disease is quite another matter. Suppose you are told that you have been diagnosed with prostate cancer and must choose among three options: surgery, radiation, and 'watchful waiting' (which means do nothing for now). Each of these options comes with a complex set of possible outcomes regarding side effects of treatment, quality of life, length of life, and so forth. Comparing the options involves making such trade-offs as the following: Would I be willing to risk a one-third chance of impotence or incontinence in order to increase my life expectancy by 3.2 years? This is a hard decision at two levels. First, the patient is unlikely to know these trade-offs, and second, he is unlikely to be able to imagine what life would be like if he were incontinent. Yet here are two scary facts about this scenario. First, most patients decide which course of action to take in the very meeting at which their doctor breaks the bad news about the diagnosis. Second, the treatment option they choose depends strongly on the type of doctor they see.[3] (Some specialize in surgery, others in radiation. None specialize in watchful waiting. Guess which option we suspect might be underutilized?)

The comparison between ice cream and treatment options illustrates the concept of mapping. A good system of choice architecture helps people to improve their ability to map and hence to select options that will make them better off. One way to do this is to make the information about various options more comprehensible, by transforming numerical information into units that translate more readily into actual use. If I am buying apples to make into apple cider, it helps to know the rule of thumb that it takes three apples to make one glass of cider.

Take the example of choosing a digital camera. Cameras advertise their megapixels, and the impression created is certainly that the more megapixels the better. This assumption is itself subject to question, because photos taken with more megapixels take up more room on the camera's storage device and a computer's hard drive. But what is really problematic for consumers is translating megapixels (not the most intuitive concept) into what they care about. Is it worth paying an additional hundred dollars to go from four to five megapixels? Suppose instead that manufacturers listed the largest print size recommended for a given camera. Instead of being given the options of three, five, or seven megapixels, consumers might be told that the camera can produce quality photos at 4×6 inches, 9×12, or 'poster size.'

Often people have a problem in mapping products into money. For simple choices, of course, such mappings are trivial. If a Snickers bar costs one dollar, you can easily figure out how much it costs to have a Snickers bar every day. But do you know how much it costs you to use your credit card? Among the fees you may be paying are: (a) an annual fee for the privilege of using the card (common for cards that provide benefits such as frequent flyer miles); (b) an interest rate for borrowing money (that depends on your deemed credit worthiness); (c) a fee for making a payment late (and you may end up making more late payments than you anticipate); (d) interest on purchases made during the month that is normally not charged if your balance is paid off but begins if you make your payment one day late; and (e) a charge for buying things in currencies other than dollars.

Credit cards are not alone in having complex pricing schemes that are neither transparent nor comprehensible to consumers. Think about mortgages, cell phone calling plans, and auto insurance policies, just to name a few. For these and related domains, we propose a very mild form of government regulation, a species of libertarian paternalism that we call RECAP: Record, Evaluate, and Compare Alternative Prices.

Here is how RECAP would work in the cell phone market. The government would not regulate how *much* issuers could charge for services, but it would regulate their disclosure practices. The central goal would be to inform customers of every kind of fee that currently exists. This would not be done by printing a long unintelligible document in fine print. Instead, issuers would be required to make public their fee schedule in a spreadsheet-like format that would include all relevant formulas. Suppose you are in Toronto and your cell phone rings. How much is it going to cost you to answer it? What if you download some email? All these prices would be embedded in the formulas. This is the price disclosure part of the regulation.

The usage disclosure requirement would be that once a year, issuers would have to send their customers a complete listing of all the ways they had used the phone and all the fees that had been incurred. This report would be sent two ways, by mail and, more important, electronically. The electronic version would also be stored and downloadable on a secure Web site.

Producing the RECAP reports would cost cell phone carriers very little, but the reports would be extremely useful for customers who want to compare the pricing plans of cell phone providers, especially after they had received their first annual statement. Private Web sites similar to existing travel sites would emerge to allow an easy way to compare services. With just a few quick clicks, a shopper would easily be able to import her usage data from the past year and find out how much various carriers would have charged, given her usage patterns.* Consumers who are new to the product (getting a cell phone for the first time, for example) would have to guess usage information for various categories, but the following year they could take full advantage of the system's capabilities. We will see that in many domains, from mortgages and credit cards to energy use to Medicare, a RECAP program could greatly improve people's ability to make good choices.

STRUCTURE COMPLEX CHOICES

People adopt different strategies for making choices depending on the size and complexity of the available options. When we face a small number of well-understood alternatives, we tend to examine all the attributes of all the alternatives and then make trade-offs when necessary. But when the choice set gets large, we must use alternative strategies, and these can get us into trouble.

Consider, for example, Jane, who has just been offered a job at a company located in a large city far from where she is living now. Compare two choices she faces: which office to select and which apartment to rent. Suppose Jane is offered a choice of three available offices in her workplace. A reasonable strategy for her to follow would be to look at all three offices, note the ways they differ, and then make some decisions about the importance of such attributes as size, view, neighbors, and distance to the nearest rest room. This is described in the choice literature as a 'compensatory' strategy, since a high value for one attribute (big office) can compensate for a low value for another (loud neighbor).

Obviously, the same strategy cannot be used to pick an apartment.

---

* We are aware, of course, that behavior depends on prices. If my current cell phone provider charges me a lot to make calls in Canada and I react by not making such calls, I will not be able to judge the full value of an alternative plan with cheap calling in Canada. But where past usage is a good predictor of future usage, a RECAP plan would be very helpful.

In a large city like Los Angeles, thousands of apartments are available. If Jane ever wants to start working, she will not be able to visit each apartment and evaluate them all. Instead, she is likely to simplify the task in some way. One strategy to use is what Amos Tversky (1972) called 'elimination by aspects.' Someone using this strategy first decides what aspect is most important (say, commuting distance), establishes a cutoff level (say, no more than a thirty-minute commute), then eliminates all the alternatives that do not come up to this standard. The process is repeated, attribute by attribute (no more than $1,500 per month; at least two bedrooms; dogs permitted), until either a choice is made or the set is narrowed down enough to switch over to a compensatory evaluation of the 'finalists.'

When people are using a simplifying strategy of this kind, alternatives that do not meet the minimum cutoff scores may be eliminated even if they are fabulous on all other dimensions. So, for example, an apartment that is a thirty-five-minute commute will not be considered even if it has a dynamite view and costs two hundred dollars a month less than any of the alternatives.

Social science research reveals that as the choices become more numerous and/or vary on more dimensions, people are more likely to adopt simplifying strategies. The implications for choice architecture are related. As alternatives become more numerous and more complex, choice architects have more to think about and more work to do, and are much more likely to influence choices (for better or for worse). For an ice cream shop with three flavors, any menu listing those flavors in any order will do just fine, and effects on choices (such as order effects) are likely to be minor because people know what they like. As choices become more numerous, though, good choice architecture will provide structure, and structure will affect outcomes.

Consider the example of a paint store. Even ignoring the possibility of special orders, paint companies sell more than two thousand colors that you can apply to the walls in your home. It is possible to think of many ways of structuring how those paint colors are offered to the customer. Imagine, for example, that the paint colors were listed alphabetically. Arctic White might be followed by Azure Blue, and so forth. While alphabetical order is a satisfactory way to organize a dictionary (at least if you have a guess as to how a word is spelled), it is a lousy way to organize a paint store.

Instead, paint stores have long used something like a paint wheel, with color samples ordered by similarity: all the blues are together, next to the greens, and the reds are located near the oranges, and so forth. The problem of selection is made considerably easier by the fact that people can see the actual colors, especially since the names of the paints are spectacularly uninformative. (On the Benjamin Moore Paints Web site, three similar shades of beige are called 'Roasted Sesame Seed,' 'Oklahoma Wheat,' and 'Kansas Grain.')

Thanks to modern computer technology and the World Wide Web, many problems of consumer choice have been made simpler. The Benjamin Moore Paints Web site not only allows the consumer to browse through dozens of shades of beige, but it also permits the consumer to see (within the limitations of the computer monitor) how a particular shade will work on the walls with the ceiling painted in a complementary color. And the variety of paint colors is small compared to the number of books sold by Amazon (millions) or Web pages covered by Google (billions). Many companies such as Netflix, the mail-order DVD rental company, succeed in part because of immensely helpful choice architecture. Customers looking for a movie to rent can easily search movies by actor, director, genre, and more, and if they rate the movies they have watched, they can also get recommendations based on the preferences of other movie lovers with similar tastes, a method called 'collaborative filtering.' You use the judgments of other people who share your tastes to filter through the vast number of books or movies available in order to increase the likelihood of picking one you like. Collaborative filtering is an effort to solve a problem of choice architecture. If you know what people like you tend to like, you might well be comfortable in selecting products you don't know, because people like you tend to like them. For many of us, collaborative filtering is making difficult choices easier.

A cautionary note: surprise and serendipity can be fun for people, and good for them too, and it may not be entirely wonderful if our primary source of information is about what people like us like. Sometimes it's good to learn what people *un*like us like – and to see whether we might even like that. If you like the mystery writer Robert B. Parker (and we agree that he's great), collaborative filtering will probably direct you to other mystery writers (we suggest trying Lee Child, by the way), but why not try a little Joyce Carol Oates, or maybe even Henry James? If you're a Democrat, and you like books that fit your predilections, you might want to see what Republicans think; no party can possibly have a monopoly on wisdom. Public-spirited choice architects – those who run the daily newspaper, for example – know that it's good to nudge people in directions that they might not have specifically chosen in advance. Structuring choice sometimes means helping people to learn, so they can later make better choices on their own.[4]

INCENTIVES

Our last topic is the one with which most economists would have started: prices and incentives. Though we have been stressing factors that are often neglected by traditional economic theory, we do not intend to suggest that standard economic forces are unimportant. This is as good a point as any to state for the record that we believe in supply and demand. If the price of a product goes up, suppliers will usually produce more of it and consumers will usually want less of it. So choice architects must think about incentives when they design a system. Sensible architects will put the right incentives on the right people. One way to start to think about incentives is to ask four questions about a particular choice architecture:

Who uses?
Who chooses?
Who pays?
Who profits?

Free markets often solve all of the key problems by giving people an incentive to make good products and to sell them at the right price. If the market for sneakers is working well, there will be a lot of competition; bad sneakers will be driven from the market and the good ones will be priced in accordance with people's tastes. Sneaker producers and sneaker purchasers have the right incentives. But sometimes incentive conflicts arise. Consider a simple case. When we go for our weekly lunch, each of us chooses his own meal and pays for what he eats. The restaurant serves us our food and keeps our money. No conflicts here. Now suppose we decide to take turns paying for lunch. Sunstein now has an incentive to order something more expensive on the weeks that Thaler is paying, and vice versa. (In this case, though, friendship introduces a complication; one of us may well order something cheaper if he knows that the other is paying. Sentimental but true.)

Many markets (and choice architecture systems) are replete with incentive conflicts. Perhaps the most notorious is the U.S. health care system. The patient receives the health care services that are chosen by his physician and paid for by the insurance company, with everyone from equipment manufacturers to drug companies to malpractice lawyers taking a piece of the action. Those with different pieces have different incentives, and the results may not be ideal for either patients or doctors. Of course, this point is obvious to anyone who thinks about these problems. But as usual, it is possible to elaborate and enrich the standard analysis by remembering that the agents in the economy are Humans. To be sure, even mindless Humans demand less when they notice that the price has gone up. But will they notice? Only if they are really paying attention.

The most important modification that must be made to a standard analysis of incentives is salience. Do the choosers actually notice the incentives they face? In free markets, the answer is usually yes, but in important cases the answer is no. Consider the example of members of an urban family deciding whether to buy a car. Suppose their choices are to take taxis and public transportation or to spend ten thousand dollars to buy a used car, which they can park on the street in front of their home. The only salient costs of owning this car will be the weekly stops at the gas station, occasional repair bills, and a yearly insurance bill. The opportunity cost of the ten thousand dollars is likely to be neglected. (In other words, once they purchase the car, they tend to forget about the ten thousand dollars and stop treating it as money that could have been spent on something else.) In contrast, every time the family uses a taxi the cost will be in their face, with the meter clicking every few blocks. So a behavioral analysis of the incentives of car ownership will predict that people will underweight the opportunity costs of car ownership, and possibly other less salient aspects such as depreciation, and may overweight the very salient costs of using a taxi.* An analysis of choice architecture systems must make similar adjustments.

Of course, salience can be manipulated, and good choice architects can take steps to direct people's attention to incentives. The telephones at the INSEAD School of Business in France are programmed to display the running costs of long-distance phone calls. If we want to protect the environment and to increase energy independence, similar strategies could be used to make costs more salient. Suppose the thermostat in your home was programmed to tell you the cost per hour of lowering the temperature a few degrees during the heat wave. This would probably have more effect on your behavior than quietly raising the price of electricity, a change that will be experienced only at the end of the month when the bill comes. Suppose in this light that government wants to increase energy conservation. Increases in the price of electricity will surely have an effect; making the increases salient will have a greater effect. Cost-disclosing thermostats might have a greater impact than (modest) price increases designed to decrease use of electricity.

In some domains, people may want the salience of gains and losses treated asymmetrically. For example, no one would want to go to a health club that charged its users on a 'per step' basis on the Stairmaster. However, many Stairmaster users enjoy watching the 'calories burned' meter while they work out (especially since those meters seem to give generous estimates of calories actually burned). Even better, for some, might be a pictorial display that indicated the

---

* Companies that specialize in short-term rentals could profitably benefit by helping people solve these mental accounting problems.

calories one had burned in terms of food: after ten minutes one had earned only a bag of carrots but after forty minutes a large cookie.

We have sketched six principles of good choice architecture. As a concession to the bounded memory of our readers, we thought it might be useful to offer a mnemonic device to help recall the six principles. By rearranging the order, and using one small fudge, the following emerges.

> iNcentives
> Understand mappings
> Defaults
> Give feedback
> Expect error
> Structure complex choices

Voilà: NUDGES.

With an eye on these NUDGES, choice architects can improve the outcomes for their Human users.

PART II

Money

Not surprisingly, Humans differ dramatically from Econs in how they deal with money. Econs are sensible spenders and savers. They put money away for a rainy day, and for retirement, and they invest that money as if they had MBAs. When they borrow, Econs have no trouble choosing between fixed- and variable-rate mortgages, and they pay their credit card bills on time every month. If you are an Econ, you can skip this section of the book, unless you want to understand the behavior of your spouse, kids, and other Humans. A major goal of the next four chapters is to explore how people can do a better job at the difficult tasks of saving, investing, and borrowing. We also offer some suggestions about how private and public institutions might nudge people in directions that will make them a bit wealthier and more secure.

6

Save More Tomorrow

In many industrialized countries around the world, governments provide pension plans in order to ensure that people have enough money for old age. The future of many of these plans is threatened by two demographic changes: people are living longer and having fewer children. In most systems, retired workers' pensions are paid for by current workers' taxes. But as the ratio of current workers to retirees falls, either taxes have to go up or benefits have to fall. If benefits are cut, workers will have to save to make up the difference. Changes in the design of private retirement plans are also putting more demands on workers to determine for themselves how much to save and how to invest it properly. Many Humans are ill-equipped for this daunting task.

What can be done to help? We will be offering two central suggestions. The first is automatic enrollment in savings plans; the second is the Save More Tomorrow program. To understand why these nudges would work, and why they are not part of the usual economics repertoire, we need to step back a bit.

The standard economic theory of saving for retirement is both elegant and simple. People are assumed to calculate how much they are going to earn over the rest of their lifetime, figure out how much they will need when they retire, and then save up just enough to enjoy a comfortable retirement without sacrificing too much while they are still working.

As a guideline for how to think sensibly about saving, this theory is excellent, but as an approach to how people actually behave, the theory runs into two serious problems. First, it assumes that people are capable of solving a complicated mathematical problem in order to figure out how much to save. Without good computer software, even a trained economist would find this problem daunting. The truth is that we know few economists (and no lawyers) who have made a serious attempt at doing it (even with software).*

The second problem with the theory is that it assumes that people have enough willpower to implement the relevant plan. Under the standard theory, flashy sports cars or nice vacations never distract people from their project of saving up for a condo in Florida. In short, the standard theory is about Econs, not Humans.

For most of their time on earth, Humans did not have to worry much about saving for retirement, because most people did not live long enough to have much of a retirement period. In most societies, those who did make it to old age were cared for by their children. In the twentieth century, the combination of rising life expectancies and geographical dispersion of families made it necessary for people to think about providing for their own retirement income rather than depending on their children to do it. Both employers and governments began to take steps to help with this problem, with Bismarck's early Social Security program in Germany leading the way in 1889.[1]

Early pension plans tended to be defined-benefit plans. In such plans, participants are entitled to a benefit that depends on a specific formula, typically based on the participant's salary and the number of years the participant was a member of the plan. In a typical private plan, a worker is entitled to receive a benefit that is a proportion of the salary paid over the last few years of work, the proportion depending on years of service. Most public Social Security systems, including that of the United States, are also defined-benefit plans.

From the perspective of choice architecture, defined-benefit plans have one large virtue: they are forgiving to even the most mindless of Humans. In the American Social Security system, for example, the only decision a worker has to make is when to start receiving benefits. The only form to fill out is the one where you write down

---

* There are good software products available from many mutual fund companies as well as from such independent firms as Financial Engines and Morningstar, but many Humans find using these programs both difficult and boring.

your Social Security number, and you have to fill it out if you want to get paid! In the private sector, defined-benefit plans are also easy and forgiving, as long as the worker keeps working for the same employer, and the employer stays in business.

While a defined-benefit world can be an easy one for someone who stays in one job her entire life, employees who change jobs frequently can end up with virtually no retirement benefits, because there is often a minimum employment period (such as five years) before any benefits are vested (that is, owned by the employee). Defined-benefit plans are also expensive for employers to administer. Many old firms are switching over to defined-contribution plans, and in America nearly all new firms offer only defined-contribution plans. Under a defined-contribution plan, employees, and sometimes employers, make specific contributions to a tax-sheltered account in the employee's name. The benefits received by employees in retirement depend on the decisions they make about how much to save and how to invest.

Defined-contribution plans have many desirable features for modern workers. The plans are completely portable, so a worker is free to move from one job to another. The plans are also flexible, giving employees the opportunity to adjust their savings and investment decisions to reflect their own financial situation and tastes. However, defined-contribution plans are not very forgiving. Employees have to get around to joining, to figuring out how much to save, to managing their portfolio over a period of years, and then to deciding what to do with the proceeds when they finally retire. People can find the whole process frightening, and many seem to be making a mess of the task.

ARE PEOPLE SAVING ENOUGH?

Of course, a key question is whether people are saving enough. Are they?

This turns out to be a complex and controversial question, and the answers differ from one country to another. For one thing, economists do not agree about how much saving is appropriate, because they do not agree on the right level of post-retirement income. Some economists argue that people should aim to have retirement income that is at least as high as the income enjoyed when working, because retirement years offer the opportunity for such time-intensive expensive activities as travel. Retired people also have to worry about growing health care costs. Others claim that retirees can use their greater time to live a more economical lifestyle: saving the money once spent on business clothes, taking the time to shop carefully and prepare meals at home, and taking advantage of senior discounts.

We do not take a strong position on this debate, but consider a few points. It seems clear that the costs of saving too little are greater than the costs of saving too much. There are many ways to cope with having saved too much – from retiring earlier than expected, to taking up golf, to traveling to Europe, to spoiling the grandchildren. Coping in the opposite direction is less pleasant. Second, we can say for sure that *some* people in our society are definitely saving too little – namely, those employees who are not participating at all in their retirement plan, or are saving a low percentage of their income after having reached their forties (or older). These folks could clearly use a nudge.

For what it is worth, many employees say that they 'should' be saving more. In one study, 68 percent of the participants in a defined-contribution savings plan said that their savings rate is 'too low,' 31 percent said that their savings rate is 'about right,' and only 1 percent said their savings rate is 'too high.' Economists tend to belittle such statements, and partly for good reason. It is easy to say that you 'should' be doing many good things – dieting, exercising, spending more time with your children – and people's actions may tell us more than their words. After all, few of the participants who say they should be saving more make any changes in their behavior. But such statements are not meaningless or random. Many people announce an intention to eat less and exercise more next year, but few say they hope to smoke more next year or watch more sitcom reruns. We interpret the statement 'I should be saving (or dieting, or exercising) more' to imply that people would be open to strategies that would help them achieve these goals. In other words, they are open to a nudge. They might even be grateful for one.

ENROLLMENT DECISIONS: NUDGING PEOPLE TO JOIN

The first step in participating in a defined-contribution plan is to enroll. Most workers should find joining the plan very attractive. Contributions are tax deductible, accumulations are tax deferred (in some cases tax free), and in many plans the employer matches at least part of the contributions of the employee. For example, a common plan feature is that the employer will match 50 percent of the employee's contributions up to some threshold, such as 6 percent of salary.

This match is virtually free money. Taking full advantage of the match should be a no-brainer for all but the most impatient or cash-strapped households. Nevertheless, enrollment rates in such plans are far from 100 percent. In the United States, roughly 30 percent of employees eligible to join a pension plan fail to enroll.[2] Typically, younger, less-educated, and lower-income employees are less likely to join, but even high-paid workers sometimes fail to sign up.

To be sure, there are situations, say for young workers with other pressing financial needs, in which it could be sensible not to join even with an employer match. But in many cases, the failure to join is simply a blunder. One extreme example comes from the United Kingdom, where some defined-benefit plans do not require any employee contributions and are fully paid for by the employer. They do require employees to take action to join the plan. Data on twenty-five such plans reveal that scarcely half of the eligible employees (51 percent) signed up![3] This is equivalent to not bothering to cash your paycheck.

Some older American workers are also turning down 'free money.' To have this free money option, a worker must meet three qualifications: he needs to be more than 59½ years old, so that he faces no tax penalty when he withdraws funds from his retirement account; his firm has to offer a matching contribution (meaning that the firm contributes something if the employee does); and his employer has to allow employees to withdraw funds from their retirement accounts while still working. For such employees, joining the plan is a sure profit opportunity because they can join, then immediately withdraw their contributions without any penalty, yet keep the employer match. Nonetheless, a study finds that up to 40 percent of eligible workers either do not join the plan at all or do not save enough to get the full match.[4]

These extreme examples are just the clearest cases in which people's failure to join a plan is foolish beyond a doubt. In many other cases, workers take months or years to join the plan, and it is a reasonable assumption that most of these workers are just spacing out or procrastinating rather than making a reasoned decision that they have a better use for their money. How can we nudge these people to join more quickly?*

MAKING SAVINGS AUTOMATIC

An obvious answer is to change the default rule. As things now stand, the default is nonenrollment; you have to do a little work to get into a retirement plan. When workers are first eligible to join (sometimes immediately upon employment), they usually receive a form to fill out. Employees who want to join must decide how much to put aside, and how to allocate their investments among the funds offered in the plan. Forms can be a headache, and many employees just put them aside.

An alternative is to adopt automatic enrollment. Here's how it works. When an employee first becomes eligible, she receives a form indicating that she will be enrolled in the plan (at a specified savings

---

* By the way, are you contributing the maximum to your retirement plan, or at least contributing enough to get the full match from your employer? Are your grown children doing so? If not, stop reading and get busy. You have more important things to do than read this book.

rate and asset allocation), unless she actively fills out a form asking to opt out. Automatic enrollment has proven to be an extremely effective way to increase enrollment in US defined-contribution plans.[5]

In one plan studied in an early paper by Brigitte Madrian and Dennis Shea (2001), participation rates under the opt-in approach were barely 20 percent after three months of employment, gradually increasing to 65 percent after thirty-six months. But when automatic enrollment was adopted, enrollment of new employees jumped to 90 percent immediately and increased to more than 98 percent within thirty-six months. Automatic enrollment thus has two effects: participants join sooner, and more participants join eventually.

Does automatic enrollment merely overcome workers' inertia, helping them make the choice they would actually prefer? Or does automatic enrollment somehow seduce workers into saving when they would prefer to be spending? One telling bit of evidence is that under automatic enrollment, very few employees drop out of the plan once enrolled. In a study of four companies that adopted automatic enrollment, the fraction of participants who dropped out of the plan in the first year was only 0.3 to 0.6 percentage points higher than it had been before automatic enrollment was introduced.[6] Although the low dropout rate is, of course, partly due to inertia, the fact that so few people drop out does suggest that workers are not suddenly discovering, to their dismay, that they are saving more than they had wanted.

FORCED CHOOSING AND MORE SIMPLICITY

An alternative to automatic enrollment is simply to require every employee to make an active decision about whether to join the plan. If a worker is eligible when he is first hired, he might be required to check a 'yes' or a 'no' box for participation in order to get paid. With required choosing in place, employees have to state their preferences, and there is no default option. As compared with the usual opt-in approach (you are not enrolled unless you decide to fill out the forms), required choosing should increase participation rates. One company switched from an opt-in regime to active decisions and found that participation rates increased by about 25 percentage points.[7]

A related strategy is to simplify the enrollment process. One study tested this idea by analyzing a simplified enrollment form.[8] New employees were handed enrollment cards during orientation with a 'yes' box for joining the plan at a 2 percent savings rate and a pre-selected asset allocation. Employees did not have to spend time choosing a savings rate and asset allocation; they could just check the 'yes' box for participation. As a result, participation rates during the first four months of employment jumped from 9 percent to 34 percent. These simplified enrollment procedures are very much in the spirit of the 'channel factors' we mentioned in Chapter 3. People really do want to join the plan, and if you dig a channel for them to slide down that removes the seemingly tiny barriers that are getting in their way, the results can be quite dramatic.

While automatic enrollment or 'quick' enrollment makes the process of joining a retirement plan less daunting, expanding the number of funds available to participants can have the opposite effect. One study finds that the more options in the plan, the lower the participation rates.[9] This finding should not be surprising. With more options, the process becomes more confusing and difficult, and some people will refuse to choose at all.

CHOOSING CONTRIBUTION RATES

Both automatic enrollment programs and forced choosing plans typically adopt a relatively low default savings rate of 2 or 3 percent, and a very conservative investment choice, such as a money market account. It turns out that many employees continue saving at the default rate of 2 percent. This rate is usually far too low to provide enough money for retirement. Many employees also remain in the default investment fund, and they lose a lot of money as a result. We will turn to investment strategies in the next chapter. Here let's see how we can help nudge the people who are saving too little.

One indication that people need help in picking a savings rate and don't realize that they need the help is that most people spend very little time on this important financial decision. One survey found that 58 percent spent less than one hour determining both their contribution rate and investment decisions.[10] Most people spend more time than that picking a new tennis racket or television set. Apparently, many people are using some simple shortcuts. In many plans, participants are asked to state a desired savings rate as a percentage of pay. Many people simply pick a 'round number,' typically 5, 10, or 15 percent of income. Of course, there is no sensible reason why the correct percentage of your income to save would be an exact multiple of 5.

Another common rule of thumb is to contribute to a retirement account the minimum amount necessary to get the full employer match. If the employer matches employees' contributions up to 6 percent of pay, then many employees contribute 6 percent. If participants are behaving this way, then firms wanting to encourage employee savings might alter their matching formula to help workers. Changing the match formula from 50 percent on the first 6 percent of pay to 30 percent on the first 10 percent of pay would probably increase contribution rates. Those who use the match threshold as a rule of thumb would save more with a higher matching threshold. And by picking a round number as the threshold, the company would nudge those who use the 'multiple of 5' heuristic.

EDUCATION

What else can employers do, if they want more employees to enroll in retirement plans, contribute an amount that will build a reasonable retirement nest egg, and allocate the funds among assets in an appropriately diversified way? Education is the obvious answer, and many employers have tried to educate their employees to make better decisions. Unfortunately, the evidence does not suggest that education is, in and of itself, an adequate solution.

One large employer, having offered its employees the chance to switch from a defined-benefit to a defined-contribution plan, provided a free financial education program.[11] The employer measured the effectiveness of this education by administering a before-and-after test of financial literacy. The quiz used a true/false format, so random answers would receive, on average, a score of 50 percent. Before the education, the average score of the employees was 54; after the education, the average score crept up to 55. Teaching is hard!

Employees often leave educational seminars excited about saving more but then fail to follow through on their plans. One study found that at the seminar everyone expressed an interest in saving more, but only 14 percent actually joined the savings plan. This was an improvement, but not a large one, over the 7 percent of comparable employees who did not attend a seminar and joined the savings plan.[12] Studies of the effects of attendance at a 'benefit fair' also find only a small effect on participation in a tax-deferred savings account.[13]

SAVE MORE TOMORROW

Although automatic enrollment is effective at getting new and young workers to enroll sooner than they would have otherwise, participants tend to stick with the default contribution rate, which is typically quite low. To mitigate this problem, consider a program of automatic escalation of contributions, developed by Thaler and his frequent collaborator Shlomo Benartzi, called Save More Tomorrow.

Save More Tomorrow is a choice architecture system that was constructed with close reference to five psychological principles that underlie human behavior:

- Many participants say that they think they should be saving more, and plan to save more, but never follow through.
- Self-control restrictions are easier to adopt if they take place some time in the future. (Many of us are planning to start diets soon, but not today.)
- Loss aversion: people hate to see their paychecks go down.

- Money illusion: losses are felt in nominal dollars (that is, not adjusted for inflation, so a dollar in 1995 is seen as worth the same as a dollar in 2005).
- Inertia plays a powerful role.

Save More Tomorrow invites participants to commit themselves, in advance, to a series of contribution increases timed to coincide with pay raises. By synchronizing pay raises and savings increases, participants never see their take-home amounts go down, and they don't view their increased retirement contributions as losses. Once someone joins the program, the saving increases are automatic, using inertia to increase savings rather than prevent savings. When combined with automatic enrollment, this design can achieve both high participation rates and increased savings rates.

The first implementation of Save More Tomorrow occurred in 1998, at a midsized manufacturing firm. Employees were given the opportunity to meet one-on-one with a financial consultant. The consultant had a laptop with software designed to compute suggested savings rates based on relevant information provided by each employee (such as past savings and the retirement plan of a spouse). About 90 percent of the employees accepted the offer to meet with the financial consultant. Many were a bit surprised by what they heard. Because most employees were saving at very low rates, the adviser told almost every employee that he needed to save a lot more. Often the software suggested a savings rate equal to the maximum allowed in the plan, 15 percent of pay. But the consultant quickly realized that such suggestions were immediately rejected as infeasible, so he generally suggested increasing the savings rate by 5 percentage points of pay.

About 25 percent of the participants accepted this advice and immediately increased their savings rates by the recommended 5 percentage points. The rest said that they could not afford the cut in pay; these reluctant savers were offered the Save More Tomorrow program. Specifically, they were offered a plan in which their savings rates would go up by 3 percentage points every time they got a pay raise. (A typical pay raise was about 3.25 to 3.50 percent.) Of this group of employees who were unwilling to increase their savings rate immediately, 78 percent joined the program to increase their contribution with every pay raise.

The results provide a dramatic illustration of the potential power of choice architecture. Compare the behavior of three groups of employees. The first group consists of those who chose not to meet with the consultant. This group was saving about 6 percent of their income when the program started, and that percentage did not budge over the next three years. The second group contains the employees who accepted the advice to increase their savings rates by 5 percentage points. Their average savings rate jumped from just over 4 percent to just over 9 percent after the first raise occurred. This rate was then essentially constant over the next few years. The third group includes those who joined the Save More Tomorrow plan. That group started with the lowest savings rate of the three groups, around 3.5 percent of income. Under the program, however, their savings rates steadily rose, and three and a half years and four pay raises later, their savings rate had almost quadrupled, to 13.6 percent – considerably higher than the 9 percent savings rate for those who accepted the consultant's initial recommendation to raise savings by 5 percentage points.

Most of the people who enrolled in the Save More Tomorrow program stuck with it for the full four raises, whereupon the increases were halted because the employees had reached the maximum they were allowed to contribute in the plan. The few employees who did leave the program did not ask that their savings rates be dropped back to their earlier low levels. Instead, they just stopped increasing their contribution rates.

In the years since this pilot program, many retirement-plan administrators have adopted the Save More Tomorrow idea, including Vanguard, T. Rowe Price, TIAA-CREF, Fidelity, and Hewitt Associates. Save More Tomorrow is now available in thousands of employer plans. The Profit Sharing Council of America reports that as of 2007, 39 percent of large employers in the United States have adopted some type of automatic escalation plan. As the plan is implemented in various ways, we have been able to learn more about what makes the program work.

In the first implementation, as we have seen, participation was more than 80 percent, but this was in an environment in which each employee was approached individually by the financial consultant, and the consultant was able to fill out the relevant forms on the spot. In contrast, participation rates have been small in some cases in which employees have had to hunt for an obscure location on a financial services Web page in order to sign up. Our main conclusion should not be surprising to anyone who has read this far into the book: participation rates jump when enrollment is easy. Holding a seminar to explain the plan helps; having the forms there to fill out helps even more. (Have we mentioned that channel factors matter?)

The most effective way to increase enrollment in a Save More Tomorrow plan is to combine it with automatic enrollment. The Safelite Group was the first to implement automatic enrollment in a Save More Tomorrow plan. The program was introduced to employees in June 2003. Ninety-three percent of participants took no action and thus were automatically enrolled in the program. In the year following the implementation of the program, only 6 percent actively opted out. Those who stayed in the program will have significantly more money available for retirement.

THE ROLE OF THE GOVERNMENT

The initiatives discussed thus far have been entirely a private-sector phenomenon. Firms have tried automatic enrollment without any nudging from the government. The primary role government needed to play was getting out of the way by reducing the barriers to adoption of these programs. To an increasing extent, the United States government has done exactly that. Beginning in June 1998, Mark Iwry, then a Treasury Department official in charge of national pension policy, directed the Internal Revenue Service to issue a series of rulings (and official pronouncements) that defined, approved, and promoted the use of automatic enrollment in retirement savings plans.

In the summer of 2006 Congress passed the Pension Protection Act, with enthusiastic backing from both parties. The details are complex and boring, so we will put those in an endnote and simply point out that the law offers employers an incentive to match employee contributions, automatically enroll them in the plan, and automatically increase their contribution rates over time.[14] The incentive is that the employer is given a waiver from an annoying regulation. Although reasonable people can quibble with the specific provisions of the act (which represent the usual sort of political compromises), we think that it is an excellent example of nudging. Employers are not required to change their plans, but if they do, they get a reward that actually saves the taxpayers money (because no one has to read or check the form that no longer has to be completed).

It is also possible to incorporate nudges directly into government-run pension schemes. New Zealand has been one pioneer in this effort. In 2007, that nation launched the aptly named KiwiSaver program. People were given some financial incentives to join, including an initial subsidy of one thousand New Zealand dollars. But on top of that, the government automatically enrolled all workers (starting a new job) in the plan. The initial results are interesting. In the first month that the program was launched, a majority of the enrollees were actively opting into the program. However, within two months the number of participants being automatically enrolled began to outstrip the opt-ins, and by six months into the program automatic enrollment became the main method of enrollment. It is also interesting to note that two-thirds of those who opted into the program also made an active choice of investment scheme, whereas of those who were automatically enrolled, only 8 percent made an active investment choice.[15]

Automatic enrollment has also been incorporated in the National Pension Savings Scheme (NPSS) that will be launched in the United Kingdom in 2012. In this plan, workers will contribute 4 percent of their salary and employers will contribute 3 percent, so joining will be highly attractive to workers on economic grounds. But Lord Adair

Turner, who led the commission that designed the NPSS, was aware of the risk that people would nonetheless neglect to join, and he sought to eliminate that risk. For that reason, people are automatically enrolled.

Of course, it would also be possible to incorporate a Save More Tomorrow feature into national savings programs of this kind. Workers might be automatically enrolled in a pension plan in which the amounts devoted to savings would increase with increases in wages. We hope some country tries that approach soon.

7

Naïve Investing

We have been exploring the first part of saving for retirement: joining a plan and deciding how much to invest. We now turn to the all-important second part: how to invest the money.

Once again the emerging switch from defined-benefit to defined-contribution plans has given employees more control, more options, and more responsibility. Although solving the problem of how much to save is hard, choosing the right portfolio is even harder. In fact, in an effort to make what we say about it comprehensible, we will simplify the actual problems people face. Just take our word for it that things are really even harder than we are letting on.

The first question investors face is this: how much risk to take? As a rule, riskier investments such as stocks (also called equities) earn higher rates of return than safer investments such as government bonds or money market accounts. Choosing the appropriate mix of stocks and bonds (and possibly other assets such as real estate) is called the asset-allocation decision. If an investor is willing to allocate more of her money to risky assets, then she will usually make more money, but of course more risk means taking the chance that returns will actually be lower. And the decision of how much to save is related in complex ways to the willingness to bear risk. Someone who insists on investing everything in a safe money market account that earns a modest rate of interest had better be saving quite a bit if she wants to have enough to have a comfortable retirement.

Suppose an investor chooses to invest 70 percent of her money in stocks and 30 percent in bonds. That choice still leaves open many specific questions of how the money is to be invested. In retirement accounts, most investors do not choose stocks individually but rather invest via mutual funds. The funds themselves differ in how risky they are, and how much they charge for their services. Some funds are specialized (investing only in companies in a particular industry or country, for example) while others invest broadly. There are also funds designed for one-stop shopping, blending a mix of stocks and bonds together. Should investors form their own blend or choose a fund blended for them? Further complicating the mix is that some companies offer employees the opportunity to invest in the company's own shares. Should workers want to own shares in the company they work for?

Making all these decisions is hard work (or should be if done carefully), and participants might be excused for thinking that having made these choices they can relax and look forward to a wonderful retirement. However, all these decisions should be revisited periodically. An investor who chose to invest half her money in stocks and half in bonds could find that stocks have shot up and two-thirds of her portfolio is now invested in stocks. Should something be done? Should some of the stocks be sold to get back to the 50–50 allocation? Or should she put more of her money in stocks, because they seem to be doing so well? Econs have no trouble with all these decisions, but Humans can easily become flummoxed. As we will see, Human investors are making all kinds of mistakes in this domain, and could benefit from a more helpful and forgiving investment choice architecture.

STOCKS AND BONDS

How should you decide how much of your portfolio should be invested in stocks? (Do you know how much of your portfolio is invested in stocks?) Of course you know that stocks have historically earned higher rates of return, but by how much?

Consider the eighty-year period from 1925 to 2005. If you had invested a dollar in U.S. Treasury bills (short-term, completely safe, bonds issued by the government), you would have turned your dollar into $18, a 3.7 percent rate of return per year. That does not seem bad until you realize that just to keep up with inflation you had to earn 3.0 percent per year. If you had invested your money in longer-term bonds, your dollar would have become $71, a 5.5 percent rate of return, which is quite a bit better. But if you had invested in mutual funds that held shares in the largest American companies (such as an S&P 500 index fund), your dollar would have grown into $2,658, a 10.4 percent rate of return, and if you had invested in a broad portfolio of the stocks of smaller companies, you could have earned even more. Stocks have earned more than bonds in most other countries around the world as well, roughly by similar magnitudes.

In economics jargon, in which stocks are referred to as equities, the difference in the returns between Treasury bills and equities is called the 'equity premium.' This premium is considered to be compensation for the greater risk associated with investing in stocks. Whereas Treasury bills are guaranteed by the federal government, and are essentially risk free, investments in stocks are risky. Although the average rate of return has been 10 percent, there have been years when stocks have fallen by more than 30 percent, and on October 19, 1987, stock indexes fell 20 percent or more all around the world in a single day.

How would Econs decide how much of their portfolio to invest in stocks? An Econ would make a trade-off between risk and return that would be based on his preferences about retirement income. That is, he would decide whether the possibility of being, say, 25 percent richer is worth the risk of being 15 percent poorer. Needless to say, even if it occurred to Humans to think about the problem this way, they would not know how to make the necessary calculations. The decisions they do make will differ from those of Econs in two ways. First, they will be unduly influenced by short-term fluctuations, and second, their decisions are likely to be based on rules of thumb. Let's consider each in turn.

COUNTIN' YOUR MONEY WHILE
SITTIN' AT THE TABLE

Recall from Chapter 1 that Humans are loss averse. Roughly speaking, they hate losses about twice as much as they like gains. With this in mind, consider the behavior of two investors, Vince and Rip. Vince is a stock broker, and he has constant access to information about the value of all of his investments. By habit, at the end of each day, he runs a little program to calculate how much money he has made or lost that day. Being Human, when Vince loses five thousand dollars in a day he is miserable – about as miserable as he is happy at the end of a day when he gains ten thousand dollars. How does Vince feel about investing in stocks? Very nervous! On a daily basis, stocks go down almost as often as they go up, so if you are feeling the pain of losses much more acutely than the pleasure of gains, you will hate investing in stocks.

Now compare Vince with his friend and client Rip, a scion of the old Van Winkle family. In a visit to his doctor Rip is told that he is about to follow the long-standing family tradition and will soon go to sleep for twenty years. The doctor tells him to make sure he has a comfortable bed, and suggests that Rip call his broker to make sure his asset allocation is where it should be. How will Rip feel about investing in stocks? Quite calm! Over a twenty-year period, stocks are almost certain to go up. (There is no twenty-year period in history in which stocks have declined in real value, or have been outperformed by bonds.) So Rip calls Vince, tells him to put all his money in stocks, and sleeps like a baby.

The lesson from the story of Vince and Rip is that attitudes toward risk depend on the frequency with which investors monitor their portfolios. As Kenny Rogers advises in his famous song 'The Gambler': 'You never count your money when you're sittin' at the table, / There'll be time enough for countin' when the dealin's done.' Many investors do not heed this good advice and invest too little of their money in stocks. We believe this qualifies as a mistake, because if the investors are shown the evidence on the risks of stocks and bonds over a long period of time, such as twenty years (the relevant horizon for many investors), they choose to invest nearly all of their money in stocks.[1]

MARKET TIMING:
BUY HIGH, SELL LOW

Throughout the 1990s, people were increasing the proportion of their retirement money invested in stocks, both in terms of the percentage of money contributed each year and the account balances held. What produced this shift in behavior? One (rather remote) possibility was that investors had spent the decade poring over finance and economics journals, had learned that stock returns had been substantially higher than bond returns over the past century or so, and so decided to invest more in stocks. The other (considerably more likely) possibility is that investors had come to believe that stocks only go up – or that even if stock prices fall, that is just another buying opportunity because they quickly rise again. The stock market provided an opportunity to test these competing hypotheses during the 2000–2002 market turndown.

One way to analyze the market-timing ability of investors is to see how their asset-allocation decisions (that is, the proportion of their portfolios invested in stocks) changed over time. The problem with this approach is that, as we have already mentioned, most people hardly ever change their portfolios unless they change jobs and have to fill out a new set of forms. So a better way to judge what people are thinking is to look at the percentage of money being invested in stocks by new participants who have just made the decision. We have data on one large group of such participants who were customers of plans administered by the Vanguard mutual fund company. In 1992 new participants were allocating 58 percent of their assets to equities, and by 2000 that percentage had risen to 74. In the next two years, however, the allocation to equities for new participants fell back to 54 percent. Their market timing was backward. They were heavily buying stocks when stock prices were high, and then selling stocks when their prices were low.

We observe similar behavior in the asset allocations within equities. Some plans allow investors to choose funds that specialize in particular industries or sectors. We have data from one such plan that offered its employees the option of investing in a technology fund. In 1998, in the early phase of the rapid run-up in the shares of technology companies, only 12 percent of employees invested in the technology fund. By 2000, when technology share prices were peaking, 37 percent of employees had money invested in that fund. After the fall in these share prices, the number of new participants investing in the technology fund had dropped back down to 18 percent by 2001. Again, participants were buying into the technology fund most aggressively at the peak, and selling after prices had fallen.

RULES OF THUMB

Even the most sophisticated investors can sometimes find the decision about how to invest their money daunting, and they resort to simple rules of thumb. Take the example of the financial economist and Nobel laureate Harry Markowitz, one of the founders of modern portfolio theory. When asked about how he allocated his retirement account, he confessed: 'I should have computed the historic covariances of the asset classes and drawn an efficient frontier. Instead, I split my contributions fifty–fifty between bonds and equities.'[2]

Markowitz was not alone. In the mid-1980s most educators had a defined-contribution pension plan provided by a company that goes by its initials, TIAA-CREF. At that time the plan had only two options – TIAA, which invests in fixed-income securities such as bonds, and CREF, which invests mostly in stocks. More than half of the participants in this plan, many of them professors of some sort, selected exactly a 50–50 split between these two options. One of these 50–50 investors was Sunstein. Notwithstanding his long-standing friendship with Thaler, who many years ago told him that over the long haul CREF was a better bet than TIAA, he hasn't changed a thing. It is on his list of things to do, right after canceling those magazine subscriptions.

Of course, an even split between stocks and bonds is not a self-evidently dumb portfolio, but if the initial allocation is never changed (or 'rebalanced,' in the finance parlance), then over time the mix of assets will depend on the rates of return. For example, Sunstein has been investing equal amounts into TIAA and CREF for more than twenty-five years, and he now has well over 60 percent of his money in CREF. The reason is that stocks have significantly outperformed bonds over the time period he has been a professor. If he had invested most of his money in stocks, he would have done a lot better.

Markowitz's strategy can be viewed as one example of what might be called the diversification heuristic. 'When in doubt, diversify.' Don't put all your eggs in one basket. In general, diversification is a great idea, but there is a big difference between sensible diversification and the naïve kind. A special case of this rule of thumb is what might be called the '1/n' heuristic: 'When faced with "n" options, divide assets evenly across the options.'[3] Put the same number of eggs in each basket.

Naïve diversification apparently starts young. Consider the following clever experiment conducted by Daniel Read and George Loewenstein on Halloween night.[4] The 'subjects' were trick-or-treaters. In one condition, the children approached two adjacent houses and were offered a choice between the same two candy bars (Three Musketeers and Milky Way) at each house. In the other condition, they approached a single house, where they were asked to 'choose whichever two candy bars you like.' Large piles of both candies were displayed to ensure that the children would not think it was rude to take two of the same. The two conditions produced quite different results. In the house with both kinds of candy, every child selected one of each candy. In contrast, only 48 percent of the children picked one of each candy when they were choosing in sequence in two houses.

Although the consequences of picking two different candies are minimal (Three Musketeers and Milky Way are both pretty good), naïve diversification in portfolio selection can have more significant consequences on what people do, and on how much money they end up having. In a revealing study, university employees were asked how they would invest their retirement money if they had just two funds to choose from.[5] In one condition, one of the funds invested entirely in stocks, the other in bonds. Most of the participants chose to invest their money half and half, achieving an asset allocation of 50 percent stocks. Another group was told that one fund invested entirely in stocks and the other 'balanced' fund invested half in stocks and half in bonds. People in this group could have also invested 50 percent of their money in stocks by putting all their money in the balanced fund. Instead, they followed the 1/n rule and divided their money evenly between the two funds – ending up with mostly stocks. People in a third group were given a choice between a balanced fund and a bond fund. Well, you can guess what they did.

This result implies that the set of funds offered in a particular plan can greatly influence the choices participants make. To test this prediction, Benartzi and Thaler (2001) examined behavior in retirement saving plans of 170 companies. They found that the more stock funds the plan offered, the greater was the percentage of participants' money invested in stocks.

Many plans have attempted to help participants deal with the difficult problem of portfolio construction by offering 'lifestyle' funds that blend stocks and bonds in a way designed to meet the needs of different levels of risk tolerance. For example, an employer might offer three lifestyle funds: conservative, moderate, and aggressive. These funds are already diversified, so individuals need pick only the fund that fits their risk preference. Some funds also adjust the asset allocation with the age of the participant.

Such a fund assortment is a good idea and represents an excellent set of default options (if the fees are reasonable). But when the funds are just included in a mix of other funds, many people appear not to understand how to use them. For example, few participants put all of their money into one of these funds, even though that is the mission for which they were designed. This is the equivalent of a not-particularly-hungry diner going to a restaurant that offers a set five-course menu and ordering the set menu plus the roast duck and a dessert. One study investigated the behavior of participants in a plan that offered three lifestyle funds and six other funds (an index fund, a growth fund, a bond fund, and so on).[6] Curiously, the participants who invested in the conservative lifestyle fund allocated just 31 percent to that fund, dividing the rest among the other funds. Because the menu of other funds is dominated by stock funds, the resulting stock exposure for those investing in the conservative fund was 77 percent. These participants end up with a fairly aggressive portfolio, probably without being aware of it.

NUDGES

Through better choice architecture, plans can help their participants on many dimensions. Attention to choice architecture has become increasingly important over the years because plans have greatly increased the number of options they offer, making it even harder for people to choose well.

Defaults

Historically, most defined-contribution plans did not have a default option. Participants who joined the plan would be given a list of options, with the instructions to allocate their money as they wished among the funds offered. No default option was necessary until plans began to adopt automatic enrollment, a regime that requires a default: if participants are enrolled automatically, they have to be enrolled into some specific asset allocation. Traditionally, firms have selected their most conservative investment option as the default, usually a money market account.

Most specialists consider a 100 percent allocation to a money market account to be too conservative. The combination of the low rates of return earned (barely above inflation) and the low savings rates by many employees is simply a recipe for poverty in your golden years. Firms chose this option not because they thought it was smart, but because they were worried about lawsuits if they defaulted employees into something more sensible (but riskier). In a rational world, this choice would be irrational. It is as irresponsible to nudge people toward investments that are too safe (and thus earn tiny returns) as it is to nudge them toward investments that are too risky.

Fortunately, many good default options are available. One alternative is to offer a set of model portfolios that have varying degrees of risk. We have noted that some plan sponsors offer conservative, moderate, and aggressive 'lifestyle' portfolios. All a participant needs to do is select the lifestyle fund that best fits his risk preferences. Another option available to plan sponsors is to offer plan participants 'target maturity funds.' Target maturity funds typically have a year in their name, like 2010, 2030, or 2040. A participant simply selects the fund that matches her expected retirement date. Managers of the target maturity funds select the degree of risk and gradually shift the allocation away from stocks and toward conservative investments as the target date approaches.

Some vendors and plan sponsors have started to offer automated solutions for portfolio selection. In particular, some plan sponsors automatically assign participants to a target maturity fund based on a standard retirement age. Others are defaulting participants into 'managed accounts,' which are typically portfolios of stocks and bonds whose allocations are based on the age of the participants and possibly other information.

Structuring Complex Choices

A defined-contribution plan like a 401(k) plan is an excellent domain in which to offer a process for making decisions that fit the needs of participants who have various levels of interest and sophistication. Here is an outline of a promising approach. New enrollees would be told that if they do not want to select their own investment plan, they can choose the default fund that has been selected with some care by knowledgeable experts. This might be the managed account discussed above. Participants who want to be somewhat more involved would be offered a choice among a small set of balanced or life-cycle funds (with the intention that each participant would invest all her money in a single fund). For those who wanted to get really involved, a full menu of mutual funds would be offered, allowing sophisticated investors (or those who believe themselves to be sophisticated) the ability to invest as exotically as they choose. Many firms are starting to implement plans much like this.

Expect Error

To help those who would not get it together to join, we encourage automatic enrollment, which we would combine with Save More Tomorrow to help people achieve an adequate savings rate.

Mappings and Feedback

Most employees have difficulty understanding how numbers like savings rates, expected rates of return, and volatility translate into changes in their lifestyle when they are old. These abstract concepts can be brought into focus by offering translations into concepts anyone can understand. For example, one might create pictures of various housing options that would be available with alternative levels of retirement income. For the lowest outcome, the participant would be shown a very small, possibly run-down apartment. For higher outcomes, larger homes with swimming pools. These visual displays could be incorporated into regular feedback to participants about how they are doing in reaching their retirement savings goals. So a participant could be told in his annual report that he is currently headed for the hovel, but if he increases his savings rate now (or joins Save More Tomorrow), he could still get to the two-bedroom condo.

Incentives

The primary incentive problems in this context are possible conflicts of interest between the employer and the employee. The issues regarding company stock are a good example. The ERISA laws already require firms to act in the best interest of the employees. These laws should be enforced.

Forming and managing an investment portfolio over a long period of years is difficult. Most firms ask a team of internal experts, helped by outside consultants, to perform this task for the assets they manage. But individual participants typically undertake this task on their own, or with the help of a coworker or relative who may have intuition but lack training for the job. The end result is similar to what might be expected if most of us tried to cut our own hair – a mess. Most people need some help; good choice architecture and carefully selected nudges can go a long way.

8

Credit Markets

It should not be surprising to learn that Human consumers are not any more sophisticated about their borrowing than they are about their investing. Consider Homer Simpson's experience when leasing a recreational vehicle called a Canyonero.

CANYONERO SALESMAN: Okay, here's how your lease breaks down. This is your down payment, then here's your monthly, annnnnnnnnd, there's your weekly.

HOMER: And that's it, right?

SALESMAN: Yup ... oh, then after your final monthly payment there's the routine CBP, or Crippling Balloon Payment.

HOMER: But that's not for a while, right?

SALESMAN: Right!

HOMER: Sweet![1]

Homer's naïveté is less unusual, and more revealing, than it might seem. Let's examine two important lending markets – mortgages, and credit cards – to see whether some nudges might help the many Homers among us.

MORTGAGES

Once upon a time shopping for a mortgage was pretty easy. Most mortgages had a fixed rate for the life of the mortgage, typically thirty years. Most borrowers provided a 20 percent down payment. In this regime, comparing loans was a snap – just pick the loan with the lowest interest rate. In the United States, this task was made especially easy with the passage of the choice-friendly Truth in Lending Act which required all lenders to report interest rates the same way, using what is called the annual percentage rate (APR). At the time, the Truth in Lending Act was an excellent bit of choice architecture because it made it easy to compare loans. In the absence of a simple way, such as APR, to judge loans, evaluating various mortgage options is quite difficult. A study by Suzanne Shu (2007) finds that even MBA students at a top school had difficulty picking out the best loans, and this was in a task that was much simpler than the one they would encounter in the real world.

In the United States, mortgage shopping has now become much more complicated. Borrowers can choose from a variety of fixed-rate loans (for which the interest rate does not change over the life of the loan), and also numerous 'variable-rate' loans in which the interest rate goes up and down according to movements in the market. Borrowers might also consider such exotic products as interest-only loans, under which the borrower makes no payments toward the principal on the loan, meaning that it is never paid off unless the house is sold (with luck, at a profit) or the borrower either wins the lottery or refinances the loan. Many variable-rate mortgages are further complicated by so-called teaser rates – a low interest rate applies for a period of a year or two, after which the rate (and payments) go up, sometimes dramatically. Then there is the matter of fees, which can vary greatly; points, which are fixed payments the borrower makes in order to receive a lower interest rate; and prepayment penalties that must be paid if the loan is repaid early. In this world, choosing a mortgage makes picking a retirement portfolio look easy. And the stakes are just as big.

Here as elsewhere, the addition of more options has the potential to make people better off, but this potential is realized only if they are able to do a good job of picking the loan that is best suited to their situation and preferences. How do people do in shopping for mortgages? A study by the economist Susan Woodward (2007) examined more than seven thousand loans insured by the Federal Housing Administration (FHA), a government agency that insures smaller loans and allows low down payments. Woodward studied which kinds of borrowers got the best deals, and under what circumstances, after controlling for risk and other factors. Here are some of her key findings:

- African-American borrowers pay an additional $425 for their loans. Latino borrowers pay an additional $400. (The average fee for all borrowers was $3,133 on loans that averaged about $105,000.)
- Borrowers who live in neighborhoods where adults have only a high school education pay $1,160 more for their loans than borrowers who live in neighborhoods where adults have a college education.
- Loans made by mortgage brokers are more expensive than those made by direct lenders by about $600.
- Sources of loan complexity such as points and seller contributions to closing costs (which can make comparing loans more difficult) are expensive for borrowers, and the additional cost is greater on brokered loans than on direct loans.

We can take some general lessons from this analysis. When markets get more complicated, unsophisticated and uneducated shoppers will be especially disadvantaged by the complexity. The unsophisticated shoppers are also more likely to be given bad or self-interested advice by people serving in roles that appear to be helpful and purely advisory. In this market, mortgage brokers who cater to rich clients probably have a greater incentive to establish a reputation for fair dealing. By contrast, mortgage brokers who cater to the poor are often more interested in making a quick buck.*

These factors are exacerbated in the segment of the market that caters to the poorest and highest-risk borrowers, the so-called subprime market. As is often the case, there are two extreme views about

---

* One brief aside here: economists often argue that when the stakes go up, people will have an incentive to get expert advice. That statement is surely true, but it does not follow that they will actually ask for and get helpful advice. In the mortgage market, many people mistakenly think that the mortgage broker is providing this service, but the broker is hardly an unbiased source. In no way do we mean to single out mortgage brokers in this respect. The poor are often fleeced by people pretending to be providing a service.

subprime loans. Some, particularly those left of center or in the news media, label all such loans with the derogatory term *predatory*. This broad brush fails to recognize the obvious fact that higher-risk loans will have to have higher interest rates to compensate the people who lend the money. The fact that poor and risky borrowers pay higher interest rates does *not* make these loans 'predatory.' In fact, the microfinance loans in developing countries that led to a well-deserved Nobel Peace Prize for Muhammad Yunus in 2006 often come with interest rates of 200 percent or more, yet the borrowers are made better off by these loans.[2] On the other side, some observers think that the hue and cry about predatory lending is based entirely on the failure of left-leaning journalists and others to understand that risky loans require higher interest rates. As usual, the truth lies somewhere between the two extremes. Subprime lending is neither all good nor all bad.

The good feature of subprime lending is that it offers credit to those who could not otherwise borrow, and makes it possible for some poor or high-risk families to become homeowners (or business owners). Subprime loans also give people a valuable second chance. Subprime lenders provide funding for any large purchase. More often than not, these purchases help people achieve an American dream – *better* home ownership. In fact, the vast majority of subprime loans are either refinanced mortgages or home equity loans.

In what sense then are subprime loans really predatory? Subprime borrowers are often unsophisticated, and they are sometimes exploited by brokers. A front-page story in the *Wall Street Journal* described in some detail the behavior of one such broker, Altaf Shaikh, a onetime professional cricket player turned pushy mortgage lender.[3] Shaikh, who jumped from one mortgage company to another, made a long series of loans that greatly profited him but were generally less beneficial to his customers. For the type of borrowers Shaikh favored, here is the typical pattern. The borrowers are approached by the broker, who acts like he is doing them a favor, and so they may not do much shopping. Solicitation can be in person or via mail or nearly any other medium. For example, a home-improvement contractor might stop by a house to suggest a renovation, and then conveniently refer the residents to a mortgage broker.

At the follow-up meeting, the broker suggests different mortgages to the prospective borrower. Here the borrower can 'choose' the interest rate, monthly payment, and number of points she wants to pay. This last choice is particularly confusing: points allow borrowers to pay a fee (an amount that is added to the loan because the borrower typically borrows money to pay for the points) in exchange for a lower interest rate, but few borrowers are capable of figuring out whether the points are worth paying. (Hint: usually they are not.)

Once the borrower agrees to a particular mortgage, the law requires that a 'good-faith estimate' be presented, spelling out all the costs of the loan, including the fee being paid to the broker. Although this estimate must be shown to the borrower within three days of the initial application, it is sometimes withheld until right before the borrower signs the mortgage. At that point, the estimate will be part of a huge pile of papers that are more often shuffled than read. This defeats the whole purpose of the estimate. The same problem occurs at closing. The broker brings a stack of papers for the borrower to look through and sign. Even though these forms describe the terms and conditions of the mortgage, signing the paperwork is a formality for most people. At such a late stage, most borrowers are not in any position to rethink (or, for that matter, think).

Ironically, part of this problem was brought on by good intentions. The Truth in Lending Act was originally intended to summarize the terms of the loan in clear language. But it is hard to see 'truth' when it is buried in a mountain of fine print. For high-risk loans, a Home Ownership and Equity Protection Act disclosure is supposed to give extra warning to the borrower. But the disclosure form doesn't explicitly say 'high-risk,' and the borrower simply needs to sign the form and buyers often just start signing without doing much reading.

Other confusing forms make it difficult for a borrower to distinguish between the loan itself and the fees involved. Mortgage forms have hundreds of lines, and the numbers that clutter the form can obscure various charges. Many of the fees aren't defined. Some borrowers do not know that they will be charged more if they pay off their mortgage ahead of time – that is, they will face a prepayment penalty. And it doesn't help that most subprime loans have variable rates that further complicate the problem of understanding the transaction.

In 2007, an eruption of subprime foreclosures began in the United States, causing ripples throughout global financial markets, and eventually leading to the financial crisis of 2008. The crisis has prompted many governments to think much harder about how to help. Of course markets, left alone, might solve part of the problem, because investors who had bought up subprime loans would learn the hard way that the loans were riskier than they seemed. (In many ways, the mortgage brokers were deceiving the investors who bought up the loans as well as the people who borrowed the money.) But market forces did not prevent the problem from occurring, so there have been calls for more intervention. Some demand an end to predatory lending, but because loans do not come stamped 'predatory,' it is hard to implement any such ban without depriving many deserving but high-risk borrowers from any source of financing. And to be sure, everyone recognizes that regulation can do some good in this complex domain; indeed, a dose of regulation may be highly desirable. But even if this is so, we libertarian paternalists would like to consider nudges as well. A valuable step would be an improvement in choice architecture to help people make better choices and avoid loans that really are predatory – loans that exploit people's ignorance, confusion, and vulnerability. In fact, we think that the entire mortgage market could benefit from a major upgrade in choice architecture.

The basic problem is that the old Truth in Lending Act is now hopelessly inadequate. When interest rates vary and there are myriad fees to pay, just looking at the APR is far from enough. The law professor Lauren Willis (2006) suggests one strategy for reform, which is to limit the set of permissible mortgages in order to make comparison easier. This would involve banning mortgages with such features as negative amortization or balloon payments; in these mortgages, large payments are due at the end because the mortgage and interest have not been fully paid over the term. The idea is that if there were fewer types of mortgages – for example, only thirty-year fixed-rate loans – then borrowers would have an easier time choosing wisely. Willis thinks that the costs of these exotic mortgages outweigh the benefits. Willis also proposes that the loan estimate must remain valid for thirty days and that the borrower must wait before purchasing a loan. Although we see some merit in this proposal, and are sympathetic with the goal of making shopping easier, Willis's proposal does not qualify as libertarian paternalism because it prohibits contracts that may be mutually beneficial. Variable-rate mortgages, even with teaser rates, are not inherently bad. For those who are planning to sell their house or refinance within a few years, these mortgages can be highly attractive.

Instead, we think that a version of our RECAP plan can help. We have in mind two versions of RECAP in this domain. In the simplified form, mortgage lenders would be required to report lending costs in two categories: fees and interest. In a version of such a report suggested by Willis all the different types of fees would be reported, but they would be added up into a single salient number.

Woodward's research finds that the people who get the best deals – by a lot! – are those who pay no fee up front. (This just means that the broker pays all the fees out of his commission. There may be occasional free lunches, but there is no such thing as a free mortgage.) The likely explanation for this result is that when the fee is zero, it is simpler for borrowers to compare terms, because the interest rate is the only thing they have to look at. The interest rate disclosure would include the rate, of course, but also a schedule of payments over a period of years, assuming that the underlying interest rates do not change. This would ensure that borrowers at least know what their payments will be when the teaser rate ends. It would be a good idea to add some kind of worst-case scenario information so that borrowers can see how much their payments could go up in the future.

Lenders would also have to provide a machine-readable detailed RECAP report, one that incorporates all the fees and interest rate provisions, including teaser rates, what the variable-rate changes are linked to, caps on the changes per year, and so forth. This information would allow independent third parties to offer much better advice. Our strong hunch is that if the RECAP data were made available, third-party services would emerge to compare lenders. Care would need to be taken that the system did not foster collusion, but we think this would be easy enough to monitor and prevent.

RECAP data would thus make it much easier to shop for mortgages online, which should make the mortgage market more competitive. Online shopping is especially likely to help women and minority groups. A study of automobile shopping found that women and African-Americans pay about the same amount as white males when they buy a car online, but at the dealership they pay more, even after you account for other factors, such as income.[4]

CREDIT CARDS

The credit card is a ubiquitous feature of modern life. It is nearly impossible to function in society without one. Try checking into a hotel, renting a car, or renting a set of golf clubs without a credit card. Good luck. Credit cards serve two functions. First, they provide a mode of payment in lieu of cash, and have largely replaced checks for that purpose in face-to-face transactions – thankfully – although occasionally you still get stuck behind someone in a grocery store checkout line who wants to write a check for a $7.37 purchase. The second purpose of a credit card is to provide a ready source of liquidity if you want to spend more than you currently have in cash. Debit cards, which look just like credit cards, serve only the first function, because they are linked to a bank account and do not allow for borrowing unless linked also to a line of credit. (Warning: some debit cards offer lines of credit at high fees. If you use a debit card to borrow, you should make sure that the fees you pay are lower than they would be with a credit card.)

Credit cards are blessedly convenient. Paying with a credit card is often faster than paying with cash, and lets you avoid struggling with change; digging into your pocket to find the correct change and managing the large jar of pennies at home are vexations from which you are liberated. Not to mention the frequent flyer miles! But if you are not careful, credit cards can be addicting. Consider some numbers from the United States:

- The U.S. Census Bureau reported that there were more than 1.4 billion credit cards in 2004 for 164 million cardholders – an average of 8.5 cards per cardholder.
- Currently, 115 million Americans carry a month-to-month credit card debt.
- In 1989 the average American family owed its credit card companies $2,697; by 2007 that number had grown to about $8,000. And these figures are probably too low because they are generally self-reported. Using Federal Reserve data, some researchers suggest that American households may have an average credit card debt of $12,000. At typical interest rates of 18 percent per year, that translates into more than $2,000 a year in interest payments alone.[5]

Comparable figures can be found in many other nations, and in some ways, the situation seems to be getting worse over time. Looking back at the problems of self-control discussed in Chapter 3, we can see how credit cards create serious problems for some people. In the pre-credit card era, households were pretty much forced to use a pay-as-you-go accounting system. That is why people used jars of money labeled according to purpose or payee. Now if you don't have the cash to fill your car up with gas, there is always your credit card. Credit cards inhibit self-control in other ways. One study by Drazen Prelec and Duncan Simister (2001) found that people were willing to pay twice as much to bid on tickets to a basketball game if they could pay with their credit card rather than cash. There is no telling how much money people pay with the cards in order to get those precious frequent flyer miles. And when the spending limit on one card is reached, there is always another card to use, or a new account can be opened using one of the solicitations that arrive almost daily in the mail announcing that you have been 'preapproved.'

Can libertarian paternalism help? As with mortgages, we think this is a perfect area for RECAP. We suggest that credit card companies should be required to send an annual statement, both hard copy and electronic, that lists and totals all the fees that have been incurred over the course of the year. This report would serve two purposes. First, credit card users could use the electronic version of the report to shop for better deals. By knowing their precise usage and fee payments, customers would get a better sense of what they are paying for.

Here is one example. One way credit card companies have slyly raised prices is by reducing the number of days you have between the time you get your bill and the day your payment is due. If you miss that payment you not only pay a penalty, but you also pay interest on all the purchases you make next month, even if you normally pay off your bill in full. For a heavy credit card user, such as a frequent business traveler, missing a five-thousand-dollar payment by one day can result in an extra payment of more than one hundred dollars.

Second, the report would make more salient to users just how much they are paying over the course of the year. Some credit cards now issue an annual summary of purchases, listed by category, which can help for tax preparation, but the RECAP requirement would force the card issuers to include information on their own fees in this document. Often those fees are hidden. For example, if you make a purchase in a foreign currency, the credit card company tacks on a fee for converting the purchase into dollars (something that costs banks virtually nothing). On your RECAP statement you would be told how much you paid for the privilege of using your card on your vacation to Mexico. Because interest on credit cards is not deductible, there is no particular reason for users to check how much they paid in interest last year on all their credit cards, and fees are likely to be buried and ignored altogether. Imagine the wakeup call for a credit card user who is told that over the past year he paid $2,153 in interest, $247 in late fees, and $57 in currency transaction fees.

Some other nudges could help as well. For example, credit cards always mention the minimum payment you can make when you receive your monthly bill. This can serve as an anchor, and as a nudge that this minimum payment is an appropriate amount.* Of

---

* Similarly, credit card limits, which are nominally in place to limit spending, may serve as high anchors that actually encourage spending.

course, because the minimum payments are tiny relative to the total bill, paying this amount just maximizes the interest payments over time. Credit card companies even make it hard to commit yourself to paying the card off in full each month. Try to set up an automatic payment feature with your credit card and your bank. Chances are the only default option offered is to pay the minimum payment, not the entire bill. We think that companies should be required to allow automatic payment of the full bill.

We have covered a number of topics in this chapter, but the unifying message is simple. For mortgages and credit cards, life is far more complicated than it needs to be, and people can be exploited. Often it's best to ask people to take care of themselves, but when people borrow, standard human frailties can lead to serious hardship and even disaster. Here as elsewhere, government should generally respect freedom of choice; but with a few improvements in choice architecture, people would be far less likely to choose badly.

9

Privatizing Social Security: Smorgasbord Style

In the 2000 U.S. presidential campaign, George W. Bush called for a partial privatization of the Social Security system. According to his plan, a portion of the payroll tax would be designated for individual savings accounts. At the same time that this issue was being debated in the United States, Sweden was launching a system similar to President Bush's proposal. Although Bush's plan did not get much attention in the early years of his administration, it resurfaced prominently in 2005. Though it failed in Congress, some version of this proposal is likely to be considered again before long, either in the U.S. or in another country. Important lessons can be learned from the Swedish experience – lessons, above all, about the limitations of any simple celebration of freedom of choice.

We shall see that Sweden's officials did quite well on some aspects of their choice architecture but made at least one important error that led its citizens to choose portfolios that are not nearly as good as they could have been. A better set of nudges would have helped. By understanding why, we can learn a lot about Social Security reform, and about much else besides.

DESIGN OF THE SWEDISH PRIVATIZATION PLAN

If we were to pick a single phrase to characterize the design of the Swedish plan, it would be 'pro-choice.' In fact, the plan is a good example of the Just Maximize Choices strategy. Give people as many options as possible, and then let them do whatever they want. At almost every stage, the designers opted for a laissez-faire approach. In particular, the plan had the following key features:

1. Participants were allowed to form their own portfolios by selecting up to five funds from an approved list.
2. One fund was chosen (with some care) to be a default fund for anyone who, for whatever reason, did not make an active choice.
3. Participants were encouraged (via a massive advertising campaign) to choose their own portfolios, rather than rely on the default fund.
4. Any fund meeting certain fiduciary standards was allowed to enter the system. Thus market entry determined the mix of funds from which participants could choose. As a result of this process, there were initially 456 (!) available funds. (As of August 14, 2007, there were 783 funds in the plan, but since inception there have been more than 1,000, so some funds come and go rather rapidly.)
5. Information about the funds, including fees, past performance, and risk, was provided in book form to all participants.
6. Funds (except for the default fund) were permitted to advertise to attract money.

If Swedish citizens were all Econs, none of these design choices would be controversial. The combination of free entry, unfettered competition, and lots of choices seems great. But if Swedes are Humans, then maximizing choice may not lead to the best possible outcome. As it turns out, it didn't.

THE DEFAULT FUND

There are two sets of issues relating to the default fund. What should be in the portfolio? And what status should it get from the government – that is, does the government want to encourage people to take up the fund, to discourage them from doing so, or what? Here are a few of the many possible options that might have been selected:

A. Participants are given no choice: the default fund is the only fund offered.
B. A default is picked, but its selection is discouraged.
C. A default is picked, and its selection is encouraged.
D. A default is picked, and its selection is neither encouraged nor discouraged.
E. Required choosing. There is no default option; participants must make an active choice or they forfeit their contributions.

Which of these would a good choice architect select? That depends on the architect's level of confidence in the ability and willingness of the participants to do a good job of choosing portfolios on their own. Option A is hardly a nudge. It eliminates all choice, and so is inconsistent with libertarian paternalism. We don't recommend it.

At the other extreme, plan designers could avoid picking a default fund entirely by forcing everyone to choose a portfolio for themselves – option E, required choosing. If the designers are confident that people will do a good job picking portfolios for themselves, then they might consider this policy. Although required choosing can be attractive in some domains, we think that the Swedish government was right not to insist on it in this particular setting.[1] Inevitably some participants will fail to respond to attempts to reach them (maybe because they are out of the country, ill, preoccupied, unable to communicate, or just clueless). Cutting such people off from all benefits is harsh, and probably unacceptable as a matter of politics or principle. In any case it isn't easy to choose among more than four hundred funds; why should a government force its citizens to make that choice, when some would prefer to rely on what experts say, as captured in the default?

So we are left with the three middle options. If we are to have a default option as well as other choices, should we encourage or discourage its use? Clearly there is a wide variety of choices along the continuum from strongly discouraging the default to strongly encouraging it. What's best? Option D has obvious appeal: simply designate a default but neither encourage nor discourage it. But it is an illusion to think that this alternative fully solves the problem.

What does it mean to be neutral? If we notify people that the plan was designed by experts and has low fees (both true about the actual default chosen), does this constitute encouragement? We don't mean to split hairs here. Our point is simply that designers will have to make a decision about how to describe the default plan, and these decisions will help determine the market share this plan attracts.

In analyzing the middle options, we need to know something about the competence of those who design the default and the competence and diversity of those who might depart from it. If the designers are terrific, if the default fits all, and if the choosers are likely to blunder, then it might make sense to encourage people to select the default. If the designers are essentially guessing, if the choosers know a lot, and if the situations of different choosers are relevantly different, then it might be best to err on the side of official neutrality.

In any case, the Swedish plan adopted a version of plan B. Participants were actively encouraged to choose their own portfolios via an extensive advertising campaign. This advertising effort seems to have had the desired effect, because two-thirds of participants did select portfolios on their own. Participants were more likely to make active choices if they had more money at stake, and, holding money constant, women and younger participants were more likely to make active choices. (We have a theory about why women were more likely to make active choices: we think that women were less likely to lose the enrollment forms, and more likely to remember to mail them in. We admit to having no data to support this theory, and plead guilty to the possibility that we are being overly influenced – via the availability bias – by the fact that our significant others are considerably more organized than we are.)

Of course, one-third of the participants ended up with the default fund, and that figure might well seem high. It was, in fact, the largest market share of any fund. But the government campaigned hard to get people to choose actively, and a sense of the impact of the campaign can be inferred by what has occurred in the years since the plan was started. The upshot is that as the government's campaign diminished in intensity, people became significantly less likely to choose their own portfolios.

Here are a few details. When the plan was launched in the spring of 2000, every participant who was then in the workforce was asked to choose a portfolio. In the years following the launch, new workers (mostly young people) have joined the plan, and they were also asked to choose a portfolio. But soon after the initial enrollment period, the government ended its advertising campaign encouraging participants to make an active choice. Moreover, private funds themselves greatly reduced their advertising aimed at attracting investments. Probably as a result of both these factors, the proportion of people choosing their own portfolios fell as well. For those workers joining the plan in April 2006 (the most recent enrollment period for which we have data), only 8 percent selected their own portfolios!* Because these new participants are primarily young workers, this percentage is most usefully compared with that of workers who were under age twenty-two when the plan was launched in 2000. That group chose their own portfolios 56.7 percent of the time in 2000, much more than now.

DID ACTIVE CHOOSERS MAKE GOOD CHOICES?

Were people made better off by choosing their own portfolios? Of course, we do not have any way of knowing the preferences of individual participants, and we also do not know what assets they may be holding outside the Social Security system, so it is not possible for us to say anything definitive about how good a job they did picking a portfolio. But we can nonetheless learn a lot by comparing the portfolios people actively constructed with the default fund on dimensions that sensible investors should value – such as fees, risk, and performance. To make a long story short, the active choosers didn't do so great.

The default fund appears to have been chosen with some care (see

* In fact, the percentage of active choosers has declined steadily, from 17.6 percent in 2001, the first year after the launch.

Table 9.1). The asset allocation is 65 percent foreign (that is, non-Swedish) stocks, 17 percent Swedish stocks, 10 percent fixed-income securities (bonds), 4 percent hedge funds, and 4 percent private equity. Across all asset classes, 60 percent of the funds are managed passively, meaning that the portfolio managers are simply buying an index of stocks and not trying to beat the market. One good thing about index funds is that they are cheap. The fees they charge investors are much lower than those charged by funds that try to beat

Table 9.1. *Comparison of the default fund and the mean actively chosen portfolio*

Asset allocation	Default (%)	Mean actively chosen portfolio (%)
Equities	82	96.2
Sweden	17	48.2
Americas	35	23.1
Europe	20	18.2
Asia	10	6.7
Fixed-income securities (bonds)	10	3.8
Hedge funds	4	0
Private equity	4	0
Indexed	60	4.1
Fee	0.17	0.77
Returns for the first three years	−29.9	−39.6
Returns through July 2007	+21.5	+5.1

Note: The table compares the default fund and the mean actively chosen portfolio. The data on the asset allocations are from data on funds' holdings from Morningstar. Fee is the yearly expense ratio as a percentage of fund assets. Ex post performance is returns over a three-year postreform period (October 31, 2000 through October 31, 2003). Funds' market shares following the portfolio choices in year 2000 have been used as weights to calculate the characteristics of the mean actively chosen portfolio.

the market. These low fees for the index funds helped keep the costs in the default fund very low, 0.17 percent. (This means that for every $100 invested, the investor is charged 17 cents per year.) Overall, most experts would consider this fund to be very well designed.

To see how the active choosers did as a group, we can examine the comparable figures for the aggregate portfolio selected initially by the participants who made their own choices. There are three points of interest in this comparison. First, although the allocation to stocks in the default plan was quite high, it is even higher in the portfolios actively chosen: 96.2 percent. People probably chose to invest so heavily in stocks because the stock market had been booming for the previous few years.

Second, the active choosers elected to invest nearly half their money (48.2 percent) in the stocks of Swedish companies. This reflects the well-known tendency of investors to buy stocks from their home country, something that economists refer to as the home bias.[2] Of course you might think that investing at home makes sense: buy what you know! But when it comes to investing, buying what you think you know does not necessarily make sense.

Consider the following fact. Sweden accounts for approximately 1 percent of the world economy. A rational investor in the United States or Japan would invest about 1 percent of his assets in Swedish stocks. Can it make sense for Swedish investors to invest 48 times more? No.*

Third, only 4.1 percent of the funds in the selected portfolios were indexed. As a result, the fees paid by the active choosers are much higher: 0.77 percent compared with the 0.17 percent charged by the default fund. This means that if two people invest $10,000 each, the active investor is paying $60 a year more in fees than the one who took the default portfolio. Over time, these fees add up.† In summary, those who selected portfolios for themselves selected a

---

* If you are worried about currency risk, that is a problem easily solved, and in fact the default fund did solve it, by hedging in the currency markets (essentially a type of insurance).

† The fees we report here are the ones that were advertised. Later some funds offered discounts, so fees fell.

higher equity exposure, more active management, much more local concentration, and higher fees.

At the time these investments were made, it would have been hard to make the case that the actively selected portfolios were better investments than the default fund. And although a few years of returns do not prove anything, not only was the default fund designed better at the start, but it has also performed better. Because of the decline in the market that followed the launch of this plan, investors did not do well for the first three years (from October 31, 2000, through October 31, 2003), but those who invested in the default fund suffered less. The default fund lost 29.9 percent in those three years, while the average portfolio of those participants who picked their funds actively lost 39.6 percent.

In subsequent years the default fund has continued to outperform people's choices. Through July 2007 the default fund is up 21.5 percent while the average actively managed portfolio is up only 5.1 percent. Indeed, the performance of the default fund has been so good over this period that the fund rating service Morningstar has given the fund its highest, five-star, rating (compared with other 'global' funds) since 2003. In contrast, the aggregate portfolio selected by participants would probably have received three stars if it were considered a single global fund.

An interesting feature of the Swedish experience is that the launch of the fund occurred just as the bull market in stocks (and the bubble in technology stocks) was ending. Although it is impossible to specify the precise effect of this accident of timing on people's choices (or even on the decision to launch the privatization program), the data provide some strong hints. We have already noted that the actively chosen portfolios had more than 96 percent of their money in stocks. Had the launch occurred just two years later, the proportion invested in stocks would almost certainly have been lower. As we saw in Chapter 7, individual investors tend to be trend followers, rather than good forecasters, in their asset-allocation decisions.

In a period in which technology stocks had been soaring, it is not surprising that the investments were also tilted toward those stocks. To give one illustrative example, the fund that attracted the largest market share (aside from the default fund) was Robur Aktiefond Contura, which received 4.2 percent of the investment pool. (This is a huge market share: keep in mind that there were 456 funds, and that one-third of the money went into the default fund.) Robur Aktiefond Contura invested primarily in technology and health care stocks in Sweden and elsewhere. Over the five-year period leading up to the choice, its value increased by 534.2 percent, the highest of all the funds in the pool. In the first three years after the launch of the program, it lost 69.5 percent of its value. In the subsequent three years, the returns have continued to be volatile.

In retrospect, it cannot be a surprise that a fund like Robur Aktiefond Contura would get a large percentage of the investments in the pool. Think about what people are being asked to do. They receive a book that lists the returns for 456 funds over various time horizons, along with a lot of other important information, involving fees and risk, that they are not well equipped to understand. The one thing they are probably sure of is that high returns are good. Of course, these are past returns, but investors have traditionally had trouble distinguishing between past returns and forecasts of future returns. We can't help but imagine the following conversation going on over a kitchen table somewhere in Sweden between Mr and Ms Svenson.

MR SVENSON: Wilma, what are you doing with that book?
MS SVENSON: I am looking for the best fund to invest in, Björn. And I think I just found it. Robur Aktiefond Contura is the winner. It is up 534 percent over the past five years. If we invest in this we can retire in Majorca!
MR SVENSON: Yeah, whatever. Can you pass the gravlax?

Because the investments of participants are influenced by recent returns, the timing of the launch of the program can have a strong impact on people's choices. This effect can be long lasting, because only a tiny percentage of participants decide to alter their portfolios. Status quo bias is alive and well in Sweden. In the first three years, the percentage of participants who made at least one change to their portfolios during the year was only 1.7, 2.7, and 3.1, respectively.

This is similar to the inertia found in U.S. 401(k) (defined contribution) plans.[3] The combination of undue attention paid to recent returns and inertia in managing the portfolio thereafter means that the accident of timing (when the new system is launched) can end up having a profound impact on the investments that participants choose.

In fact, 'accident of timing' may be the wrong phrase, because a privatization plan seems most likely to be approved after a long bull market. Witness the decline in political support for the Bush plan after the bear market of 2001 and 2002. Political judgments, no less than investment decisions, can be driven by recent, available events.[4]

ADVERTISING

The decision to allow funds to advertise does not seem particularly controversial. In fact, given the rest of the design of this system, it is hard to imagine an advertising ban. If funds are free to enter this market, then presumably they should be free to court customers by all legal means, which naturally include (truthful) advertising. Still, it is interesting to see what effect advertising had on this market. What should we expect?

Consider two extreme 'dream' scenarios. In the first dream, one being dreamt by a free-market economist with a peaceful smile on his face, advertisers are helping to educate consumers by explaining the benefits of lower costs, diversification, and long-run investing, as well as the folly of extrapolating recent returns into the future. In this dream, ads help each consumer discover her own ideal location on what economists call the 'efficient frontier' – the place all rational investors want to find. In other words, the advertising helps consumers make better, smarter choices.

The other dream is more of a nightmare, one that keeps psychologists and behavioral economists tossing and turning. In this dream, advertisers are encouraging participants to think big, not to settle for average (by indexing), and to think of investing as a way to get rich. In this nightmare, ads almost never mention fees. But they do talk a lot about past performance, even though there is essentially no evidence that past performance predicts future performance. (People who like to bet on sporting events will recognize a parallel in advertisements telling people about 'locks' on upcoming games, and about the amazing and nearly infallible forecasts of, say, the past three weeks.)

How did reality turn out? A typical ad showed the actor Harrison Ford, of *Star Wars* and *Indiana Jones* fame, plugging a Swedish fund company's products. According to the ad copy, 'Harrison Ford can help you pick a better pension.' We are not sure which of Ford's roles qualifies him to provide this advice. (We do know that Indiana Jones is depicted as a professor from the University of Chicago, but, alas, he was not in the business school or the economics department.)

More generally, a study by Henrik Cronqvist (2007) shows that the ads resembled the nightmare more than the happy dream. Only a small proportion of fund advertising can be construed as directly informative about characteristics relevant for rational investors, such as funds' fees. And while funds heavily advertised past returns (for those funds that had high returns), such ads in no way forecasted good future returns. Nevertheless, fund advertising did strongly affect investors' portfolio choices. It steered people into portfolios with lower expected returns (because of higher fees) and higher risk (through a higher exposure to equities, more active management, more 'hot' sectors, and more home bias).

DOING (BADLY) WITHOUT NUDGES

The tale of privatization of Social Security in Sweden is highly revealing. The basic problem is that government planners did not choose the best choice architecture. Instead, they relied on a kind of dogmatic commitment to the Just Maximize Choices mantra, in a way that led to predictable effects from availability bias and inertia. Better choice architecture could have helped.

We have emphasized that on the key issue of choosing a default, the designers of the Swedish plan did an excellent job. The default plan was selected with care, and we think many people outside of Sweden would invest in the fund if it were available. This outcome belies the notion that governments are inherently incapable of doing anything right. The worst feature of the Swedish plan was the decision to encourage participants to choose their own portfolios. In complex situations, the government might actually be able to provide some useful hints. Recall a main lesson from Part I: if the underlying decision is difficult and unfamiliar, and if people do not get prompt feedback when they err, then it's legitimate, even good, to nudge a bit.

In this context, it would have been better for the government to say something like this: 'We have designed a program that has a comprehensive set of funds for you to choose from. If you do not feel comfortable making this decision on your own, you could consult with an expert, or you could choose the default fund that has been designed by experts for people like you.' The Swedish government seems to agree with us: it no longer actively encourages people to choose their own portfolios.

If the United States ever adopts similar partial privatization of its own Social Security system, whether as an alternative to or substitute for the traditional system, many lessons can usefully be learned from the Swedish experience. Because the US economy is more than thirty times as big as Sweden's, a similar free-entry system would probably generate thousands of funds. This might make those who believe in the Just Maximize Choices mantra happy, but most Humans would find choosing from such a long list bewildering. A better plan would start by following Sweden's lead of choosing a good default plan, containing mostly index funds with managers selected by competitive bidding. Participants would then be guided through a simplified choice process (preferably on the Web). The process would start with a yes-or-no question: 'Do you want the default fund?' For those who said yes, their task would be done (though of course they could always change their minds at a later date). Those who rejected the default would be offered a small set of blended funds, perhaps based on the age of the participant (again privately managed with competitive fees). Only participants who rejected all of these funds would get to the comprehensive list. Evidence from the private sector suggests that few participants would make use of the big list, but their right to do so would be fully protected.

An examination of the Swedish experience offers a much broader lesson. The more choices you give people, the more help with decision making you need to provide. As we will see, that is a lesson that the people who designed the American Medicare prescription drug program did not learn. It is usually good to provide people with lots of options, but when the question is complicated, sensible choice architecture guides people in the right directions.

PART III

Society

IO

Prescription Drugs:
Part D For Daunting

Many people around the world may be surprised to learn that Americans are required to pay for their own prescription drugs, either directly or by purchasing an insurance policy, often provided by their employer. Many elderly Americans rely on a government program called Medicare for their health insurance, and until recently Medicare did not cover prescription drugs. Solving this problem was one of the major issues discussed in the 2000 presidential campaign.

Democrat Al Gore, then vice president, proposed a classic government mandate. Gore wanted to add prescription drug coverage to Medicare, assemble a panel of medical experts to work out the specifics, and offer one package to all seniors. Republican George W. Bush, in contrast, offered what might be considered a good example of the theme of his campaign: compassionate conservatism. Indeed, Bush tried to combine compassionate conservatism with a major role for free markets and the private sector. He offered seniors an expensive new entitlement program – but one that featured a wide variety of drug plans devised by private health care companies and that let consumers choose whether to join and which plan to pick.

Three years later, President Bush's version passed on a narrow vote in Congress. The largest overhaul in Medicare's history, Bush's plan created a half-trillion-dollar federal subsidy for prescription drug coverage called Part D. 'The reason why we felt it was necessary to provide choices is because we want the system to meet the needs of the consumer,' President Bush told a clubhouse of Florida seniors in

2006, with the plan's rollout under way. 'The more choices you have, the more likely it is you'll be able to find a program that suits your specific needs. In other words, one-size-fits-all is not a consumer-friendly program. And I believe in consumers, I believe in trusting people.'[1]

President Bush's trust in American seniors left them with a great deal of decision-making responsibility. As such, it is an interesting and instructive example of choice architecture. A system of constrained free choice might seem like a nice example of libertarian paternalism in action. And in fact, we think that on some dimensions Bush was on the right track. As a health care delivery system, Part D met its planners' expectations reasonably well. As a piece of choice architecture, however, it suffered from a cumbersome design that impeded good decision making. It offered a menu with lots of choices, which is fine, but it had four major defects:

- It gave participants little guidance to help them make the best selections from that menu.
- Its default option for most seniors was nonenrollment.
- It chose a default at random (!) for six million people who were automatically enrolled, and it actively resisted efforts to match people and plans based on their prescription drug histories.
- It failed to serve the most vulnerable population, specifically the poor and the poorly educated.

Do not misunderstand. Part D has done a lot of good. Contrary to the charges of the critics, it has not been an unmitigated disaster. But there is plenty of room for better choice architecture.

Our discussion in this chapter will be fairly detailed; it is difficult to understand the program, and what is wrong with it, without a sense of the key choices and where they went sour. But if the four defects are kept in mind, the forest will not be lost for the trees.

DESIGN OF MEDICARE PART D

Before Part D, about half of all American seniors – approximately twenty-one million – had some form of prescription drug coverage through private plans (sometimes offered by their former employer) or a government source such as the Department of Veterans Affairs. Government officials had high hopes of covering the rest through Part D. The working principle was to provide seniors with as many federally approved choices as possible. The result was a policy with five key features.

1. For most people, Part D is a voluntary plan; you benefit only if you enroll in it. An exception applies to 6.2 million low-income seniors and disabled people who were previously covered by Medicaid (the government medical insurance program for the poor). These two groups are supposed to choose from a subset of the private plans, namely the cheapest and most basic plans meeting certain benchmarks (in 2007 states had between five and twenty basic plans). Anyone who does not make an active choice is enrolled randomly into one of these plans.

2. The initial enrollment period ran from November 2005 to May 2006, with open enrollment periods at the end of every subsequent year. Seniors who did not enroll when they became eligible, and who lacked a comparable private plan, faced a penalty on their premiums for every month they delayed.

3. Plans differ across states, from 47 stand-alone plans in Alaska to 63 in West Virginia and Pennsylvania. Most states offer between 50 and 60 plans. The total number of available plans has increased since the law was enacted.

4. During the initial enrollment period, the government sponsored a $400 million public awareness campaign encouraging people to choose a plan. Medicare officials, including the secretary of health and human services, traveled the country in a giant blue bus to promote the program. Companies also sent out their own advertisements. Currently, seniors are advised to 'rely on advice from people you know or trust,' 'choose a plan you are already familiar with,' or use a customized guide

called the Medicare Prescription Drug Plan Finder on the Medicare Web site.[2]

5. Coverage starts with the first prescription a patient needs, but then stops for a while after the patient has spent a certain amount of money, only to start up again when another spending plateau is reached. In the popular press, this coverage gap is usually described as the 'doughnut hole.' Because we know well that discussion of the details of Plan D can cause dangerous headaches even without any mention of the doughnut hole, we will consign any further discussion of this issue to the endnotes. Let's just say that no economist would ever recommend an insurance policy with this feature.

If the people eligible for these plans were Econs, none of these design features would be a problem. 'If consumers are up to this task, then their choices will ensure that the plans, and insurers, that succeed in the market are ones that meet their needs,' writes the Nobel Prize winner Daniel McFadden, a University of California–Berkeley economist who has studied Part D extensively. 'However, if many are confused or confounded, the market will not get the signals it needs to work satisfactorily.'[3] With so many complex plans to choose from, it should not be a huge surprise that seniors have had a difficult time sending the right signals.

CONFUSION AWAITING CLARITY

As the six-month window for enrolling in Part D was closing, people were struggling to sign up. Consider the experience of seniors in McAllen, Texas. Known as the City of Palms, McAllen is a town of one hundred thousand people, located in the Rio Grande valley near the Mexican border. A manufacturing hub for multinational corporations, McAllen is the kind of poor town – about one-fifth of residents sixty-five and older live in poverty – that was intended to benefit hugely from Part D.

To obtain those benefits, however, eligible residents first needed to wade through forty-seven prescription drug plans. 'Intellectually, the program is a good idea,' said Dr E. Linda Villarreal, a former president of the Hidalgo-Starr County Medical Society. 'But there's been total chaos and confusion among most of my patients, who do not understand the system and how to work it.' Ramiro Barrera, a co-owner of Richard's Pharmacy in Mission, said: 'The new Medicare program is a full-time job. We are swamped with requests for help from beneficiaries.'4

The experience in McAllen was hardly unique. Seniors everywhere were confused. So were their doctors and pharmacists. Together they overwhelmed Medicare hot lines set up to help people figure out the best plan for them. Critiquing Medicare Part D's complexity became so common that *Saturday Night Live* spoofed the maze of detail in a phony public service commercial. The commercial promised a simple and easy plan to tech-savvy seniors who had succeeded in completely mastering their computers, iPods, and satellite televisions.

President Bush sympathized with the frustration but said that the program would ultimately be worth the pain. 'I knew that when we laid out the idea of giving seniors choices, it would create a little confusion for some,' he told the Florida seniors. 'I mean, after all, up to now there hadn't been many choices in the system, and all of a sudden, [for] a senior who feels pretty good about things [here comes] old George W and all of a sudden forty-six choices pop up.'

How were seniors expected to handle all those choices? President Bush urged them to have patience and to turn to private institutions for assistance. 'We encouraged all kinds of people to help,' he said. 'AARP is helping; NAACP is helping; sons and daughters are helping; faith-based programs are helping people sort through the programs to design a program that meets their needs. I readily concede some seniors have said, there are so many choices, I don't think I want to participate. My advice is there is plenty of help for you.'

The impulse here was commendable, but you have now read enough to know that offering people forty-six choices and telling them to ask for help is likely to be about as good as no help at all. And in Medicare Part D's case, many of the groups meant to assist seniors were confused themselves. The confusion spread to medical professionals, who agreed with their patients that the number of plans in the current program bewildered everyone. Others, such as AARP, decided to go into the business of offering insurance plans as well as giving advice about which plan to select, a pretty obvious conflict of interest.

In the end, getting seniors into a plan turned out not to be the biggest problem. Organizations were ultimately successful at signing up large numbers of beneficiaries.[5] As of January 2007 fewer than 10 percent of all Medicare beneficiaries – about four million – had no drug coverage, either through Part D or an equivalent private plan.[6] One-quarter of those in a plan were probably healthy enough that they did not need to enroll immediately.[7] Their participation, however, was crucial to Part D's survival, because they helped to subsidize sick seniors. To federal health officials, the high enrollment was a sign of undeniable success. To this extent, freedom of choice has worked – a nice point for those who reject, as we do, the idea that one size fits all.

Overall, seniors seem happy about the program (as they should be, because it provides them with an enormous government subsidy!). Since the passage of the new Medicare law, disapproval of the program has steadily fallen while approval has risen, in an apparent tribute to rapid learning over time. In November 2005, just as seniors were getting their first taste of forty-plus plans, half of eighteen hundred seniors surveyed had an unfavorable view of the program, compared with 28 percent who viewed it favorably. By November 2006 the unfavorable rating had fallen to 34 percent, while the favorable rating had risen to 42 percent. When asked about their own personal experiences, three out of four held a 'very' or 'somewhat' positive view of Part D.[8]

Seeing these patterns, a vigorous defender of Part D could claim that, as with any new program, participants underwent a sometimes painful educational process, but, on the whole, were ultimately satisfied with the plan they chose. Overwhelming majorities thought they had made good choices, though for reasons to be developed shortly, we doubt that many had much basis for that evaluation.

Of course it is true that because of learning, once-complicated choices become easier. But we think that there has been a lot less learning about Part D than a casual look suggests. For starters, the high enrollment rates were achieved in part because approximately two-thirds of seniors were easily or automatically enrolled through one of a variety of routes: employer or union plans; Medicaid, Veterans Affairs, or federal employee coverage; or the special, more comprehensive Medicare program known as Medicare Advantage. Advertising campaigns and media coverage certainly boosted awareness, but no one should read the statistics and conclude that thirty-eight million seniors filled out a Part D application because the government asked them to do so.

In addition, many people are still not enrolled in the program, even though it is clear that they should be. Four million uncovered Americans is a large number, and studies suggest that this group is probably dominated by poorly educated people living just above the poverty line (and thus not eligible for Medicaid). In addition, one-quarter of the 13.2 million seniors eligible for a low-income subsidy – again, most of them poorly educated and living alone – did not take advantage of it. Because coverage for this last group is practically free when the subsidy is added in, 25 percent nonenrollment is disturbingly high.

Even when people do elect to enroll, an abundance of choice can overwhelm them. Since the new Medicare law passed, seniors have consistently told interviewers that they find Part D dumbfounding. After a year of experience in the program, only about one in ten said it was working well and needed 'no real changes.' In November 2006, once again with a year of experience and knowledge, 73 percent of seniors said Part D was 'too complicated,' and 60 percent agreed with a statement that an unnamed party, most likely the government, should 'select a handful of plans so seniors have an easier time choosing.' The consensus of the medical community was even stronger. More than 90 percent of both doctors and pharmacists, who had been bombarded with patient questions throughout the enrollment period, agreed that the program was too complicated.

These responses suggest that overall consumer satisfaction could be a lot higher with a better design. Complexity is the most glaring problem. But it is not the only one. In fact, two other pieces of Part D's choice architecture are just as puzzling.

RANDOM DEFAULT PLANS FOR THE MOST VULNERABLE

In the Introduction, we discussed the options faced by cafeteria supervisor Carolyn; one of those options was to display food items at random. We said that this option could be considered fair-minded and principled, but that it would lead to unhealthy diets at some schools. The option didn't strike us as desirable because it unfairly penalized some students by inducing them to consume a diet consisting entirely of pizza, egg rolls, and ice cream.

Still, this is the option the government adopted for six million of its poorest and sickest citizens. It automatically assigned each person who did not pick a plan on her own to a randomly chosen default plan with premiums at or below certain benchmarks for her specific region. As a result of plan restructuring, another 1.1 million people were eligible for random assignment in 2007. One state, Maine, shrewdly resisted this system in favor of an 'intelligent assignment' process for 45,000 people. We will return to shrewd Maine shortly; for now, we focus on the other forty-nine states.

The poorest and sickest enrollees are those people eligible for both Medicare and Medicaid (and so are called the 'dual eligibles'). These people are disproportionately African-American, Latino, and female. Dual eligibles are more likely to have diabetes and strokes than other Medicare beneficiaries, and they use, on average, ten or more prescription drugs.[9] They include the most severely disabled Americans, physically and cognitively handicapped men and women of all ages, and elderly patients suffering from dementia and requiring full-time care. The government has not said exactly how many dual eligibles actively chose a plan, but the evidence we have suggests that very few did. Dual eligibles are able to switch plans at any time – but if few are actively choosing plans, we suspect that few are taking advantage of the flexible switching option.

Random assignment can cause random harm to unlucky people placed in plans that don't fit their needs. For the drugs that dual eligibles take most often, and that are in categories covered by the law, plans varied considerably in their coverage, from as low as 76 percent to as high as 100 percent. This means that some dual eligibles were defaulted into a plan that did not cover the drugs they use most. They could switch, of course, but being Human, most stayed with the plan that had been lovingly picked at random for them. And given the patchy drug access, it is not surprising that random plan defaults impaired people's health. In a recent survey of dual eligibles, 10 percent reported improved medication access, while more than 22 percent said they had stopped taking medications temporarily or permanently because of problems in managing the new plan.[10]

The government's official reason for rejecting intelligent assignment in favor of random assignment is that people's prescription needs change. Someone's past use is no guarantee of her future use. In the health care community, there has been a lot of head scratching about this argument. Especially for the elderly, who are often on several long-term medications, last year's drug use is often an excellent predictor of next year's, and certainly it is a better predictor than picking a plan out of a hat.

It seems somewhere between callous and irresponsible to assign plans without even looking at people's specific needs. Random assignment is also inconsistent with the market-based philosophy of the plan. In markets, better products get a higher share, and most free-market economists consider this a good feature. We do not think that every automobile manufacturer should get the same market share any more than we think that families should pick their cars at random. Why should we want randomness for insurance plans?

How costly were the mistakes and misallocations caused by this random assignment? One way to examine this issue is to see how many people chose to switch plans after the first year. (Every November there is an open enrollment period when participants can switch plans.) Unfortunately, we don't know as much as we'd like to about plan switching because the government has not been very forthcoming about releasing the data. It did announce that during the open enrollment period for 2007, about 2.4 million – 10 percent of Part D enrollees – changed plans. But of those who changed, 1.1 million were low-income beneficiaries, most of whom were moved unilaterally by the government so that they would not have to pay increased premiums. That means that excluding dual eligibles, only 6 percent actively changed plans. (We suspect that the percentage of active switchers is even lower if we include the entire population of enrollees.)[11]

There are two possible interpretations of these low switching rates. One interpretation, favored by defenders of the plan, and the one that would be correct if we were studying a population of Econs, is that all is going well – the wide variety of plans is handling diverse health conditions, and seniors have chosen the best plan for their needs. The second interpretation, more plausible if the participants are Humans, is that inertia and the status quo bias are keeping people from switching. How can we tell which interpretation is right? One way is by comparing the participants who actively chose their own plan with those who had a plan picked at random for them. For the latter group there can be no presumption that the plan they started with is the best one. And the fact that we find low switching rates for both groups suggests that the second interpretation is right. Most participants seem to find that the burden of switching – the time and energy it takes to decide on the best plan – is just not worth the effort.

Is it worth that effort? The answer depends on how varied the plans are, and how costs differ depending on the set of drugs people use. Consider a comparative study of the prices of drugs covered by basic plans (the kind poor beneficiaries would be defaulted into) in three regions of the country. The study reported savings between $5 and $50 per drug per month when individuals are assigned to the lowest-cost, best-fitting basic drug plan.[12] More data comparing entire plans, as opposed to individual drugs, should be available soon, and we think they will confirm results that other academic teams are beginning to find. Kling's team has estimated almost a $700 annual difference between a randomly chosen plan and the lowest-cost plan. Choosing the right plan, rather than a random plan, has the potential to save both seniors and the government a lot of money. If hundreds of dollars are at stake for every person, many seniors would find it worthwhile to spend at least an hour or two sorting out the best plan (much as they would in choosing a new washing machine or putter).

NOT USER-FRIENDLY

Unfortunately, spending an hour or two is not going to get the job done. The chief tool people have to help choose a plan is the Medicare Web site. 'This will help people make competent decisions,' said the head of federal Medicare offices. 'They'll have an un-precedented array of tools that will help them find a drug plan.'[13] But there is an obvious problem with relying heavily on a Web site. Most seniors do not yet use the Internet, let alone the Medicare Web site, and those who do are rarely Web-savvy (though this will change over time). Most seniors get their information about Part D passively from mailings by insurers, the government, and groups like AARP. Those mailings are highly unlikely to contain personalized information. So the Web site is the best source for help. To whom does the job of navigating the site fall? To seniors' adult children, of course.

An economist friend of ours, Katie Merrell, is one adult who does research on health coverage and took it upon herself to choose plans for both her elderly parents. She found that the task took hours, even for an expert like herself. Katie allowed us to see how painful choosing a plan would be by kindly providing a list of the drugs her mother takes. Thaler logged onto the Medicare Part D Web site and tried his luck. What a nightmare! Just to give one example, the site does not have a spell checker. If you type 'Zanax' instead of 'Xanax,' you don't get any help (unlike at Google, for example). This is a problem because drug names resemble strings of random letters, so typing errors are to be expected. Getting all the dosages right is also tricky. You need to know both the size of the pill (for example, 25 mg) and how frequently it is taken. The Web site assumes you take a generic drug, if it is available, and gives you the option of keeping the premium brand drug. Many people, however, take generics while calling them by their brand name, which requires paying close attention to every drug selection.

Contrast this process with a free piece of software called Epocrates R.x. which helps you find a drug even if you've forgotten its entire name. The software, which loads easily onto an iPhone or another mobile device, allows you or a doctor to figure out the drug through the color, size, and shape of the pills. A formulary reference also contains a library of information about dosages, warnings, prices, and possible interactions with other drugs. Back on the Medicare Web site, once a user manages to get all the data entered, three plans are suggested with annual cost estimates. (Technophobic seniors can call 1–800-MEDICARE and have a customer service representative give them the three plan suggestions and prices, but no explanation is offered for how these plans have been chosen.)[14]

Eventually (with help from Katie that bordered on psychotherapy), Thaler managed to get some answers, though not the same ones that Katie got. Still, because Thaler is nearing Medicare age himself, he thought perhaps someone younger would have an easier time of it. So we asked one of our graduate student research assistants to give it a try. Being younger and more patient helped, but he got yet another set of answers. We then pulled out all the stops and put the youngest and smartest member of our team on the job, our student intern (and *Teen Jeopardy* whiz), who is now studying at a top college. Even she, who normally finds everything easy, was befuddled at times in this process. And no two of us, though armed with the same data, ended up with the same cost estimates or the same recommended plans.*

At first, we were stumped. But it turns out that even four Econs couldn't have mimicked each other perfectly. We all got different estimates because prescription drug plans are constantly updating their drug prices. There is no guarantee that the cheapest plan for your mother today would be the cheapest plan for your mother

---

* Katie tells us we shouldn't feel bad. She used the exercise of picking a plan for her mom in a talk she gave to a group of experts in the field and found a similar range of different answers and comparable frustration.

tomorrow. In fact, Consumers Union has tracked price differences in five large states and found continuous monthly changes. Sometimes these fluctuations are only a few dollars; sometimes more. Nearly 40 percent of the 225 plans underwent changes of more than 5 percent, which can add up to several hundred dollars per year.[15] Frequent price changes are one more hurdle for Humans to jump, and in light of our experience, they can be a rude awakening to those who don't know about them.

DID CHOOSERS MAKE GOOD CHOICES? NOT ALWAYS

What is it like to pick a prescription drug plan? How hard is it to choose the right one? The short answer is: really hard. For the sake of argument, ignore decisions about whether to enroll in Medicare Part D, or whether to enroll in a stand-alone drug plan or a Medicare Advantage plan. Assume that you, like most enrollees, are picking a stand-alone plan. You'll need to compare plans along fifteen major dimensions. (If you doubt that this is confusing, read the endnote, which offers some details, but we suggest taking two aspirin before you start reading.)[16]

True, the Medicare Web site tries to help seniors sort plans across some of these dimensions. But we have already pointed to the pain and suffering that accompany using this Web site, and even if you arrive at the concluding page and see the three cheapest plans available, you shouldn't breathe easy. You will not be able to tell from the Web site whether prior authorization will be hard to obtain in your situation, or what the quantity limit on a particular drug will be. This information is probably available only after you sign up for a plan and attempt to fill the particular prescription.

Figuring out whether seniors are making good choices would require information about their health characteristics and their plans. Given the obvious concerns about privacy, the government has not released these data. But it apparently believes, and even says, that seniors are making good choices. We are not so sure. A good choice is one that meets a person's specific needs. In an experiment, the economist Daniel McFadden and his team have attempted to evaluate how good (or bad) seniors' choices turn out to be. In his study nearly two-thirds of enrollees failed to choose the plan that minimized their out-of-pocket costs.[17]

POSSIBLE NUDGES

As libertarian paternalists, we applaud the Bush administration for insisting on freedom of choice in Part D. We leave it to others to debate the pros and cons of a single-payer plan. But like any plan with lots of options, better choice architecture can help a lot.

Intelligent Assignment

Random default plan assignment is a terrible idea. If a poor person is assigned to a bad plan and does not switch, her drug bills may rise, or she may decide to stop taking an expensive drug, as some already have. This may save the government money in the short run, but it will be costly in the long run, especially for diseases such as diabetes, for which a failure to keep on the drug regime can lead to numerous complications. The government also pays more if it assigns someone to one plan if a different plan covers all that person's drugs and costs 15 percent less.

The most obvious response is to end random assignment in favor of what has been dubbed intelligent assignment. As we have noted, Maine is the only state that uses an intelligent assignment system for placing its dual eligibles in a prescription drug plan.[18] Random assignment 'resulted in a poor fit for many dual eligible beneficiaries in Maine,' according to a Government Accountability Office report. Under random assignment, only one-third of the beneficiaries were placed in plans that covered all of their recently used drugs, and one-quarter were in plans that covered fewer than 60 percent of those drugs.[19]

In Maine, to match each eligible participant with a plan, the ten plans meeting state coverage benchmarks were evaluated according to three months of historical data on prescription use. Participants in plans covering fewer than 80 percent of their required drugs were switched automatically (with participants retaining the option to cancel the reassignment). Another set of participants received letters informing them that better matches existed, and were advised to contact state officials for more information. Intelligent assignment switched more than ten thousand people – 22 percent of all the dual eligibles – and produced dramatic results. Although incomplete data and technology malfunctions created some initial problems, Maine officials now say that every dual eligible is in a plan that covers 90–100 percent of her required drugs.[20]

Maine was not the only state interested in intelligent assignment. In 2005 two leading pharmaceutical groups, the National Association of Chain Drug Stores and the National Community Pharmacists Association, collaborated with a Tampa, Florida, health care information technology company, Informed Decisions, to develop software that matched people with plans. The consortium's presentations to federal government officials were met politely but coolly. (Perhaps its advocates should have called it 'intelligent design.') As a result of skepticism from Washington and legal challenges from insurers, intelligent assignment is used to place dual eligibles only in Maine. Other states should clearly be encouraged, not discouraged, from experimenting with similar methods, and more important, the law mandating random assignment should be revised.

RECAP

Seniors could be helped a lot if our RECAP system were applied to Medicare. RECAP would also make using the Medicare Web site a snap (well, relatively speaking).

Here's how RECAP would work. Once a year, just before the enrollment period opens, companies would send seniors a complete, itemized list of all the drugs used over the previous year and all the fees incurred. Insurers would also have to provide an electronic summary of their complete pricing schedule to anyone who wanted it. The information would be made available online, so it could be imported into both the Medicare Web site and comparison pricing programs that could now easily be offered by third parties. The purpose of the information would be to nudge seniors away from a status quo bias and encourage comparison shopping by making prescription drug costs as salient as possible. Because the costs of delay are high for large majorities of seniors, similar nudges could be used on nonenrollees. Price disclosures could be sent to those seniors who delayed enrollment, with a clear delineation of the recent and current premiums for a sample of popular plans. One goal would be to highlight for seniors how much money a delay costs them.

We believe that in this domain, as elsewhere, the requirement that providers offer a RECAP report would lead private sector firms to offer services allowing participants to input their data to help choose the best plan. In fact, a Massachusetts company called Experion Systems has already developed an online Prescription Drug Plan Assistant tool that is a more user-friendly version of the government Web site's form. An early version of the tool asks people questions that guide better decision making. Experion has also joined with the pharmacy chain CVS/pharmacy to make it possible to import usage information of the sort that would be found on a RECAP report. If a RECAP rule were in place, then Experion could import the relevant usage data no matter where people obtain their prescriptions.

The RECAP information could also be used to improve intelligent assignment programs. One research team has produced some preliminary evidence that a RECAP-style nudge has promise. In a study of Wisconsin beneficiaries, the team estimated that if people moved from their current plan to the lowest-cost plan that continued to meet their drug needs, they could save, on average, about five hundred dollars a year.[21] To see whether people would take advantage of these savings with a slight nudge, the researchers mailed a personal letter to a random sample of study participants who had agreed to share their personal drug histories. The letter explained the costs in their current plan, the cheapest comparable plan, and the savings they could realize by switching plans. Another random sample of participants received generic Part D brochures instead. Both mailings contained the Internet address of the Medicare plan finder Web site and information about how to use it. The personal letters appear to have nudged more people to pick lower-cost plans. The overall switch rate among seniors receiving letters was 27 percent – 10 percentage points higher than among those receiving brochures. More than three times as many letter receivers as brochure receivers picked the cheapest plan – the one mentioned in the letter (although the overall percentages were still in single digits). These results are consistent with other studies showing that people are making errors in their choices among plans, and that simple, clear information can reduce those errors.

The lesson of Part D is similar to that of the Swedish Social Security reform. In complex situations, the Just Maximize Choices mantra is not enough to create good policy. The more choices there are, and the more complex the situation, the more important it is to have enlightened choice architecture. To produce a user-friendly design, the architect needs to understand how to help Humans. Software and building engineers live by a time-honored slogan: keep it simple. And if a building has to be complicated to be functional, then it is best to offer plenty of signs to help people navigate. Choice architects need to incorporate these lessons.

11

How to Increase Organ Donations

The first successful organ transplant took place in 1954, when a man offered his twin brother a kidney. The first transplant of a kidney from a deceased donor occurred eight years later. As they say, the rest is history.

Since 1988 more than 360,000 organs have been transplanted, with nearly 80 percent of the organs coming from deceased donors. Unfortunately, the demand for organs greatly exceeds the supply. As of the end of 2008 there were more than 97,000 on waiting lists for organs, mostly for kidneys, in the United States alone, and hundreds of thousands world wide. Many (possibly as many as 60 percent) will die while on the list, and in the United States the waiting list is growing at a rate of 12 percent per year.* Although this topic is both interesting and important enough to deserve an entire book, we will comment only briefly on the potential effect of better choice architecture in increasing available organs.[1] We think that

---

* Of course, economists have a simple solution to this problem, which is to permit a market in organs. Although the idea has obvious merit, it is also spectacularly unpopular for reasons that are not well understood. We will not address the issue here. For a good summary of the argument in favor of introducing markets see Becker and Elias (2007). Although explicit markets appear to be politically infeasible now, a type of barter exchange does seem to be acceptable. Suppose that each of us needs a kidney, and each has a sibling who is willing to donate but does not have the same blood type (which is essential). If Sunstein's sister was a match for Thaler and Thaler's brother was a match for Sunstein, then a trade could be set up. Much work is now being done in an effort to orchestrate such matches, using techniques similar to those we discuss below involving school choice. A question to ponder: Why is it socially acceptable for Sunstein and Thaler to arrange this trade but unacceptable for Sunstein to offer to buy Thaler's brother a new car in exchange for his kidney?

some simple interventions would save thousands of lives every year – and do so while imposing essentially no new burdens on taxpayers.

The primary sources of organs are patients who have been declared 'brain dead,' meaning that they have suffered an irreversible loss of all brain function but are being maintained temporarily on ventilators. In the United States, roughly twelve thousand to fifteen thousand potential donors are in this category each year, but fewer than half become donors. Because each donor can be used for as many as three organs, getting another thousand donors could save as many as three thousand lives. The major obstacle to increasing donations is the need to get the consent of surviving family members. It turns out that good default rules can increase available organs and thus save lives. Let us consider the possible approaches.

EXPLICIT CONSENT

In the United States, most states use what is called an explicit consent rule, meaning that people have to take some concrete steps to demonstrate that they want to be donors. It is clear that many people who are willing to donate organs fail to take the necessary steps. A study of Iowa residents by Sheldon Kurtz and Michael Saks confirms the point. 'Ninety-seven percent of respondents indicated their general support for transplantation. Sizeable majorities said they were interested in donating their own organs and those of their children (should the tragic circumstances arise that would make them eligible).' However, people's stated willingness to become donors did not translate into the necessary action. 'Of those who expressed their support, only 43% had the box checked on their driver's license. Of those who stated they personally wanted to donate their organs, only 64% had marked their driver's license and only 36% had signed an organ donor card.'[2]

In short, the concrete steps necessary to register as an organ donor appear to deter otherwise willing donors from registering. Many Americans who fail to register as organ donors at least profess to be willing donors. As in other domains, the default rule has a big impact, and inertia exerts a strong influence. Changes in choice architecture would help to ensure that more organs are available, in a way that would not only save lives but also fit with the wishes of the potential donors.

ROUTINE REMOVAL

The most aggressive approach, which is more than a default rule, is called routine removal. Under this regime, the state owns the rights to body parts of people who are dead or in certain hopeless conditions, and it can remove their organs without asking anyone's permission. Though it may sound grotesque, routine removal is not impossible to defend. In theory, it would save lives, and it would do so without intruding on anyone who has any prospect for life.

Although this approach is not used comprehensively by any state, many states do use the rule for corneas (which can be transplanted to give some blind patients sight). In some states, medical examiners performing autopsies are permitted to remove corneas without asking anyone's permission. Where this rule has been used, the supply of corneal transplants has increased dramatically. In Georgia, for example, routine removal increased the number of corneal transplants from twenty-five in 1978 to more than one thousand in 1984.[3] The widespread practice of routine removal of kidneys would undoubtedly prevent thousands of premature deaths, but many people would object to a law that allows government to take parts of people's bodies when they have not agreed, in advance, to the taking. Such an approach violates a generally accepted principle, which is that within broad limits, individuals should be able to decide what is to be done with and to their bodies.

PRESUMED CONSENT

A policy that can pass libertarian muster by our standards is called presumed consent. Presumed consent preserves freedom of choice, but it is different from explicit consent because it shifts the default rule. Under this policy, all citizens would be presumed to be consenting donors, but they would have the opportunity to register their unwillingness to donate, and they could do so easily. We want to underline the word *easily*, because the harder it is to register your unwillingness to participate, the less libertarian the policy becomes. Recall that libertarian paternalists want to impose low costs, and if possible no costs, on those who go their own way. Although presumed consent is, in a sense, the opposite of explicit consent, there is a key similarity: under both regimes, those who don't hold the default preference will have to register in order to opt out.

Let's suppose, for the sake of argument, that both explicit consent and presumed consent could be implemented with 'one-click' technology. Specifically, imagine that the state could successfully contact every citizen (and the parents of minors) by email, asking them to register. In a world of Econs, the two policies would produce identical outcomes. Because the costs of registering are trivial, everyone would click the preferred choice. But even in a one-click world, the default will matter if the population is made up of Humans.

Of course that is how the population is composed, and thanks to an important experiment conducted by Eric Johnson and Dan Goldstein (2003), we know something about how much the choice of the default matters in this domain. Using an online survey, the researchers asked people, in different ways, whether they would be willing to be donors. In the explicit consent condition, participants were told that they had just moved to a new state where the default was not to be an organ donor, and they were given the option of confirming or changing that status. In the presumed consent version, the wording was identical but the default was to be a donor. In the third, neutral, condition, there was no mention of a default – they

SOCIETY

just had to choose. Under all three conditions, the response was entered literally with one click.

As you will now expect, the default mattered – a lot. When participants had to opt in to being an organ donor, only 42 percent did so. But when they had to opt out, 82 percent agreed to be donors. Surprisingly, almost as many people (79 percent) agreed to be donors in the neutral condition.

Although nearly all states in the United States use a version of explicit consent, many countries in Europe have adopted presumed consent laws (though the cost of opting out varies, and always involves more than a click). Johnson and Goldstein have analyzed the effects of such laws by comparing countries with presumed consent to those with explicit consent. The effect on consent rates is enormous. To get a sense of the power of the default rule, consider the difference in consent rates between two similar countries, Austria and Germany. In Germany, which uses an opt-in system, only 12 percent of the citizens gave their consent, whereas in Austria nearly everyone (99 percent) did.

SOME COMPLEXITIES

So far, presumed consent looks awfully good, but we must stress that this approach is hardly a panacea. A program that successfully gets organs from deceased donors to needy transplant recipients requires a complete infrastructure. Currently, Spain is the world's leader in developing that infrastructure, achieving a donation rate of nearly thirty-five donors per million people, compared with a bit more than twenty donors per million in the United States. But the U.S. donation rate is higher than in many presumed consent countries because of the superiority of the American medical system in quickly matching consenting donors with recipients, delivering the organs, and performing successful transplants. The default consent rule, therefore, is not the only thing that matters. Still, careful statistical analyses by the economists Abadie and Gay (2004) find that, holding everything else constant, switching from explicit consent to presumed consent increases the donation rate in a country by roughly 16 percent. Johnson and Goldstein obtain a slightly smaller but similar effect. Whatever the precise figure, it is clear that the switch would save thousands of lives every year.

Determining the exact effect of changing the default rule is difficult because countries vary widely in how they implement the law. France is technically a presumed consent country, but physicians routinely ask the family members of a donor for their permission, and they usually follow the family's wishes. This policy blurs the distinction between presumed consent and explicit consent.

Still, the default rule does matter. In the United States, if there is no explicit donor card for survivors to see, families reject requests for donations about half the time. The rejection rate is much lower in countries with presumed consent rules, even though there is typically no record of the donor's wishes. In Spain the rate is about 20 percent, and in France it is about 30 percent.[4] As one report put it: 'The next of kin can be approached quite differently when the decedent's silence is presumed to indicate a decision to donate rather than when it is presumed to indicate a decision not to donate. A system of presumed consent allows organ procurement organizations and hospital staff to approach the family as the family of a "donor" rather than as the family of a "nondonor." This shift may make it easier for the family to accept organ donation.'[5]

MANDATED CHOICE

Having families overrule the 'implied' consent of donors is just one problem with presumed consent. Another is that it is a hard sell politically. More than a few people object to the idea of 'presuming' anything when it comes to such a sensitive matter. For these reasons, we think that the best choice architecture for organ donations is mandated choice.

Mandated choice can be implemented through a simple addition to the driver's license registration scheme used in many states. With mandated choice, renewal of your driver's license would be accompanied by a requirement that you check a box stating your organ donation preferences. Your application would not be accepted unless you had checked one of the boxes. In 2008 the state of Illinois adopted a version of this procedure. When drivers go to get their photo taken for their new license they are asked if they want to be a donor. If they say yes, they are reminded that becoming a donor means that family members will not be allowed to overrule their wishes and asked if they want to reconsider. The early results of this program are highly encouraging.

NORMS

We hope more states and countries follow Illinois' lead in adopting mandated choice, on the grounds that it is likely to save many lives while also preserving freedom. But even under a system of explicit consent, states could take a few simple steps that would do a great deal of good. Before adopting mandated choice Illinois had implemented a plan to spur donor enrolment that showed a terrific intuitive understanding of choice architecture.

The key part of the plan was the Illinois First Person Consent registry, enacted in 2006, which has helped to attract more than 4 million registered donors by the end of 2008. A central feature of the registry is that after a person gives her consent, additional consent from the donor's family is not required at the relevant time. (This feature is retained in the new mandated choice plan.) Under the previous Illinois system, the only way to be sure that your wishes would be honored was to sign a donor card, or to submit a document signed by two witnesses. The First Person Consent registry greatly reduced the cost of consent by allowing people to register online.

We think that the Web page (see Figure 11.1) used to attract donors is an excellent example of good nudging. First, the state stresses the importance of the overall problem (97,000 people on the waiting list) and then brings the problem home, literally (4,700 in Illinois). Second, social norms are directly brought into play, in a way that builds on the power of social influences: '87 percent of adults in

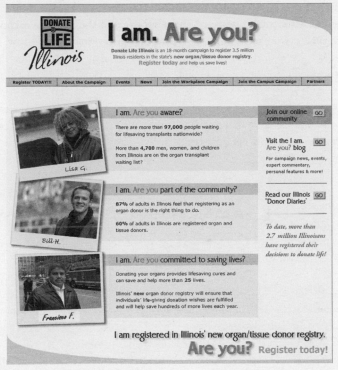

Figure 11.1. *Online promotion of organ donation in Illinois (Used with permission of Donate Life Illinois)*

Illinois feel that registering as an organ donor is the right thing to do' and '60 percent of adults in Illinois are registered.' Recall that people like to do what most people think it is right to do; recall too that people like to do what most people actually do. The state is enlisting existing norms in the direction of lifesaving choices – and doing so without coercing anyone. Third, there are links to MySpace, where people can signal that they are concerned citizens. In the context of environmental protection, people often do what they believe is right in part because they know that other people will actually see them doing what they believe is right. The same might well be true for organ donations.

The Web site is almost certainly saving a significant number of lives, and the combination of the Web site and the mandated choice plan offers two excellent models for other governments to follow.

12

Saving the Planet

In recent decades, governments all over the world have been taking aggressive steps to protect the environment. Concerned about air and water pollution, the spread of pesticides and toxic chemicals, and the loss of endangered species, governments have expended significant resources, hoping to improve human health and to reduce the harmful effects of human activities on wildlife and on pristine areas. Many of their actions have done a lot of good; efforts to reduce air pollution have prevented hundreds of thousands of premature deaths and millions of illnesses as well. But many regulatory efforts have been costly and wasteful, and some of them have aggravated the very problems that they were meant to solve. Aggressive controls of new sources of air pollution, for example, can extend the life of old, dirty sources, and thus increase air pollution, at least in the short run.

In recent years, the focus has shifted to international environmental problems, including depletion of the ozone layer, now controlled by a range of international agreements, which have succeeded in banning ozone-depleting chemicals. But above all, public attention is focused on climate change, which is not yet subject to effective international controls, and on which we shall have a few things to say here. Might nudges and improved choice architecture reduce greenhouse gases? Definitely; we will sketch some promising possibilities.

Most of the time, governments seeking to protect the environment and to control the harmful health effects of pollution have gone well beyond a nudge, and their steps have not been libertarian. In this domain, freedom of choice has hardly been the guiding principle. Regulators have often chosen some kind of command-and-control regulation, by which they reject free choices and markets entirely and allow people little flexibility in promoting environmental goals. Command-and-control regulation is sometimes embodied in technological mandates, through which government effectively requires the environmentally friendly technologies that it prefers; catalytic converters for cars are one example.

More often, government officials do not specify technologies, but require across-the-board reductions in emissions. They might say, for example, that in ten years, all new cars must emit 90 percent less carbon monoxide, on average, than they now do, or that power plants must not exceed certain levels of sulfur dioxide emissions. Or the government might establish a national ambient air quality standard, insisting that every state must meet it by a specified date, and must not allow pollution levels to exceed the standard (except, perhaps, rarely).

In many countries, national emissions limitations imposed on major pollution sources have been the rule, not the exception. Such limitations have sometimes been effective; the air is much cleaner than it was in 1970. Philosophically, however, such limitations look uncomfortably similar to Soviet-style five-year plans, in which bureaucrats announce that millions of people have to change their conduct in the next five years. Sometimes people do change, but sometimes they don't, or the costs of making the changes turn out to be unexpectedly high, and then the bureaucrats have to go back to work. If the goal is to protect the environment, might good choice architecture be able to help?

We are all too aware that for environmental problems, gentle nudges may appear ridiculously inadequate – a bit like an effort to capture a lion with a mousetrap. When the air or the water is too dirty, the standard analysis says that it is because polluters impose 'externalities' (that is, harms) on those who breathe or drink. Even libertarians tend to agree that when externalities are present, markets alone do not achieve the best outcomes. Those who pollute (meaning all of us) do not pay the full costs that we impose on the environment, and those of us who are harmed by pollution (again, all of us) usually lack any feasible way to negotiate with polluters to get them to clean up their acts. People who celebrate freedom of choice are well aware that when 'transaction costs' (the technical term for the costs of entering into voluntary agreements) are high, there may be no way to avoid some kind of government action, even of the coercive kind. When people are not in a position to make voluntary agreements, most libertarians tend to agree that government might have to intervene.

It helps to think about the environment as the outcome of a global choice architecture system in which decisions are made by all kinds of actors, from consumers to large companies to governments. Markets are a big part of this system, and for all their virtues, they face two problems that contribute to environmental problems. First, incentives are not properly aligned. If you engage in environmentally costly behavior next year, through your consumption choices, you will probably pay nothing for the environmental harms that you inflict. This is what is often called a 'tragedy of the commons.' Each dairy farmer has an incentive to add more cows to his herd, because he obtains the benefits of the additional cows while suffering only a fraction of the costs; but collectively the cows ruin the pasture. Dairy farmers need to find some way to avert this tragedy, perhaps through an agreement to limit the number of cows that each will be permitted to add. Similar problems plague the fishing industry, and they help to explain air pollution and the problem of climate change.

The second problem that contributes to excessive pollution is that people do not get feedback on the environmental consequences of their actions. If your use of energy produces air or water pollution, you are unlikely to know or appreciate that fact, certainly not on a continuing basis. Even if you know about the connection, it is probably not salient to your behavior. Those who turn up the air conditioning and leave it on for a few weeks are unlikely to think, moment-by-moment or even day-by-day, about all of the personal and social costs. We thus begin our discussion of environmental problems with these two aspects of choice architecture: incentives and feedback.

BETTER INCENTIVES

When incentives are badly aligned, it is appropriate for government to try to fix the problem by realigning them. In the environmental area, two broad approaches have been proposed. The first is to impose taxes or penalties on those who pollute. In the domain of climate change, a tax on greenhouse gas emissions, favored by many environmentalists (and economists too), is a simple example. The second approach is called a cap-and-trade system. In such systems those who pollute are given (or sold) 'rights' to pollute in certain amounts (the 'cap') and these rights are then traded in a market. Most specialists believe that incentive-based systems such as these should usually displace command-and-control regulation. We agree. Incentive-based approaches are more efficient and more effective, and they also increase freedom of choice.[1]

We freely acknowledge that such proposals are not original, but the fact that we agree with most economists on this issue does not seem a sufficient reason to reject the idea! (We offer some behavioral elaborations below that incorporate the fact that agents in the economy are Humans.) Furthermore, we think that despite its coercive features, this basic approach is in a sense a cousin of libertarian paternalism, because people can avoid paying the tax by not creating pollution. Especially when compared with command-and-control systems, economic incentives have a strong libertarian element. Liberty is much greater when people are told, 'You can continue your behavior, so long as you pay for the social harm that it does' than when they are told, 'You must act exactly as the government says.' Companies much prefer cap-and-trade systems to rigid government commands, because such systems allow more freedom and impose lower costs. If a polluter wants to increase its level of activity, and hence its level of pollution, it isn't entirely blocked. It can purchase a permit via the free market. Assuming that greenhouse gases are to be regulated, many companies have been arguing for a cap-and-trade system for exactly this reason. And if the problem of climate change is to be seriously addressed, the ultimate strategy will be based on incentives, not on command-and-control.

Much of the time, the best approach to pollution problems is to impose a tax on the harmful behavior and to let market forces determine the response to the increased cost. The price of the harm-producing good will go up, and consumption will decline. Many European nations recognize the point. Of course none of us likes taxes. But raising the tax on gasoline, for example, would eventually induce drivers to buy more fuel-efficient cars, drive less, or both. As a result, emissions of carbon dioxide, the leading contributor to global warming, would decline. And if gas taxes were increased, automobile manufacturers would have plenty of incentives to develop new technologies to meet the demand for more fuel-efficient cars. In Europe, unlike in the United States, there has been considerable interest in the use of 'green taxes.'

The alternative cap-and-trade system is similar in spirit and approach. In the pollution context, people who reduce their pollution below a specified level are allowed to trade their 'emissions rights' for cash. In one stroke, such a system creates market-based disincentives to pollute and market-based incentives for pollution control. Such a system also rewards rather than punishes technological innovation in pollution control, and does so with the aid of private markets. Trading systems, based on market principles, are proving increasingly popular at the international level. The Kyoto Protocol, designed to control greenhouse gases, contains a trading mechanism specifically designed to decrease the costs of emissions reductions.[2]

The European Union has shown a great deal of interest in the climate change problem, and many of its nations have contrasted their concern, and their behavior, with that of the United States. And indeed, the EU has created an ambitious program, the Emissions Trading System, which covers about 40 percent of greenhouse gas emissions in the EU. Originally designed to assist the countries of the European Union in meeting their Kyoto requirement, the Emissions Trading System is a cap-and-trade system where fixed emissions allowances are allocated to industry via national allocation plans in each country.[3] An allowance must be surrendered for each ton of CO_2 emitted annually.[4] The allowances are set for multi-year periods known as trading periods; the first trading period ran from 2005 to 2007, and the second will continue through 2012.[5] Currently covered industries include energy, minerals (glass, ceramix, cement), iron and steel, and paper and pulp.[6]

The ETS has been at least modestly successful so far: the increase in verified emissions, adjusted for the entry of new installations, between 2005 and 2006 was only 0.3%, while the increase in the EU's gross domestic product was 3 percent. In 2006, 99 percent of installations were in compliance with the regulations.[7] It has been estimated that the ETS caused a reduction in CO_2 of between 50 and 100 megatons per year, equivalent to 2.5 percent to 5 percent abatement – far less than what is required or sought, but certainly a start.

Incentive-based systems of this kind, including the ETS, have not always lived up to their promise, and have not always gained political traction – in part, we think, because they make the costs of cleaning up the environment transparent. Announcing a new fuel efficiency standard sounds misleadingly 'free,' whereas imposing a carbon tax sounds expensive, even if it is actually a cheaper way of achieving the same goal. One solution to the political problem of getting such bills passed may be to use some mental accounting. For example, the revenues from a carbon tax might be paired with a cut in personal tax rates, the funding of Social Security and Medicare, or the provision of universal health insurance. Similarly, the 'rights' to pollute in a cap-and-trade system can be auctioned off, and the revenues used in the same way. This linking of costs and benefits might help the pill go down more easily.

In the United States, the most dramatic program of economic incentives can be found in the 1990 amendments to the Clean Air Act. Pushed by President George H. W. Bush, and broadly supported by both Republicans and Democrats, the act relies on an emissions trading system for the control of acid deposition ('acid rain'). Indeed, much of corporate America was willing to accept the system on the ground that the ability to trade emissions rights would drive down the cost. With this program, Congress made a specific decision about the 'ceiling' or 'cap' – the aggregate emissions level – for pollutants that produced acid deposition. Polluters are explicitly permitted to trade their allowances. Because pollution reduction can be turned into cash, strong incentives are created for environmentally beneficial behavior.

The acid deposition program has turned out to be a terrific success.[8] Compliance with the program has been nearly perfect. Considerable trading has occurred; an effective market in permits has developed, just as anticipated. Since enactment of the program, the price of transporting coal has been reduced dramatically because of deregulation, and the program has proved able to handle this surprise, with permits trading for far less than anticipated. As compared with a command-and-control system, the trading mechanism is estimated to have saved $357 million annually in its first five years. For its first twenty years, the mechanism was projected to save $2.28 billion annually, for an overall savings in excess of $20 billion.

Indeed, it is fair to say that the acid deposition program ranks among the most spectacular success stories in all of American environmental regulation. Because the costs of the program have been so much lower than anticipated, the cost-benefit ratio seems especially good, with compliance costs of $870 million compared to estimates of annual benefits ranging from $12 billion to $78 billion – including reductions of nearly 10,000 premature deaths and more than 14,500 cases of chronic bronchitis.

It is reasonable to hope that for greenhouse gases, many nations will either rely on carbon taxes or (more likely) build on the acid deposition model, using economic incentives to reduce aggregate emissions. Indeed, much attention has already been given to the possibility of creating worldwide markets in greenhouse gas emissions rights, with a cap on global emissions.[9] A central advantage of such a system is that it would ensure that reductions would be made by those who could do so most cheaply – and that those with a real need for emissions licenses would pay people, perhaps especially in poor nations, who would prefer to have the money.

FEEDBACK AND INFORMATION

Although we think that the most important step in dealing with environmental problems is getting the prices (that is, incentives) right, we realize that such an approach is politically difficult. When voters are complaining about the high price of gasoline, it can be hard for politicians to unite on a solution that raises this price. A key reason is that the costs of pollution are hidden, while the price at the pump is quite salient. So we suggest that along with getting the prices right (or while we are waiting for the political courage to set the prices right), we should take other nudge-like steps that can help to reduce the problem in politically more palatable ways.

An important and highly libertarian step would be an improvement in the process of feedback to consumers through better information and disclosure. Such strategies can improve the operation of markets and government alike, and are also far less expensive, and less intrusive, than the command-and-control approaches that national legislatures have so often favored. To be sure, many environmentalists fear that disclosure by itself will accomplish too little. They might be right. But sometimes information is a surprisingly strong motivator.

All over the world, disclosure is being used as a regulatory tool. In the United States, mandatory messages about risks from cigarette smoking, first established in 1965 and modified in 1969 and 1984, are perhaps the most familiar example of a disclosure policy. The Food and Drug Administration has long maintained a policy of requiring risk labels for pharmaceutical products. The Environmental Protection Agency (EPA) has done the same for pesticides and asbestos. Before the phaseout of ozone-depleting chemicals, warning labels were required for products containing such chemicals. Congress requires warnings on products with saccharin. Under President Reagan, no fan of regulation, the Occupational Safety and Health Administration issued a Hazard Communication Standard (HCS). All employers must adopt a hazard-communication program – including individual training – and inform workers of the relevant risks. The HCS has made workplaces significantly safer, and, aside from mandating disclosure, it has done so without requiring employers to alter their behavior in the slightest.

Some disclosure statutes are designed to trigger political rather than market mechanisms; here the goal is not to give consumers feedback on their decisions but to inform voters and their representatives. In American law, the most famous of these statutes is the National Environmental Policy Act, enacted in 1972. The principal goal of the act is to require government to compile and disclose environmentally related information before it goes forward with any projects having a major effect on the environment. The purpose of disclosure is to activate political safeguards, coming from the government's own judgments once the environmental effects are made clear, or from external pressure on the part of citizens who have learned about those effects. The idea behind the statute is that if the public gets riled up, the government will be pressured to give some weight to environmental effects, but if the public reacts to the disclosures with a yawn, the government would be justified in doing nothing. Many nations have adopted similar statutes, requiring careful consideration of the environmental consequences of proposed courses of action.

One significant success story for disclosure requirements is the Emergency Planning and Community Right to Know Act, a law enacted by Congress in 1986 in the aftermath of the Chernobyl nuclear reactor disaster in Ukraine.[10] Originally a modest and uncontroversial measure, the law was not designed to produce environmental benefits by itself. It was essentially a bookkeeping measure, intended to give the Environmental Protection Agency a sense of what was out there. The statute turned out to do a lot more. In fact, the requirement of disclosure, captured in the Toxic Release Inventory, may be the most unambiguous success story in all of environmental law.

To create the Toxic Release Inventory, firms and individuals must report to the national government the quantities of potentially hazardous chemicals that have been stored or released into the environment. The information is readily available on the EPA Web site to anyone who wants it. More than 23,000 facilities now disclose detailed information on more than 650 chemicals, covering more than 4.34 billion pounds of on-site and off-site disposal or other releases. Users of hazardous chemicals must also report to their local fire departments about the locations, types, and quantities of stored chemicals. And they must disclose information about potential adverse health consequences.

The surprising fact is that without mandating any behavioral change, this law has had massive beneficial effects, spurring large reductions in toxic releases throughout the United States.[11] This unanticipated consequence suggested that all by themselves, disclosure requirements might be able to produce significant emissions reductions.* (We will shortly see how the success of the Toxic Release Inventory might be repeated in the context of climate change.) Lists are used in other environmental areas and countries, such as Italian sea resort cleanliness and recycling, and a climate index for Swedish municipalities.

Why, exactly, has the Toxic Release Inventory had such beneficial effects? A major reason is that environmentally concerned groups, and the media in general, tend to target the worst offenders, producing a kind of 'environmental blacklist.'[12] This is a nice example of a social nudge. No company likes to be on the Toxic Release Inventory list. The bad publicity can result in all sorts of harms, including lower stock prices.[13] Companies that end up on the list are likely to take steps to reduce their emissions. Even better, companies are motivated to ensure that they do not end up on the list. The result is a kind of competition, in which companies enact more and better measures to avoid appearing to be significant contributors to toxic pollution. If companies are able to reduce emissions at low cost, they will do so, simply in order to avoid the bad publicity and the resulting harms.

---

* A paper by Ginger Zhe Jin and Phillip Leslie (2003) documents a similar finding for restaurants. In 1998 Los Angeles County introduced hygiene quality grade cards that had to be displayed in restaurant windows. The researchers found that the grade cards caused the restaurant health inspection scores to improve, consumers' sensitivity to hygiene in restaurants to increase, and hospitalizations for food-borne illnesses to decrease.

With this example in mind, we can now sketch an initial, low-cost nudge for the problem of climate change. The governments of many nations should be creating a Greenhouse Gas Inventory (GGI), requiring disclosure by the most significant emitters. The GGI would permit people to see the various sources of greenhouse gases in the relevant nation and to track changes over time. Seeing that list, governments could respond by considering legislative measures. In all likelihood, interested groups, including members of the media, would draw attention to the largest emitters. Because the climate change problem is salient, a Greenhouse Gas Inventory might well be expected to have the same beneficial effect as the Toxic Release Inventory. To be sure, an inventory of this kind might not produce massive changes on its own. But such a nudge would not be costly, and it would almost certainly help.

Other information-disclosure efforts could be adopted. Since 1975 Congress has required new automobiles to meet fuel economy standards. A helpful disclosure mandate, accompanying the economy standards requirement, was designed to promote competition by requiring companies to post in large print the expected fuel economy buyers can expect from each car (see Figure 12.1).

But what, exactly, do mileage numbers mean? For most of us, the

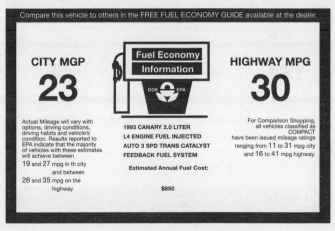

Figure 12.1. *Fuel economy sticker (Environmental Protection Agency)*

answer isn't at all obvious. The goal of promoting competition could be accomplished far more effectively by translating the mileage data into dollars, solving the mapping problem. In fact, the EPA is revising its fuel economy label to highlight the estimated annual fuel cost, as well as the methodology for determining that number. The new label also shows graphically where the specific vehicle falls within the range of mpg ratings for vehicles in its class (see Figure 12.2). The regulations go into effect starting with model year 2008 vehicles.

We applaud the new stickers, though we think they might be even more powerful if they computed a five-year figure for money spent on fuel. Imagine the sticker on a Hummer! Even better would be to post these numbers on the back of the car for other drivers to see. Richard Larrick and Jack Soll of Duke University think labels should display gallons-per-mile instead of miles-per-gallon because the latter obscures the value of gas savings as fuel efficiency improves. One additional mile of efficiency at 10 mpg saves more gas than one additional mile of efficiency at 50 mpg. Humans don't realize this (Econs do), and instead undervalue the mpg improvements when moving from an inefficient car like a Hummer to a moderately

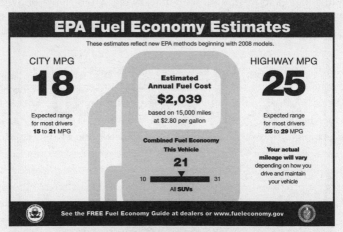

Figure 12.2. *Revised fuel economy sticker (Environmental Protection Agency)*

efficient car like a Ford station wagon, while overvaluing similar jumps between already efficient cars, say from a Honda Civic to a Toyota Prius.[14]

Fuel efficiency, by the way, is not the only reason for the Toyota Prius' commercial success, especially compared with other hybrid cars. Another reason is that the Prius is sold only as a hybrid (unlike, say, a Camry, which is sold in both conventional and hybrid versions). People who want to signal their green credentials are much happier in a Prius than a hybrid Camry because no one will know that the Camry is a hybrid unless she carefully examines some labeling on the car.

Labeling shows enormous potential for tackling environmental challenges, precisely because the concepts involved are so abstract and inscrutable to most of us. Numbers, imagery, and product comparisons help to translate and demystify the larger issues. Alert to this point, Japan is planning to label consumer goods to show carbon footprints in a bid to raise public awareness about global warming. Under the plan, a select range of products from beverages to detergent will carry markings on their carbon footprints – or on how much gas responsible for global warming has been emitted through production and delivery. Similar labels have been introduced in other developed countries, including Britain and France. 'We hope that displaying carbon footprints will raise awareness among consumers as well as companies of their emissions and motivate them to emit less CO_2,' said trade ministry official Shintaro Ishihara.[15]

Similar labeling and disclosure requirements might produce greener housing. In the European Union, where buildings account for 40 percent of energy consumption, information about energy audits and ratings are becoming a required disclosure as part of the home sale or lease process. Incentive problems have long permeated the home-building industry because the costs of making a home more energy efficient are borne up front by the builder, whereas the costs of heating and cooling are later paid by the owners. It is not surprising to find that homes do not have the kinds of energy-saving devices that are common when the building is designed by the ultimate user (and utility bill payer). Take one example from the hotel business.

Many hotel rooms, especially in Europe, require that the plastic room key used to enter the room be inserted in a slot by the door in order to turn on the lights. When the key is removed, the lights and air conditioning go off, but the power to the clock radio does not. Why are rooms designed this way? Because the hotel company has to pay the utility bills, and management knows that customers have no incentive to turn out the lights. Hotel companies are willing to pay the extra cost up front to include this feature.

But why don't we have a similar switch in our homes? Wouldn't you like to be able to flip one switch as you walk out the door that would turn off all the lights but not all the clocks?

AMBITIOUS ENVIRONMENTAL NUDGES

Here is a more ambitious idea. What if a way could be found to ensure that people see, each day, how much energy they have used? Clive Thompson (2007) has explored the efforts of Southern California Edison to encourage its consumers to conserve energy – and its creative, nudgelike solution. Past attempts to notify people of their energy use with emails or text messages did no good, but what worked was to give people an Ambient Orb, a little ball that glows red when a customer is using lots of energy but green when energy use is modest. In a period of weeks, users of the Orb reduced their use of energy, in peak periods, by 40 percent. That flashing red ball really gets people's attention and makes them want to use less energy. (We think it might work even better if, when energy use went over a certain threshold, the device made annoying sounds, such as cuts from ABBA's *Gold: Greatest Hits*.)

As Thompson notes, the underlying problem is that energy is invisible, so people do not know when they are using a lot of it. The genius of the Orb is that it makes energy use visible. Emphasizing the importance of feedback, Thompson suggests that we might find a way to see our daily consumption of energy – and perhaps even to put the relevant figures in a public place, such as a Facebook page.

In fact, a design firm, DIY Kyoto (based on the Kyoto Protocol, the international effort to control emissions of greenhouse gases), already sells the Wattson, a device that displays your energy use and allows you to transmit the data to a Web site, thus permitting comparisons with Wattson users elsewhere. And in Sweden, a group of design engineers and investors have patented a power cord that shows the intensity of the electric current running through it with glowing pulses of light. The longer the light has been on, the brighter the cord glows. Thompson suggests that approaches like these could produce 'a cascade of conservation.'

One way this cascade might unfold is through a bit of friendly competition. John Tierney, a columnist for the *New York Times*, has suggested that people might choose to wear a piece of jewelry, perhaps a lapel pin, with a little glowing footprint, that would change color perhaps from red to yellow to green – depending on their carbon footprint – how much electricity and gasoline they use, how many airplane trips they take (and whether they travel by private jet). Tierney held a contest on his blog to pick a name for this gadget. The winning entry was the iPed (though we liked The AlGoreRhythm best). Here is how Tierney makes his case for the iPed:

Of course, it would be a chore to set up monitors for energy use, but plenty of greens are willing to give lots of time to the cause. Some are accused of being religious zealots – global warmists. But one of the advantages of religion is that it inspires people to acts of selflessness for the common good. Why not reward devout conservationists by letting them display their virtue?

Besides putting the enthusiasm of greens to practical use, this fashion statement might also inject some realism into the debate about global warming. Once you start keeping track of all the energy you use, you begin to see the difficulties of making drastic reductions – and the difference between effective actions and ritual displays. Installing a solar-powered hot-water heater or a windmill at your place in the country is not going to erase the carbon footprint of maintaining and traveling to a second home. Recycling glass bottles and avoiding plastic bags at the grocery store will not offset your car's emissions.[16]

Thanks to technological innovation, we should expect feedback devices to grow more sophisticated every year. Take the Prius, for example, whose interior dashboard display encourages drivers to alter their behavior to save even more gas by avoiding the brakes and accelerating gently.

Gentle acceleration was the goal of automotive giant Nissan when it took a step beyond feedback with an elegantly simple device: an acceleration pedal that literally pushes back when a driver starts to speed. Dubbed ECO Pedal, the system detects excess pressure on the accelerator, and nudges the lead-footed driver by showing her that she could save gas if she eased up just a bit. In-house tests by the company have indicated that the pedal can increase fuel efficiency by 5–10 percent. Drivers have the option of skipping the ECO Pedal, and of course, they can still 'floor it' if they have to make an evasive maneuver.

It's not clear how many people would actually want to make their energy use public or to buy cars that have their own ideas about what good driving looks like. As libertarian paternalists, we don't want public officials to require them to do so. But if people want to get into a kind of competition to conserve more, who could object? The most straightforward point is that if we can find ways to make energy use visible, we'll nudge people toward reducing their energy use without mandating any such reductions.

Here's a related idea: voluntary participation programs designed to assist not individual consumers but companies both large and small. With such programs, public officials do not require anyone to do anything. Instead, they ask companies whether they would be willing to follow certain standards that are expected to have desirable effects on the environment.[17] The basic idea is that even in a free market, companies often fail to use the latest products, and sometimes government can help them to make money while also reducing pollution.

In 1991, for example, the EPA adopted its Green Lights program, which was designed to increase energy efficiency, a goal that (in the agency's view) was simultaneously profitable and good for the environment. The EPA entered into a series of voluntary agreements with both for-profit and nonprofit firms (including hospitals and universities). Through these agreements, firms pledged to implement energy-saving lighting improvements. In 1992 the EPA adopted a similar innovation, the Energy Star Office Products program, also intended to promote energy efficiency, but with a focus on printers, copiers, computer equipment, and appliances in general. The EPA set out voluntary performance standards and allowed participating firms to use the agency's Energy Star logo. In addition, the agency publicized the cooperation of industry groups, adopted substantial media campaigns, and offered awards to companies showing particular gains in energy efficiency.

One of the EPA's major goals has been to show that energy efficiency is not merely good for the environment; it produces significant savings as well. But from the standpoint of standard economic theory, no such savings should be predicted. Here's why. If companies could actually save money while protecting the environment, they would already have done that. In a market economy, firms should not need the government's help to cut their own costs. Competitive pressures should ensure that those that don't cut costs soon find themselves losing money – and out of the market.

In practice, however, things don't always turn out this way. Managers in firms are busy and can't pay attention to everything. To implement some change, someone in the firm has to champion the change. In most firms, managers do not think that being the guy who pushes an energy cost-saving policy is the route to the CEO office, especially when the cost savings are small relative to the bottom line. The project sounds boring and penny-pinching, and the manager who suggests it might be destined for a job in accounting rather than the president's office.

In theory, the EPA's programs shouldn't have worked. So much for theory. As it turned out, both programs have succeeded in promoting greater use of low-cost energy-efficient technologies. As a result, such technologies have become far more broadly diffused than they had previously been. Because of Green Lights, cost-saving lighting programs have been adopted in numerous places. Energy Star Office Products has led to substantial improvements in energy

efficiency, yielding cost savings for those who use the relevant equipment. Government accomplished all this not with a mandate but with
a gentle nudge.

Global warming, rising energy prices, and energy market reforms
have turned many European utility companies into conservation
innovators as they develop approaches that promise simultaneously
to lower emissions and charge customers more precisely based on
their actual consumption. A 2007 research study forecasts that there
will be 60 million smart meters throughout Europe by 2012, which
means one in four customers bills will be calculated by them.[18] Italy
has been at the forefront of these devices, with the country's largest
utility company, Enel SpA, first rolling out the meters back in 2000.
Sweden expects to achieve complete installation by 2009, with large-
scale installations ongoing in Denmark, Finland, and Austria.

The success of these programs offers broad lessons for environmental protection. For those especially concerned about the problem
of climate change, the lesson is clear. Whether or not governments
choose some kind of incentive-based system, they can help to reduce
energy use, and thus reduce greenhouse gas emissions, with a nudge.
Public officials are often ignorant, to be sure, but sometimes they
have useful information, and companies can literally profit from it.
All over the world, they can both do good and do well.

13

Privatizing Marriage

We hope that the idea of libertarian paternalism will offer some new ways of thinking about many old problems. We now turn to the very old institution of marriage, and explore some of the questions that have recently been raised about marriage and same-sex relationships.

We begin by offering a proposal that is highly libertarian, that would protect freedom, including religious freedom, and that should, in principle, prove acceptable to all sides. We recognize that many people in many nations, including members of many religious groups, strongly object to same-sex marriage. Religious organizations insist on their right to decide for themselves which unions they are willing to recognize, with attention to gender, religion, age, and other factors. We also know that many members of same-sex couples want to make lasting commitments to one another. To respect the liberty of religious groups while protecting individual freedom in general, we propose that marriage, as such, should be completely privatized. Under our proposal, the word *marriage* would no longer appear in any laws, and marriage licenses would no longer be offered or recognized by any level of government. The state would do its business, while religious organizations would do theirs. We would eliminate the ambiguity created by the fact that the word *marriage* now refers both to an official (legal) status and to a religious one.

Under our approach, the only legal status states would confer on couples would be a civil union, which would be a domestic partnership agreement between any two people.* Marriages would be

---

* We duck the question of whether civil unions can involve more than two people.

strictly private matters, performed by religious and other private organizations. Within broad limits, marriage-granting organizations would be free to choose whatever rules they like for a marriage conducted under their auspices. So, for example, a church could decide that it would marry only members of that church, and a scuba diving club could decide that it would restrict its ceremonies to certified divers. Instead of channeling every partnership into the same one-size-fits-all arrangement of state marriage, couples could choose the marriage-granting organization that best suits their needs and desires. Government would not be asked to endorse any particular relationships by conferring on them the term *marriage*. We spell out the details of how this would work below.

Our more limited proposal, for those who find this idea too radical, is in line with an approach now taken by a number of nations: make the civil union form available to both opposite-sex and same-sex couples. We think that at a minimum, many nations should be proceeding in this fashion.

We then turn to questions of choice architecture. Using the principles that have helped us analyze savings policies and other aspects of life, we ask: How can nations design good rules to govern contractual arrangements between domestic partners (who will sometimes also be husband and wife as a result of a private ceremony)? How can governments protect children and vulnerable parties?

WHAT IS MARRIAGE?

As a matter of law, marriage is no more and no less than an official status, created by the state and accompanied by government entitlements and mandates. When you are married, you get many material benefits, economic and noneconomic.[1] The law varies from nation to nation, but as a general rule, these benefits fall into six major categories.[2]

1. Tax benefits (and burdens). In some nations, the tax system offers big rewards to many couples as a result of marriage – at least if one spouse

earns a great deal more than the other. (There can be a big marriage penalty if both spouses earn substantial incomes.)

2. Entitlements. The law often benefits married couples through a number of entitlement programs. In the United States, for example, the Family and Medical Leave Act requires employers to allow unpaid leave to workers who seek to care for a spouse; employers need not do so for 'partners.'[3] Many nations grant similar advantages to members of married couples.

3. Inheritance and other death benefits. A member of a married couple obtains a number of benefits at the time of death. In some nations, a husband or wife can give his or her entire estate to the spouse without incurring any estate taxes.

4. Ownership benefits. Under the law, spouses may have automatic ownership rights that mere partners lack. In some places, people have automatic rights to the holdings of their spouses, and they cannot contract around the legal rules.

5. Surrogate decision making. Members of a married couple are sometimes given the right to make surrogate decisions of various sorts in the event of the other's incapacitation. When an emergency arises, a spouse is permitted to make judgments on behalf of an incapacitated husband or wife. Partners are far less likely to obtain these benefits.

6. Evidentiary privileges. In some nations, courts recognize marital privileges, including a right to keep marital communications confidential and to exclude adverse spousal testimony.

To say the least, this is an immense and diverse set of benefits, and we have by no means listed them all. The benefits also tend to be fairly stable over time; recall that the status quo is powerful, and there are sharp political constraints on any effort to rethink it. But economic and material benefits of this kind hardly exhaust the meaning of marriage. Crucially, many nations explicitly link these material rights and obligations to the symbolic and expressive benefits associated with the status of marriage. For many people, perhaps most, these symbolic and expressive benefits are much of what it means to be married. So long as the government grants marriage licenses, the status of 'official marriage' – that is, marriage that carries with it a legal status – has immense importance. A couple that is married within a religious or other private tradition, but not with the authority of the state, lacks an important kind of validation, regardless of the strength of that couple's private commitment or the importance to them of the religious element of their marriage.

To see the importance of the official license, suppose that whites and blacks were told that they could have access to all of the material benefits of marriage but that they would be in a status called 'civil union' rather than 'marriage.' Exclusion from the institution of marriage – from the official status – would itself be an offense to interracial couples. In fact, it would violate the Constitution in many legal systems. The state cannot tell members of such couples that they receive material benefits but are not allowed to enter the legal institution of marriage. For interracial couples, it would not matter if their marriages were supported and validated by private organizations. In sum: when people marry, they receive not only material benefits but also a kind of official legitimacy, a stamp of approval, from the state.

WITHOUT STATE LICENSES

We can now see that insofar as it operates through the government, marriage is an official licensing scheme – and that when the state grants marriage licenses, it gives both material and symbolic benefits to the couples it recognizes. But why combine these two functions? And what is added by official use of the word *marriage*?

Compare marriages with other kinds of partnerships. When we decided to write this book together, we had to make a set of agreements. We jointly signed a contract with our publisher, agreeing how to divide the royalty payments we would receive if anyone chose to buy the book, and we made numerous other informal agreements about how we would write the book. The legal system will protect us through copyright laws if someone tries to republish our prose (and would also provide some rules if we had gotten into a dispute leading one of us to quit the project in disgust before the book was done).

However, nothing in the legal system says that we must or must not swear a solemn oath to be best friends, to eat lunch together at least once a week but no more than twice, or to forswear other collaborations. Book writing need not be monogamous. But even when our agreements are informal, and not backed by legal sanction, we take them seriously and will in all likelihood abide by them. Insofar as the state is concerned, why not handle domestic partnerships like any other business partnerships? Why not privatize?

STATE CONTROL OF MARRIAGE IS ANACHRONISTIC

Our basic claim here is that state-run marriage makes it difficult to protect the freedom of religious organizations to proceed as they see fit while also safeguarding the freedom of couples to make the commitments they seek without being treated as second-class citizens by the state. But we also believe that the official licensing system no longer fits modern reality. For one thing, the institution of state-run marriage has a highly discriminatory past, enmeshed as it has been in both sexual and racial inequality. This past cannot be entirely severed from the current version of the institution of marriage.[4]

Insofar as it operated through government, the marital institution was originally a means of government licensing of both sexual activities and child rearing. If you wanted to have sex or to have children, you were in a much better position if you had a license from the state. In fact you might well have needed that license, no less than you now need a license to drive. A state license was a way of ensuring that sexual activity would not be a crime; and it was difficult to adopt children outside of the marital relationship. But official marriage no longer has this role. In some nations, people now have a constitutional right to have sexual relationships even if they are not married – and people become parents, including adoptive parents, without the benefit of marriage. Now that marriage is not a legal precondition for having either sex or children, the state's licensing role seems less important.

As a matter of history, a primary reason for the official institution of marriage has been not to limit entry but to police exit – to make it difficult for people to abandon their commitments to one another. Of course, there are good reasons for this form of policing, which can operate as a nudge or as much more. Marriage might be seen, in part, as a solution to a self-control problem, in which people take steps to increase the likelihood that their relationship will endure. If divorce is difficult, then marriages are more likely to be stable. Marital stability is usually good for children (though children can also benefit from the end of a bad marriage). Marital stability can also be good for spouses, who may benefit from protection against impulsive or destructive decisions that are detrimental both to their relationships and to their long-term welfare.

Humans, as opposed to Econs, are certainly willing to consider legal protection against impulsive decisions. (If Econs have impulses, their Reflective System keeps them under control.) We can even see the legal institution of marriage as a precommitment strategy, not unlike that of Ulysses in approaching the Sirens, in which people knowingly choose a legal status that will protect them against their own errors. In the United States, some states have in fact experimented with an institution called covenant marriage, which makes exit extremely difficult. People can voluntarily enter into such marriages, just as they can take other steps to protect their long-term interests.

But in the modern era, exit is much less rigorously policed. In many nations, people can leave the marital form essentially whenever they wish to do so. And it turns out that covenant marriage has made almost no difference to the institution of marriage. Only about 1–3 percent of couples choose covenant marriage when it is available, and not surprisingly, couples who choose that option tend to be religious and to have a traditional view of marriage, child rearing, and divorce.[5] By and large, such couples already have the commitments and desires that would tend to produce stable marriages. It's hardly a bad thing that they can choose a form of marriage that fits their goals, and libertarian paternalists are glad that the option is available. But the relative unpopularity of covenant marriage, and the evident failure of the movement behind it, demonstrates that the non-covenant option is pretty 'sticky' for nearly all couples.

Increasingly, marriage is not a particularly extraordinary contract. It is dissoluble at the will of the parties, rather than a permanent status. Now that exit is neither forbidden nor rare, it is hard to contend that the official institution of marriage is essential as a way of promoting the stability of relationships. In any case, the civil union form that we endorse, along with private institutions and their diverse norms, should be able to do the desirable work in promoting such stability.

Official marriage licenses also have the unfortunate consequence of dividing the world into the status of those who are 'married' and those who are 'single,' in a way that produces serious economic and material disadvantages for the latter (and sometimes for the former). Many of these economic and material inequalities are impossible to defend. For example, is there any good reason that a person in a same-sex relationship should not be able to make medical decisions on his partner's behalf or bequeath some of his assets upon death without paying taxes? Private relationships, intimate and otherwise, might be structured in many different ways, and the simple dichotomy between 'single' and 'married' does not do justice to what people might choose. Indeed, that simple dichotomy is an increasingly imprecise description of what people actually do choose. Many people are in relationships that are intimate, committed, and monogamous – but without the benefit of marriage. Many people are in marriages that are neither intimate nor monogamous. Countless variations exist. Why not leave people's relationships to their own choices, subject to the judgments of private organizations, religious and otherwise?

IS OFFICIAL MARRIAGE BENEFICIAL?

Those who want to preserve official marriage, and those who are likely to be alarmed by our proposal, might be concerned with the interests of children or the interests of the more vulnerable partner (usually the woman). These are legitimate concerns. Let us take them up in sequence.

Marriage has often been understood as a means of protecting children, and it should be unnecessary to say that this goal is important. But the official institution of marriage is an exceedingly crude tool for providing that protection, which could easily be ensured in better, more direct ways.[6] For example, the law could do much more to ensure that absent parents provide financial help for their children. When a child's interests are involved, mandates are perfectly appropriate. Society can and does go beyond libertarian paternalism to make so-called deadbeat dads pay child support. Those who favor nudges might just add that some simple tools might help. Consider, for example, automatic enrollment (without an opt-out right in this case) of absent parents in a payment plan so that a certain amount is deducted from the relevant checking account on a monthly basis.

In any case, there is no reason to think that civil unions and private arrangements, religious and otherwise, cannot provide as much protection of children as official marriage does. If children need material support, that support can be required directly through legal institutions. If children need stable homes, the question is whether an official licensing scheme with the name *marriage* contributes enough to family stability to be worth the candle. Maybe so, but it's hard to see any basis for a confident answer.

If the concern is for dependents at risk after the dissolution of a long-term relationship, good default rules are the best place to start. A detailed literature exists on this question; some of the most helpful suggestions are both libertarian and paternalist, in the sense that they maintain freedom of choice while also steering people in desirable directions.[7] We shall have more to say on possible approaches shortly. For now we note only that the official institution of marriage is neither necessary nor sufficient for good default rules.

From the standpoint of good choice architecture, then, a central problem with the current licensing scheme is that it is not nearly libertarian enough. Of course, we recognize that no one is forced to marry, certainly not by law. In this way, the institution of marriage is altogether different from the kinds of rigid government commands that most threaten personal freedom. When democratic societies license marriage, they are doing something very different from what they would do by requiring (say) all employers to provide a specified level of health care, or all employees to save a specified amount of money. Marriage might even seem to be a way of facilitating private choices rather than eliminating them. But the licensing scheme is not merely a device for facilitation. It is very different from the law of contract. The state does not simply permit people to marry within their religions; it does not merely enforce people's agreements. It also creates a monopoly on the legal form of marriage; imposes sharp limits on who may enter and how; and accompanies the legal form with material and symbolic benefits that it alone confers. For those who believe in liberty, this is hardly an unambiguous good.

We acknowledge that many couples may benefit, in one or another way, from public statements of their commitments to each other. Many people believe that the official institution of marriage helps to secure people's commitments in a way that is both an individual and a social good. But if commitments are important, why not rely on civil unions and private institutions, including religious ones? Is government licensing with the term *marriage* necessary at all? Many commitments are stable without licenses from the state. People stay tied to their friends, their churches, their co-authors, and their employers for a long time. And even without a government licensing scheme or legal sanction, people take their private commitments seriously. Members of religious organizations, homeowners' associations, and country clubs all feel bound, sometimes quite strongly, by the structures and rules of such organizations. Recall that if some kind of commitment is desirable, nothing in our proposal prevents people from making commitments through the civil union form or purely through private institutions.

In this light, what is the balance sheet for official marriage? Its benefits are surprisingly low; in many ways it is an anachronism. The most that can be said is that official marriage *might* contribute to a kind of commitment that benefits both couples and children. On the cost side, official marriage does not do a great deal of harm. But it does produce unnecessary polarization, confusion about the relationship between state-sponsored marriage and religious marriage, and intense grappling over fundamental issues and definitions. In the current era, the most obvious difficulty is that religious organizations insist that they should be permitted to define marriage as they like, while same-sex couples insist that they should be able to make long-term commitments without having a second-class status as a matter of law. Our proposal simultaneously satisfies both of these opposing factions. The underlying problems would easily be avoided with a simple declaration that *marriage* should be for private institutions, not for the state, and that religious organizations would be free to set their own rules regarding who could marry. That declaration – a form of separation of church and state – would have an additional benefit, to which we will shortly turn.

In some nations, our proposal might seem radical, but much of the world is moving in the general direction. The consensus in favor of opposite-sex 'marriages' is breaking down in favor of a range of experiments. Many countries make some kind of civil union form available, and make it accessible to same-sex couples and sometimes opposite-sex couples as well. In New Zealand, for example, the civil union form is available for both kinds of couples. Germany, Denmark, Switzerland and the United Kingdom allow 'partnerships,' having many of the same rights as married couples. The Czech Republic maintains a Registered Partnership Act exclusively for same-sex partners, placing them essentially on the same plane as heterosexual couples. In 2006, South Africa enacted a gender-neutral marriage bill; Norway did the same in 2008. In 2003, Buenos Aires became the first city in Latin America to adopt gender-neutral civil unions.

These various initiatives can be placed in different categories, with some broadening the idea of marriage, others allowing same-sex couples to enter into an official status without the same name, and still others creating a new status, with a different name, and making it available to all. As far as we are aware, no nation goes so far as to abolish official marriage as such, but many are moving in more libertarian directions that reduce the directive and exclusionary role of the state.

NUDGING COUPLES

In our view, the official institution of marriage, and the debate over its nature and future, have deflected attention from the key question facing choice architects: What are the appropriate default rules for people who make a commitment to each other?

It is here that good choice architects can make real improvements. We cannot sort out all of the complex issues in this space, but let us sketch a few proposals, which could be applied to any form of legal domestic partnership (including marriages in their current form). Our motivation is simple: if we were starting from scratch, no sane person could possibly devise the existing system, which is so full of confusion and arbitrariness that, in many states, even experienced divorce lawyers often have no idea how disputes are likely to come out. At a minimum, the choice architecture should be changed so that people can have a clearer sense of their rights and obligations. More ambitiously, nudges should be introduced to protect those who are most vulnerable, frequently women and above all children.

As usual, the place to start is with people's actual goals and intentions. If people make explicit promises to one another, the law should generally enforce their promises. To the extent that people leave gaps or uncertainties, the law must choose a menu of default rules. Unfortunately, people are likely to need some steering when making long-term mutual commitments. As we have suggested, unrealistic optimism is at its most extreme in the context of marriage. In recent studies, for example, people have been shown to have an accurate sense of the likelihood that other people will get divorced (about 50 percent). But recall the fact that they have an absurdly optimistic sense of the likelihood that they themselves will not get divorced. It's worth repeating the key finding: nearly 100 percent of people believe that they are certain or almost certain not to get divorced![8]

It is in these circumstances, and in part for that reason, that people are immensely reluctant to make prenuptial agreements. Believing that divorce is unlikely, and fearing that such agreements will spoil the mood, most people simply take their chances with existing divorce law, which is (not to put too fine a point on it) a mess, often unintelligible even to specialists in the field. Also, it is sophisticated and wealthy couples who are most likely to enter into prenuptial agreements, to understand the law, and to obtain high-quality legal representation in the event of divorce. The result of all this is to leave most people vulnerable to the vagaries of chance – and to a legal system that has an astonishing degree of uncertainty. When pre-nuptial agreements have not been made, we believe that the relevant rules should nudge the outcome in a way that will help the weakest parties – usually women. Typically, a woman's economic prospects fall after divorce, whereas the prospects of the man increase.[9] It makes sense to adopt default rules that insure against the most severe kinds of loss.

As a presumption, people should be permitted to make their own provisions if that is what they wish to do. If men and women freely agree to an outcome that generally benefits men, the law should respect that agreement – and use other parts of the legal system, including the tax-and-transfer system, to help those who need it. Mandatory rules that forbid people to agree on their preferred terms are not likely to accomplish their intended goals; people will contract around the rules by adjusting other parts of the deal. But what people wish to do is likely to be affected by the law's default rules. If the law establishes a standard practice, many people will follow it.

If the default rule says that special help will be provided to those who have been the primary caretakers of the children, then that rule is likely to stick. If joint custody is the clear default rule when neither parent has been a negligent caretaker, people will have a plain understanding of what will happen on dissolution of the household. And if the default rule says that upon divorce the primary caretaker will continue as such, and receive financial assistance, that rule will also tend to stick. In this context, the stickiness of default rules can easily be enlisted to insulate the most vulnerable people from the worst outcomes.

Aside from helping the vulnerable, default rules should be clear in this arena, because Humans, unlike Econs, have a self-serving bias when it comes to negotiating settlements.[10] Essentially, the self-serving bias means that in difficult or important negotiations, we tend to think that both the objectively 'fair' outcome and the most likely outcome is the one that is skewed in our own favor. (After Brazil and Italy play in the World Cup, ask citizens of both nations in which direction the referees were biased.) When both sides suffer from the self-serving bias, bargaining is likely to reach an impasse, and people will spend a lot of time fighting in court, sometimes ruining their lives (at least for a time). In divorce cases, emotions are running high, and each side is likely to think itself entirely in the right, and to assume that the judge will certainly see things the same way. You might think that even if spouses are subject to self-serving bias, lawyers are not, and hence lawyers should be able to deflate their clients' expectations; but in many cases, lawyers suffer from self-serving bias as well.

The upshot is that where the law is unclear, long and intense disputes are likely. Both sides would benefit if they could be nudged toward a smaller range of expected outcomes, so that their expectations will have some overlap. Families facing divorce will gain if the law provides an anchor or range, helping people know what constitutes a fair or likely outcome.

To achieve this goal, the best solution is to introduce something not unlike criminal sentencing guidelines – a fairly narrow range of possible outcomes within which a judge has discretion to consider other factors. In many states, something similar is already in place, but for purposes of the self-serving bias, the rules are less helpful if people do not know about them. And research has shown that many couples entering marriage do not have anything like a clear idea of what generally happens, with respect to either child support or alimony payments, upon divorce.[11] (If you are married, or plan to get married, do you know how alimony and child support are calculated in your state? Oh, never mind. There is no chance that you will get a divorce.) Governments should spell out clearly what range of support is generally acceptable, as a portion of income (subjected, perhaps, to upper limits).

The best approach might be an explicit formula based on such factors as the ages of both spouses, their earning capabilities, the length of marriage, and so forth. Starting with the formula as an anchor, a judge could weigh other considerations such as the standard of living during the marriage, the health of the spouse seeking maintenance, the financial prospects of both sides, and other relevant factors. The reasons for any 'departures' from the range would have to be clearly spelled out and limited to a small number of acceptable reasons for adjustment, because the whole goal of transparency in the process is to nudge couples toward settlement within an expected range.

But let us conclude with our broader point. With respect to marriage, there are powerful arguments for privatization – for allowing private institutions, religious and otherwise, to do as they wish, subject to default rules and criminal prohibitions. We have argued that states should abolish 'marriage' as such and rely on civil unions instead. If religious institutions want to restrict 'marriage' to heterosexual couples, they should certainly be permitted to do exactly that. If such institutions want to limit divorce (that is, ending a 'marriage'), they could do that too. More modestly, nations could provide (as many do) the civil union form for all couples, and allow such couples to rely on private institutions for 'marriages.' The beauty of this approach is that it would allow a wide range of experiments – increasing freedom for individuals and religious organizations alike while at the same time reducing the unnecessary and sometimes ugly intensity of current public debates.

PART IV

Extensions and Objections

14

A Dozen Nudges

We have described a lot of nudges, but we are confident that there are countless others. Here are a dozen more – mininudges, if you will. Readers are warmly encouraged to add to the list by sending them to our Web site: www.Nudges.org.

1. Give More Tomorrow. Many people have strong charitable impulses, and we suspect that because of inertia they give far less than they actually want to give. Their Reflective System wants to be charitable, but their Automatic System doesn't get around to it. How many times have you thought that you ought to provide some help but failed to do so because the moment passed and you focused on other things?

A simple nudge would be a Give More Tomorrow program. The basic idea, modeled on Save More Tomorrow, is to ask people whether they would like to give a small amount to their favorite charities starting sometime soon, then commit to increasing their donations every year. (It would probably be impractical to link the increases to pay increases.) If people decided to opt out of Give More Tomorrow, they need only make a quick phone call or send a brief email at any time. We suspect that many people would gladly join such a program.

Anna Breman (2006) has conducted a pilot experiment using this idea in collaboration with a large charity. Donors already making monthly donations were asked to increase their donations either immediately or starting in two months. The latter group increased their donations by 32 percent. We are involved with some additional experiments in collaboration with our own university, and the initial results look promising. If the goal is to increase charitable giving, here's an easy way to do it. In fact it would not be at all surprising if the Give More Tomorrow program produced far more money for those who need it – while also pleasing the well-meaning but absent-minded donors who want to give but never get around to it.

2. The Charity Debit Card and tax deductions. A related nudge would make it easier for people to deduct their charitable contributions. Keeping track of donations and listing them on a tax return is burdensome for some Humans, who end up donating less than they would if the tax savings were automatic. An obvious solution is the Charity Debit Card – a special debit card that would be issued by banks and accepted only by charities. With the Charity Debit Card, any charitable donations are deducted from your normal account, and your bank sends you a statement at the end of the year with your donations itemized and totaled. You could also use the card to keep a record of when you donate nonmonetary items like furniture or cars, ensuring that your bank would know the value of what you donated and add it to your end-of-year statement. The statement could even be sent straight to the IRS so that the government could automatically process the appropriate deduction for you. By making donations salient, such a card could make charity simpler and more attractive.

3. The Automatic Tax Return. Speaking of taxes and automatic processing, no sensible choice architect would design the current income tax system, which is famous for its complexity. Withholding was a major advance that simplified life for everyone. Ordinary people and the Internal Revenue Service would benefit even more if the process could be made more automatic. A simple step, suggested by the economist Austan Goolsbee (2006), is the Automatic Tax Return. Under this approach, anyone who does not itemize deductions and has no income (such as tips) that is not reported to the IRS would receive a tax return that is already filled out. To file, the taxpayer would need only to sign it and mail it (or, even better, go to a secure IRS Web site, sign in and click). (Of course, the taxpayer would be required to make changes if her status changed, or if she started receiving unreported income.)

Goolsbee estimates that this proposal would save taxpayers up to 225 million hours of tax preparation time and more than $2 billion a year in tax preparation fees. True, many people don't trust the IRS, so here's one way to assure them that our tax collectors are honest: if there's an error, you get the money back, plus a bonus (say, $100).

Automatic tax returns are already being used in other countries around the world. Denmark pioneered the pre-filled tax return idea in the early 1980s, and the other Nordic countries soon followed. Finland Prime Minister Matti Vanhanen awarded his Tax Administration an award in 2006 for its automatic tax return program, with the prize jury praising it for having 'significantly reduced the time taxpayers need to complete and file their returns ... (and) substantially reduced the Tax Administration's internal costs from processing return forms.' Today, pre-filled systems of varying levels have been adopted in Australia, Norway, Sweden, Belgium, Chile, Portugal, Spain, and France, with the Netherlands planning to implement one in 2009. In Norway, taxpayers who want to alter their tax information can even request a change form through a text message.[1]

4. Stickk.com. Many people need help in achieving their goals and aspirations. Committing oneself to a specific action is one way to improve the odds of success. Sometimes it is easy to make a commitment, as, for example, by cutting up your credit cards, refusing to stock your kitchen with brownies and cashews, or having your significant other hide the TV remote until those leaves get raked. Other times it is hard. Remember the weight-loss bet we described between two graduate students in Chapter 2? Well, one of them, Dean Karlan, now a Yale economics professor, has teamed up with his Yale colleague Ian Ayres to propose a Web-based business modeled on the same concept. Ayres and Karlan call the business Stickk.com.[2]

Stickk offers two ways to make commitments: financial and non-financial. With financial commitments, an individual puts up money and agrees to accomplish a goal by a certain date. He also specifies how to verify that he has met his goal. For example, he might agree to a weigh-in at a doctor's office or a friend's house; a urine test for nicotine at a clinic; or an honor-system verification. If the person reaches his goal, he gets his money back. If he fails, the money goes to charity. He also has the option to enter into a group financial commitment, in which the group's pooled money is divided among those members of the group who reach their goals. (A tougher, more mischievous, and perhaps even more effective option is to give the money to people the would-be committer hates, such as an opposing political party, or the fan club of the home team's arch-rival – think Yankees and Red Sox.) The nonfinancial commitments include peer pressure (emails to family or friends announcing your successes or failures) and monitoring one's own goal via a group blog.

A committer's goal might be to lose weight, quit smoking, exercise more frequently, improve grades, or the like. There is even a creative section for people with idiosyncratic goals: climb Mount Kilimanjaro while there is still ice at the summit (verification by photograph), travel to Mongolia (verification by passport stamp), learn to juggle seven oranges and a watermelon (verification by video), run a marathon, save more money (less creative, to be sure), use less gas and electricity (not so creative but admirable), or whatever self-improvement people can conjure up and post on the Web site.

5. Quit smoking without a patch. Organizations already exist to help people make commitments and achieve goals. CARES (Committed Action to Reduce and End Smoking) is a savings program offered by the Green Bank of Caraga in Mindanao, Philippines. A would-be nonsmoker opens an account with a minimum balance of one dollar. For six months, she deposits the amount of money she would otherwise spend on cigarettes into the account. (In some cases, a representative of the bank visits every week to collect the deposits.) After six months, the client takes a urine test to confirm that she has not smoked recently. If she passes the test, she gets her money back. If she fails the test, the account is closed and the money is donated to a charity.

The early results from this program have been evaluated by MIT's Poverty Action Lab and look very good. Opening up an account makes those who want to quit 53 percent more likely to achieve their goal.[3] No other antismoking tactic, not even the nicotine patch, appears to have been so successful.

6. Motorcycle helmets. Many states ban people from riding motor-cycles without helmets. To libertarians, these bans are questionable. They ask: If people want to take risks, shouldn't they be allowed to do so? To date, an intense debate has separated the hardcore paternalists, who emphasize the dangers and support bans, from the fans of laissez-faire, who insist that the government should let people do what they want. The columnist John Tierney (2006) has suggested a nudge-like way that states might promote safety while maintaining freedom. The basic idea is that riders who do not want to use the helmet have to get special licenses. To qualify for the license, a rider would have to take an extra driving course and submit proof of health insurance.*

Tierney's approach imposes some costs on those who want to feel the wind in their hair; an extra driving course and proof of insurance are not exactly trivial. But requirements of this kind are less intrusive than a ban – and might do a lot of good to boot.

7. Gambling self-bans. Gambling raises complex issues, to say the least, and we will not explore in any detail what a libertarian paternalist might do in this area. (Suffice it to say that if we were in charge, we would not give state governments a monopoly on gamb-ling – especially if they choose to specialize in gambles that offer the worst odds for customers, namely state lotteries, which pay off roughly fifty cents on the dollar. Hint: if you want to gamble with decent odds, start a football pool with your friends.) However, it is clear that gambling addicts are among us, and they need real help.

Here's an ingenious solution. Over the past decade, several states, including Illinois, Indiana, and Missouri, have enacted laws enabling gambling addicts to put themselves on a list that bans them from entering casinos or collecting gambling winnings. The underlying thought is that someone who has self-control problems is aware of her shortcomings and wants to put her Reflective System in control of her Automatic System. Sometimes recreational gamblers can do this on their own or with their friends; sometimes private institutions can

---

* One reader of Tierney's column suggested in a letter to the editor that a rider with this special license should also have to display a decal certifying that he has signed up to be an organ donor.

help them. But addicted gamblers might do best if they have a way to enlist the support of the state. We think that self-bans are a great idea and suggest that research be done to explore ways to use this concept in other domains.

8. Destiny Health Plan. Insurance companies don't like paying large medical bills any more than patients do. There is room for some creative efforts on the part of such companies to work with their customers to improve people's health while reducing medical bills for all. Consider here the Destiny Health Plan now offered in four states (Illinois, Wisconsin, Michigan, and Colorado). The plan features a Health Vitality Program explicitly designed to give people an incentive to make healthy choices. A participant is able to earn 'Vitality Bucks' if he works out at a health club in a particular week, has a child join a soccer league, or completes a blood-pressure check with normal results. Vitality Bucks can be used to obtain airline tickets, hotel rooms, magazine subscriptions, and electronics. The Destiny Health Plan is a clever effort to combine health insurance with nudges designed to get people to live healthier lives.

9. Dollar a day. Teenage pregnancy is a serious problem for many girls, and those who have one child, at (say) eighteen, often become pregnant again within a year or two. Several cities, including Greensboro, North Carolina, have experimented with a 'dollar a day' program, by which teenage girls with a baby receive a dollar for each day in which they are not pregnant.[4] Thus far the results have been extremely promising. A dollar a day is a trivial cost to the city, even for a year or two, so the plan's total cost is extremely low, but the small recurring payment is salient enough to encourage teenage mothers to take steps to avoid getting pregnant again. And because taxpayers end up paying a significant amount for many children born to teenagers, the costs appear to be far less than the benefits. Many people are touting 'dollar a day' as a model program for helping reduce teenage pregnancies. (Surely there are more such programs to be invented. Consider that a nudge to think of one.)

10. Filters for air conditioners; the helpful red light. In hot weather, people depend on air conditioners, and many central air-conditioning systems need their filters changed regularly. If the filter

isn't changed, bad things can happen; for example, the system can freeze and break down. Unfortunately, it is not easy to remember when to change the filter, and not surprisingly, many people are left with huge repair bills. The solution is simple: people should be informed via a red light in a relevant and conspicuous place that the filter needs to be changed. Many contemporary cars notify people when the oil needs to be changed, and many new refrigerators have a warning light for their built-in water filters. The same can be done with air conditioners.

11. No-bite nail polish and Disulfiram. People who hope to change certain bad habits might want to buy products that make it unpleasant, or painful, to continue to indulge those habits. Through this route, the Reflective System can choose to discipline the Automatic System through products that tell the Automatic System: *Stop!*

Several products now accomplish exactly this task. Those who want to stop biting their nails can buy bitter nail polishes such as Mavala and Orly No Bite. A more extreme version of this concept is Disulfiram (antabuse), which is given to some alcoholics. Disulfiram causes alcohol drinkers to throw up and suffer a hangover as soon as they start to drink. For some people suffering from chronic alcoholism, Disulfiram has had a strong and positive effect as part of a treatment program.

12. The Civility Check. We have saved our favorite proposal for last. The modern world suffers from insufficient civility. Every hour of every day, people send angry emails they soon regret, cursing people they barely know (or even worse, their friends and loved ones). A few of us have learned a simple rule: don't send an angry email in the heat of the moment. File it, and wait a day before you send it. (In fact, the next day you may have calmed down so much that you forget even to look at it. So much the better.) But many people either haven't learned the rule or don't always follow it. Technology could easily help. In fact, we have no doubt that technologically savvy types could design a helpful program by next month.

We propose a Civility Check that can accurately tell whether the email you're about to send is angry and caution you, 'WARNING: THIS APPEARS TO BE AN UNCIVIL EMAIL. DO YOU

REALLY AND TRULY WANT TO SEND IT?' (Software already exists to detect foul language. What we are proposing is more subtle, because it is easy to send a really awful email message that does not contain any four-letter words.) A stronger version, which people could choose or which might be the default, would say, 'WARNING: THIS APPEARS TO BE AN UNCIVIL EMAIL. THIS WILL NOT BE SENT UNLESS YOU ASK TO RESEND IN TWENTY-FOUR HOURS.' With the stronger version, you might be able to bypass the delay with some work (by inputting, say, your Social Security number and your grandfather's birth date, or maybe by solving some irritating math problem!).*

The Reflective System can be nicer as well as smarter than the Automatic System. Sometimes it's even smart to be nice. We think that Humans would be better off if they gave a boost to what Abraham Lincoln called 'the better angels of our nature.'

---

* While we are waiting for this program to be invented, we have adopted a self-control device of our own as a substitute. When one of us gets really angry, he drafts the angry email, and sends it to the other one to edit. Of course, this won't work if we get angry with each other, so we are hoping the program gets invented soon.

15

Objections

Who would oppose nudges? We are aware that hard-line anti-paternalists, and possibly others, will have serious objections.[1] Let us consider the possible counterarguments in sequence. We begin with those that seem to us weakest, and then turn to those that raise more complicated issues.

THE SLIPPERY SLOPE

It is tempting to worry that those who embrace libertarian paternalism are starting down an alarmingly slippery slope. Skeptics might fear that once we accept modest paternalism for savings or cafeteria lines or environmental protection, highly intrusive interventions will surely follow. They might object that if we permit information campaigns that encourage people to conserve energy, a government propaganda machine will move rapidly from education to outright manipulation to coercion and bans.

The critics could easily envisage an onslaught of what seem, to them, to be unacceptably intrusive forms of paternalism. Governments that start with education might end with stiff fines and even prison terms. The case of cigarettes offers a possible example. Some nations have gone from modest warning labels to much more aggressive information campaigns to high cigarette taxes to bans on smoking in public places, and a smoker would not have to be paranoid to think that the day might eventually come when one or another nation heavily regulates or even bans cigarettes altogether. Indeed, many would welcome this for cigarettes, though most would not for alcohol. Where do we stop? Sliding all the way down the slippery slope is unlikely, to be sure, but faced with the risk of overreaching, critics might think it is better to avoid starting to slide at all.

We have three responses to this line of attack. The first is that reliance on a slippery-slope argument ducks the question of whether our proposals have merit in and of themselves. Surely that question is worth engaging. If our proposals help people save more, eat better, invest more wisely, and choose better insurance plans and credit cards – in each case only when they want to – isn't that a good thing? If our policies are unwise, then it would be constructive to criticize them directly rather than to rely only on the fear of a hypothetical slippery slope. And if our proposals are worthwhile, then let's make progress on those, and do whatever it takes to pour sand on the slope (assuming that we really are worried about how slippery it is).

The second response is that our own libertarian condition, requiring low-cost opt-out rights, reduces the steepness of the ostensibly slippery slope. Our proposals are emphatically designed to retain freedom of choice. In many domains, from environmental protection to marriage, we would create such freedom where it does not now exist. So long as paternalistic interventions can be easily avoided by those who seek to adopt a course of their own, the risks decried by antipaternalists are modest. Slippery-slope arguments are most convincing when it is not possible to distinguish the proposed course of action from abhorrent, unacceptable, or scary courses of action. Because libertarian paternalists retain freedom of choice, we can say, with conviction, that our own approach opposes the most objectionable kinds of government intervention.

The third point is one that we have emphasized throughout: In many cases, some kind of nudge is inevitable, and so it is pointless to ask government simply to stand aside. Just as no building lacks an architecture, so no choice lacks a context. Choice architects, whether private or public, must do *something*. With respect to pollution, rules have to be established, even if only to say that polluters face no liability and may pollute with impunity. Even if states dispensed with both marriage and civil unions, contract law would have to be available to say what disbanding couples owe each other (if anything). If the government is going to adopt a prescription drug plan, some sort of choice architecture must be put in place.

Often life turns up problems that people did not anticipate – for investments, rental car and credit card agreements, mortgages, and uses of energy. Both private and public institutions need rules to determine how such situations are handled. When those rules seem invisible, it is because people find them so obvious and so sensible that they do not see them as rules at all. But the rules are nonetheless there, and sometimes they are not so sensible.

Those who object to nudges might accept this point for the private sector. Perhaps they believe that competitive pressures can combat the worst kinds of nudges. Banks or cell phone companies that push people in bad directions might find themselves losing customers. We have raised questions about this view, and we will raise some more; but let us put those questions to one side and focus on the slippery-slope argument for government alone. Those who make this argument sometimes speak as if government can be absent – as if the default terms that set the background come from nature or from the sky. This is a big mistake. To be sure, the default terms that now apply in any particular context might be best, in the sense that they promote people's interests overall or on balance. But that view must be defended, not assumed. And it would be odd for those who generally hold government in extremely low esteem to think that in all domains, past governments have somehow stumbled onto a set of ideal arrangements.*

---

* A possible response would invoke the great British traditionalist Edmund Burke, and in particular Burke's arguments on behalf of the likely wisdom of long-standing social practices; see Burke (1993). Burke thought that such practices reflected not government action but the judgments of many people over many periods, and that the law often embodies those judgments. Many traditionalists invoke Burkean arguments against social engineering of any kind.

We agree that long-standing traditions may be quite sensible, but we do not believe that traditionalists have a good objection to libertarian paternalism. Social practices, and the laws that reflect them, often persist not because they are wise but because Humans, often suffering from self-control problems, are simply following other Humans. Inertia, procrastination, and imitation often drive our behavior. Once our

EVIL NUDGERS AND BAD NUDGES

In offering supposedly helpful nudges, choice architects may have their own agendas. Those who favor one default rule over another may do so because their own economic interests are at stake. When companies offer you a special rate for the first month, then automatically reenroll you in the program at a higher rate after the end of the introductory period, their primary motivation is not to save you the trouble of signing up for yourself. So let's go on record as saying that choice architects in all walks of life have incentives to nudge people in directions that benefit the architects (or their employers) rather than the users. But what conclusion should we draw from this observation? Real architects can have conflicts of interest with their clients as well, but we don't think they should stop designing buildings. Instead, we try to line up incentives when we can, and employ monitoring and transparency when we can't.

One question is whether we should worry even more about public choice architects than private choice architects. Maybe so, but we worry about both. Private institutions are sometimes self-serving, greedy, and incompetent, and they exploit people. On the face of it, it is odd to say that the public architects are always more dangerous than the private ones. After all, managers in the public sector have to answer to voters, and managers in the private sector have as their mandate the job of maximizing profits and share prices, not consumer welfare. Indeed, some of those who are most suspicious of governments think that the only responsibility of private managers is to maximize share prices. As we have emphasized, the invisible hand will, in some circumstances, lead those trying to maximize profits to maximize consumer welfare too. But when consumers are confused about the features of the products they are buying, it can be profit maximizing to exploit their confusion, especially in the short run but

traditions are brought down to earth, the arguments on their behalf seem stronger or weaker, depending on the context. We do not mean here to question the view that laws that really do embody the judgments of many people often deserve support for that reason.

possibly in the long run too. The financial crisis of 2008 was produced, in part, because people had too little understanding of the
agreements into which they were entering, and their ignorance was
exploited.

The invisible hand works best when products are simple and
purchased frequently. We worry very little about consumers being
ripped off by their dry cleaners. A dry cleaner who loses shirts or
suddenly doubles prices will not be in business long. But a mortgage
broker who fails to point out that the teaser rate will disappear
quickly is long gone by the time the customer gets the bad news.

The editors of the *Economist*, in a largely sympathetic treatment of
libertarian paternalism, offered this cautionary note: 'From the point
of view of liberty, there is a serious danger of overreach, and therefore grounds for caution. Politicians, after all, are hardly strangers
to the art of framing the public's choices and rigging its decisions
for partisan ends. And what is to stop lobbyists, axe-grinders and
busybodies of all kinds hijacking the whole effort?'[2]

We agree that government officials, elected or otherwise, are often
captured by private-sector interests whose representatives are seeking
to nudge people in directions that will specifically promote their
selfish goals. That is one reason that we want to maintain freedom of
choice. But if private-sector interests are just following the invisible
hand in furthering the interests of their customers, what's the
problem?[3] The more serious point is that we should be worried about
all choice architects, public and private alike. We should create rules
of engagement that reduce fraud and other abuses, that promote
healthy competition, that restrict interest-group power, and that
create incentives to make it more likely that the architects will serve
the public interest. In both the public and private sectors, a primary
goal should be to increase transparency. Our various RECAP
proposals are specifically designed to make it easier for consumers to
figure out how much of some service they are using and how much
they are paying for it. In the environmental domain, we have suggested that disclosure can be an effective, and low-cost, monitoring
device.

We would love to see similar principles used to monitor

governments. Require government officials to put all their votes, earmarks, and contributions from lobbyists on their Web sites. Require those determining the future of energy policy (to cite a random example) to reveal which profit-maximizing firms were invited to lend their all-too-invisible hands to the process of designing the rules. Require government agencies, not merely the private sector, to disclose their contributions to air and water pollution, and their greenhouse gas emissions. American Supreme Court Justice Louis Brandeis urged that 'sunlight is the best of disinfectants.' Democratic governments, as well as authoritarian ones, could use a lot more sunlight.

In emphasizing the effects of plan design on choice, we hope to encourage plan designers to become more informed. And by arguing for a libertarian check on bad plans, we hope to create a strong safeguard against ill-considered or ill-motivated plans. To the extent that individual self-interest is a healthy check on planners, freedom of choice is an important corrective.

THE RIGHT TO BE WRONG

Skeptics might argue that in a free society, people have the right to be wrong, and it is sometimes helpful for us to make mistakes, since that is how we learn. On the first point we heartily agree, which is why we insist on opt-out rights. If people really want to invest their entire retirement portfolio in high-tech Romanian stocks, we say go for it. But for unsophisticated choosers, there is little harm in putting some warning signs along the way. We approve of the signs at some ski areas warning novice and intermediate skiers: 'Don't even think about going down this trail if you are not an expert.'

We worry more about poor people who were duped into taking a mortgage they would soon be unable to afford than about the investment firms that bought portfolios of those mortgages. That latter group should have known better (though better disclosure would help here, too), and they are likely to devise improved methods of evaluating the risks of loans on their own. But how much learning do you think is good for people? We do not believe that children should learn the dangers of swimming pools by falling in and hoping for the best. Should pedestrians in London get hit by a double-decker bus to teach them to 'look right'? Isn't a reminder on the sidewalk better?

OF PUNISHMENT, REDISTRIBUTION, AND CHOICE

Some of our most extreme critics offer an objection that will strike many readers as just odd. These critics object to any forced exchanges. They don't like to take anything from Peter to give to Paul, even if Peter is very rich and Paul is very poor. They obviously oppose progressive taxes. (Well, most taxes, actually.) In the areas that concern us, these critics would disapprove of policies that explicitly benefit the weak, poor, uneducated, or unsophisticated. They would object to these policies not because they lack sympathy for these groups but because they think that any help for them should come voluntarily from the private sector, such as from charities, and that government policies would come at the expense of other groups (often the strong, rich, educated, and sophisticated). They don't like any government policy that takes resources from some in order to assist others.

We must confess that we do not share the view that all redistribution is illegitimate. We think that a good society makes trade-offs between protecting the unfortunate and encouraging initiative and self-help – between giving everyone a decent share of the pie and increasing the size of the pie. In our view, the optimal level of redistribution is not zero. But even those who hate redistribution more than we do should have little concern about our policies. Most of the time, nudging helps those who need help while imposing minimal costs on those who do not. If people are already saving for retirement, offering the Save More Tomorrow program will cause them no problems. If people are not smoking, or are naturally (or unnaturally) thin, campaigns to help smokers and the obese will do them little harm.

Some skeptics might object that some of our proposals would require the Econs to pay something (not a lot) for programs they don't need and from which they don't benefit. But if the people who need the help are also imposing costs on society – for example, through higher health costs – then having the Econs share in the costs of helping the Humans seems like a modest price to pay. Of course, some anti-redistributive types will object to a health system that forces the rest of us to pay for those who need health care. And it is true that on a relative basis the Econs may still lose out from policies that help Humans. If Peter's happiness depends, in part, on his being richer than Paul, then anything that pulls Paul up by his bootstraps makes Peter worse off. But we think, though we admit to having no evidence to support our view, that most Peters actually take pleasure in helping out the worst-off members of society (even if the Pauls are being helped by government rather than by private charity). As for those who feel miserable if their poorest neighbors close some of the gap, they have our sympathy, but not our empathy.

The most ardent libertarians have another arrow in their quiver. They are concerned about liberty and free choice rather than about welfare. For this reason, they prefer required choosing to nudges. At most, they would like to provide people with the information necessary to make an informed choice, and then tell people to choose for themselves: no nudges! This view is reflected in the campaign by the Swedish government to get citizens to choose their own investment portfolios and the idea that for organ donations, people should be asked to make their wishes clear, without any default rule. Both policies represent a deliberate decision not to nudge.

Although nudges are often unavoidable, we enthusiastically agree that required (or strongly encouraged) active choosing is sometimes the right route, and we have no problem with providing information and educational campaigns (we are professors, after all). But forced choosing is not always best. When the choices are hard and the options are numerous, requiring people to choose for themselves might be preferred and might not lead to the best decisions. Given that people would often choose not to choose, it is hard to see why freedom lovers should compel choice even though people (freely and voluntarily) resist it. If we ask the waiter to select a good bottle of wine to go with our dinner, we will not be happy if he says that we should just choose for ourselves!

As for information and educational campaigns, one of the main lessons from psychology is that it is impossible for such programs to be 'neutral,' regardless of how scrupulously designers try to achieve that goal. So to put it simply, forcing people to choose is not always wise, and remaining neutral is not always possible.

DRAWING LINES AND THE PUBLICITY PRINCIPLE

A while back Sunstein took his teenage daughter to Lollapalooza, the three-day rock festival held every year in Chicago, Illinois. On Friday night a huge sign, with changing electronic messages, often showed the schedule of performances, but interspersed that information with a message saying, 'DRINK MORE WATER.' The print was large; the message was accompanied by another one: 'YOU SWEAT IN THE HEAT: YOU LOSE WATER.'

What was the point of this announcement? Chicago had been in the midst of a terrible heat wave, and those who ran Lollapalooza were clearly trying to prevent the various health problems that are associated with dehydration. The sign was a nudge. No one was forced to drink. But those who produced the sign were sensitive to how people think. In particular, the choice of the particular words *more water* was excellent. Those words were likely to be far more effective than blander alternatives, such as 'DRINK ENOUGH WATER' or 'DRINK WATER.' The suggestion that we 'LOSE WATER' cleverly invoked loss aversion on behalf of staying hydrated. (As it happens, Sunstein wished that he had seen the sign earlier; he became very thirsty during the performance of the band Death Cab for Cutie, but the crowd was so densely packed that it was impossible to go out to find water.)

Now compare an imaginable alternative. Suppose that instead of having a visible 'DRINK MORE WATER' sign, the schedules for the day were briefly and invisibly interrupted by subliminal advertising. The subliminal advertisement might say, 'DRINK MORE WATER,' 'AREN'T YOU THIRSTY???,' or 'DON'T DRINK AND DRIVE'; 'DRUGS KILL' or 'SUPPORT YOUR PRESIDENT,'; 'ABORTION IS MURDER' or 'BUY 10 COPIES OF *NUDGE.*' Can subliminal advertising be seen as a form of libertarian paternalism? After all, it steers people's choices, but it does not make their decisions for them.

So do we embrace subliminal advertising – so long as it is in the interest of desirable ends? What limits should be placed on private or public manipulation as such? A general objection to libertarian paternalism, and to certain kinds of nudges, might be that they are insidious – that they empower government to maneuver people in its preferred directions, and at the same time provide officials with excellent tools by which to accomplish that task. Compare subliminal advertising to something just as cunning. If you want people to lose weight, one effective strategy is to put mirrors in the cafeteria. When people see themselves in the mirror, they may eat less if they are chubby. Is this okay? And if mirrors are acceptable, what about mirrors that are intentionally unflattering? (We seem to run into more of those every year.) Are such mirrors an acceptable strategy for our friend Carolyn in the cafeteria? If so, what should we think about flattering mirrors in a fast food restaurant?

To approach these problems we once again rely on one of our guiding principles: transparency. In this context we endorse what the philosopher John Rawls (1971) called the publicity principle. In its simplest form, the publicity principle bans government from selecting a policy that it would not be able or willing to defend publicly to its own citizens. We like this principle on two grounds. The first is practical. If a government adopts a policy that it could not defend publicly, it stands to face considerable embarrassment, and perhaps much worse, if the policy and its grounds are disclosed. (Those who participated in, or sanctioned, the cruel and degrading actions in the Abu Ghraib prison might have benefited from using this principle.) The second and more important ground involves the idea of respect.

The government should respect the people whom it governs, and if it adopts policies that it could not defend in public, it fails to manifest that respect. Instead, it treats its citizens as tools for its own manipulation. In this sense, the publicity principle is connected with the prohibition on lying. Someone who lies treats people as means, not as ends.

We think that the publicity principle is a good guideline for constraining and implementing nudges, in both the public and private sectors. Consider Save More Tomorrow; here people are explicitly informed of the nature of the proposal, and specifically asked whether they would like to accept it. Similarly, when firms adopt automatic enrollment, they do not make a secret of it, and can say honestly that they do so because they think that most workers will be better off joining the plan.

The same conclusion holds for legal default rules. If government alters such rules – to encourage organ donation or to reduce age discrimination – it should not be secretive about what it is doing. The same can be said for educational campaigns that enlist behavioral findings in order to provide a helpful nudge. If government officials use cleverly worded signs to reduce litter, deter the theft of petrified wood, or encourage people to register as organ donors, they should be happy to reveal both their methods and their motives. Consider an American advertisement from a few years ago, showing an egg frying on a hot stove with the voiceover, 'This is your brain on drugs.' The vivid image was designed to trigger fear of drug use. The advertisement might well be deemed manipulative, but it did not violate the publicity principle.

We readily agree that hard cases are imaginable. In the abstract, subliminal advertising does seem to run afoul of the publicity principle. People are outraged by such advertising because they are being influenced without being informed of that fact. But what if the use of subliminal advertising were disclosed in advance? What if the government openly announces that it will be relying on subliminal advertising in order, for example, to combat violent crime, excessive drinking, and the failure to pay one's taxes? Is disclosure enough?

We tend to think that it is not – that manipulation of this kind is objectionable precisely because it is invisible and thus impossible to monitor.

NEUTRALITY

We have stressed that in many situations government cannot be purely neutral, but a form of neutrality is sometimes both feasible and important. Consider the case of voting. Ballots have to list candidates in some order. It is well known that candidates benefit from being listed first. One study finds that a candidate whose name is listed first gains about 3.5 percentage points in the voting.* No one should be happy about a situation in which governments – which is to say incumbents – are allowed to choose the order of the candidates' names. With respect to ballot design, a principle of neutrality makes a lot of sense, and in that context, neutrality is often thought to require randomness.

Why, then, do we think that governments should be trusted with nudging Medicare participants toward the insurance plan that is best for them, or with paying for ads that tell people not to 'mess with Texas'? Why is randomizing ballots good and randomizing assignment to insurance policies bad?[4] Part of the answer is that sometimes people have a right, even a constitutional right, to government neutrality of a certain kind. With respect to the right to vote, the government must avoid deliberate nudging in the particular sense that its choice architecture cannot favor any particular candidate. Something similar can be said about the right to free exercise of religion and the right to free speech. Government may not encourage people to join a 'Pray to Jesus More Tomorrow' plan, or a 'Dissent Less Tomorrow' plan.

Outside the context of constitutional rights, there is a more general

* See Koppell and Steen (2004). The effect is smaller when the candidates are well known, such as in presidential elections, but when candidates have little name recognition or get low media coverage (as in many if not most local elections), the effect can be even bigger.

question about neutrality, and it extends to both the private and the public sectors. Our basic conclusion is that the evaluation of nudges depends on their effects – on whether they hurt people or help them. Skeptics might argue that in some domains, it is best to avoid nudges altogether. But how can firms do that? It is not possible to avoid choice architecture, and in that sense it is not possible to avoid influencing people. We agree that in some cases, forced choosing is best. But often it is not feasible, and sometimes it is more trouble than it is worth.

True, some kinds of nudges are not inevitable. Education and advertising campaigns are optional, and they can be avoided. Should governments educate people about the risks of smoking and drinking, unprotected sex, trans fats, spike-heeled shoes? Should employers offer educational campaigns about similar topics? To answer these questions, we need to know something about the Nudgers and the Nudgees. One question is whether an outside agent (the Nudger) is likely to be able to help an individual (the Nudgee) make a better choice. Part of this depends on how hard the choices are for the Nudgees. As we have seen, people are most likely to need nudges for decisions that are difficult, complex, and infrequent, and when they have poor feedback and few opportunities for learning.

But the potential for beneficial nudging also depends on the ability of the Nudgers to make good guesses about what is best for the Nudgees. In general, Nudgers will be able to make good guesses when they have much more expertise at their disposal, and when the differences in individuals' tastes and preferences are either not very big (nearly everyone prefers chocolate ice cream to licorice) or when differences in tastes and needs can be easily detected (as when the government deduces that you are likely to prefer a drug plan that offers low prices on the drugs you take regularly). For all the reasons we have discussed, nudging makes more sense for mortgages than for soft drinks. Mortgages are complicated, and outsiders can provide a lot of help. By contrast, no expert has much to offer about whether you are likely to prefer Coke to Pepsi that would not be better answered by taking a sip of each. So to summarize, when choices are fraught, when Nudgers have expertise, and when differences in individual preferences are either not important or can be easily estimated, then the potential for helpful nudging is high.

Of course, we need to be worried about incompetence and self-dealing on the part of Nudgers. If the Nudgers are incompetent, then they could easily do more harm than good by directing people's choices. And if the risk of self-dealing is high, then it is right to be wary of attempts to nudge. There are some who think that any decision made by a government official is likely to be incompetent and corrupt. Those who hold this view would want government-sponsored nudging to be kept to a bare minimum – that is, limited to cases in which some nudging is inevitable, such as choosing default options. But for those with less pessimistic views about government, who think politicians and bureaucrats are just Humans, not much more likely to be stupid or dishonest than (say) business executives, lawyers, or economists, we can ask whether a situation contains special risks of self-dealing. This makes it clear why leaving ballot design to politicians is an obviously bad idea, whereas letting politicians hire experts to help pick sensible default options for Medicare participants is probably a good idea (especially if politicians have to report donations from insurance companies).

WHY STOP AT LIBERTARIAN PATERNALISM?

We hope that conservatives, moderates, liberals, self-identified libertarians, and many others might be able to endorse libertarian paternalism. So far we have emphasized the criticisms of certain conservatives and the most ardent libertarians. A different set of objections can be expected from the opposite direction. Enthusiastic paternalists might well feel emboldened by evidence of Human frailties. So emboldened, they might urge that in many domains, nudging and libertarian paternalism are much too modest and cautious. If we want to protect people, why not go further? In some circumstances, wouldn't people's lives go best if we took away freedom of choice? Isn't there a legitimate place for mandate and bans? If Humans really make errors, why not protect them, by forbidding them to err?

The truth, of course, is that there are no hard-and-fast stopping points. We have defined libertarian paternalism to include actions, rules, and other nudges that can be easily avoided by opting out. We do not have a clear definition of 'easily avoided,' but we hold up 'one-click' paternalism to be as close as we can get with existing technology. (We can hope for 'one-thought' or 'one-blink' technology in the near future.) Our goal is to allow people to go their own way at the lowest possible cost. To be sure, some of the policies we have advocated impose higher costs than one click. To opt out of an automatic enrollment plan, an employee typically has to fill out and return some form – not a big cost, but more than one click. It would be arbitrary and a bit ridiculous to offer an inflexible rule to specify when costs are high enough to disqualify a policy as libertarian, but the precise question of degree is not really important. Let us simply say that we want those costs to be small. The real question is when we should be willing to impose some nontrivial costs in the interests of improving people's welfare.

A good approach to thinking about these problems has been proposed by a collection of behavioral economists and lawyers under the rubric of 'asymmetric paternalism.'[5] Their guiding principle is that we should design policies that help the least sophisticated people in society while imposing the smallest possible costs on the most sophisticated. (Libertarian paternalism is a form of asymmetric paternalism in which the costs imposed on the sophisticated are kept close to zero.) A simple example of asymmetric paternalism involves sunlamps. Sunlamps are consumer devices that let users get a tan without going to the beach. Typically a user will lie down under the lamp, close her eyes, and remain there for a few minutes. It is dangerous to stay under the lamp for more than a few minutes because serious burns are possible. (Of course, using the lamp at all may be risking skin cancer, but we will follow the lead of the users of this appliance and ignore that issue here.) It is the nature of a sunlamp that it is warm. So a choice architect who is expecting error will realize that there is a serious danger here: some users lying under a warm lamp with their eyes closed will drift off to sleep and wake up with third-degree burns.

Now suppose that for a modest cost, the sunlamp can be equipped with a timer switch set so that it can be turned on only for brief periods, after which it shuts off automatically – a design common for the warming lamps found in some hotel bathrooms. Should the government require that all sunlamps be sold with such a switch? Asymmetrical paternalists believe that the answer depends on some kind of cost-benefit analysis. If the cost of the switch is low enough and the risk of burns is high enough, then the answer is yes.

Asymmetric paternalists also endorse a class of regulations requiring 'cooling-off periods.' The rationale is that in the heat of the moment, consumers might make ill-considered or improvident decisions. Self-control problems are the underlying concern. A mandatory cooling-off period for door-to-door sales, of the sort imposed by the United States Federal Trade Commission in 1972, provides an illustration.[6] Under the Commission's rule, any door-to-door sale must be accompanied by a written statement informing the buyer of his right to rescind the purchase within three days of the transaction. The law came about because of complaints about high-pressure sales techniques and contracts with fine print. Again a cost-benefit test, looking at the benefits for those who are helped and the costs for those who are not, could be used to decide when such laws would be imposed. Using such a test, regulators would want to consider how big the imposition is on those who have to wait a few days to receive the product, and how often buyers would want to change their minds. When the costs are low (did anyone ever really need to buy an encyclopedia right away, even before Wikipedia was online?) and there are frequent changes of heart, such a regulation makes sense to us.

For certain fundamental decisions, often made on impulse, a similar strategy might well be best. Some states impose a mandatory waiting period before a couple may get divorced.[7] Asking people to pause and think before making a decision of that magnitude seems like a sensible idea, and we are hard-pressed to think of why anyone would need to divorce immediately. (True, spouses sometimes really don't like each other, but is it really terrible to have to wait a short while before the deed is done?) We could easily imagine similar restrictions on the decision to marry, and some states have moved in this direction as well.[8] Aware that people might act in a way that they will regret, regulators do not block their choices but do ensure a period for sober reflection. Note in this regard that mandatory cooling-off periods make best sense, and tend to be imposed, when two conditions are met: (a) people make the relevant decisions infrequently and therefore lack a great deal of experience, and (b) emotions are likely to be running high. These are the circumstances in which people are especially prone to making choices that they will regret.

Occupational safety and health laws go beyond asymmetric paternalism; they impose flat bans, and they undoubtedly do hurt some people.[9] Such laws do not permit individual workers to trade their right to (what the government considers to be) a safe work environment in return for a higher salary, even if sophisticated and knowledgeable people might like to do that. All over the world, pension and Social Security programs do not merely encourage savings; they require it. The laws that ban discrimination on the basis of race, sex, and religion are not waivable. An employee cannot be asked to trade the right to be free from sexual harassment in return for a higher wage. These various prohibitions are not in any sense libertarian, but perhaps some of them can be defended by reference to the kinds of Human errors that we have explored here. Non-libertarian paternalists might like to build on such initiatives to do a great deal more, perhaps in the domains of health care and consumer protection.

Many of these arguments have substantial appeal, yet we usually resist going further down the paternalistic path. What are the grounds for our resistance? After all, we have already granted that the costs imposed by libertarian paternalism may not be zero, so it would be disingenuous for us to say that we always and strongly object to regulations that raise the costs imposed from tiny to small. Nor do we personally oppose all mandates. But deciding where to stop, and when to call a nudge a shove (much less a prison), is tricky.

Where mandates are involved and opt-outs are unavailable, the slippery-slope argument can begin to have some merit, especially if regulators are heavy-handed. We agree that flat bans are justified in some contexts, but they raise distinctive concerns, and, in general, we prefer interventions that are more libertarian and less intrusive.

We are much less cool about cooling-off periods. We're even warm. In the right circumstances, the gains from such rules can be sufficient to make it worthwhile to take a few cautious steps down that possibly slippery slope.

16

The Real Third Way

In this book we have made two major claims. The first is that seemingly small features of social situations can have massive effects on people's behavior; nudges are everywhere, even if we do not see them. Choice architecture, both good and bad, is pervasive and unavoidable, and it greatly affects our decisions. The second claim is that libertarian paternalism is not an oxymoron. Choice architects can preserve freedom of choice while also nudging people in directions that will improve their lives.

We have covered a great deal of territory, including savings, Social Security, credit markets, environmental policy, health care, marriage, and much more. But the range of potential applications is much broader than the topics we have managed to include. One of our main hopes is that an understanding of choice architecture, and the power of nudges, will lead others to think of creative ways to improve human lives in other domains. Many of those domains involve purely private action. Workplaces, corporate boards, universities, religious organizations, clubs, and even families might be able to use, and to benefit from, small exercises in libertarian paternalism.

With respect to government, we hope that the general approach might serve as a viable middle ground in our unnecessarily polarized society. The twentieth century was pervaded by a great deal of artificial talk about the possibility of a 'Third Way.' We are hopeful that libertarian paternalism offers a real Third Way – one that can break through some of the least tractable debates in contemporary democracies.

Ever since Franklin Delano Roosevelt's New Deal, the Democratic

Party has shown a great deal of enthusiasm for rigid national requirements and for command-and-control regulation. Having identified serious problems in the private market, Democrats have often insisted on firm mandates, typically eliminating or at least reducing freedom of choice. Republicans have responded that such mandates are often uninformed or counterproductive – and that in light of the sheer diversity of Americans, one size cannot possibly fit all. Much of the time, they have argued on behalf of laissez-faire and against government intervention. At least with respect to the economy, freedom of choice has been their defining principle.

To countless ordinary people, the resulting debates seem increasingly tired, abstract, and unhelpful – pointless sloganeering. Many sensible Democrats are fully aware that mandates can be ineffective and even counterproductive, and that one size may not fit all. American society is simply too diverse, individuals are simply too creative, circumstances change too rapidly, and government is simply too fallible. Many sensible Republicans know that even with free markets, government intervention cannot be avoided. Free markets depend on government, which must protect private property and ensure that contracts are enforced. In domains ranging from environmental protection to planning for retirement to assisting the needy, markets should certainly be enlisted. In fact, some of the best nudges use markets; good choice architecture includes close attention to incentives. But there is all the difference in the world between senseless opposition to all 'government intervention' as such and the sensible claim that when governments intervene, they should usually do so in a way that promotes freedom of choice.

For all their differences, liberals and conservatives are beginning to recognize these fundamental points. No less than those in the private sector, public officials can nudge people in directions that will make their lives go better while also insisting that the ultimate choice is for individuals, not for the state. The sheer complexity of modern life, and the astounding pace of technological and global change, undermine arguments for rigid mandates or for dogmatic laissez-faire. Emerging developments should strengthen, at once, the principled commitment to freedom of choice and the case for the gentle nudge.

Postscript: The Financial Crisis of 2008

The first edition of this book was finished during the summer of 2007 and published in February of 2008. This edition was prepared in the summer of 2008, but we write this postscript in late November, a time of striking contradictions. The United States has just elected Barack Obama as president; he is a man of enormous talents and much of the world is celebrating. Yet Obama, along with other national leaders, faces exceedingly difficult challenges, and not just in the form of gigantic expectations.

The world is facing the most serious financial crisis since the Great Depression. It is fair to say that very few regulators or economists saw the crisis coming. In the United States, the former Federal Reserve chairman Alan Greenspan admitted that he had erred in not anticipating the crisis, and found himself in a state of 'shocked disbelief.' It is reasonable to ask whether an understanding of human behavior can help to explain what happened – and whether nudging might help to prevent future occurrences of the same sort of mess.

To simplify a long and complex story, the origins of the crisis can be found in investments in 'subprime' mortgages – loans to people who do not qualify for market interest rates. A dramatic recent increase in home prices slowly drew to a halt in 2004. By early 2008, many borrowers were delinquent and subject to foreclosure. As a result, investments in subprime mortgages turned out to be a disaster. The failure of investment firms and mortgage companies led to a massive reduction in liquidity in credit markets first in the United States and then globally. In turn, that reduction in liquidity produced significant decreases in stock values and a range of associated economic harms, including many business failures and a felt need for government rescue plans all over the globe.

The initial point is that notwithstanding the stunned surprise of the economics profession, some behavioral economists, above all Robert Shiller, anticipated the problem well before it occurred.[1] Even at an early stage, keen observers found it plain that real estate prices were inflated (judged, say, by the ratio of buying and rental prices), that the increase in home prices between 1997 and 2006 was wildly inconsistent with historical trends, and that the United States was in the midst of a speculative bubble, which was bound to pop eventually. Three characteristics of Humans, all explored in this book, help to explain how this happened: bounded rationality, limited self-control, and social influences.

HUMAN INVESTORS AND ECONOMIC CRISIS

Bounded Rationality

We have emphasized that when things get complicated, Humans can start to flounder. Which brings us to an aspect of the financial crisis that has not received the attention it deserves: the financial world has gotten much more complex over the past two decades. Not so long ago, most mortgages were of the simple, thirty-year fixed-rate variety. Shopping was simple: just find the lowest monthly payment.

Now mortgages come in countless varieties. Even experts have trouble comparing the pros and cons of different loans, and a low initial monthly payment can be a misleading guide to the total costs (and risks) of a loan.

One key cause of the subprime mortgage disaster is that countless borrowers did not understand the terms of their loans. Even those who attempted to read the pages of fine print felt their eyes glazing over, especially after their mortgage broker assured them they were getting an amazing deal.

Yet growing complexity on the borrowers' side was trivial

compared to what was going on for the investors who were providing the money. Once upon a time, mortgages were held by the banks that initiated the loans. Now they are sliced up into intricate pieces called mortgage-backed securities, which include new, arcane, derivative products such as credit default swaps and liquidity puts.

You probably do not know what liquidity puts are, and that won't hurt you, but top management at Citigroup didn't understand them either. As a result, the company ended up with massive losses, and had to be bailed out with hundreds of billions of taxpayer funds.

The Citigroup fiasco began in 2007, and it should have been a wake-up call to Wall Street in particular and international institutions in general. No such luck. It is fair to say that the top management of many of the world's largest financial firms, now in trouble or gone, did not understand the risks their employees were taking by issuing or trading these complex new securities.

Self-control

Econs do not suffer from self-control problems, and so temptation is not a word that exists in the economists' lexicon. As a result, most of the world's regulators have not thought much about the problem. But when the dessert cart comes by, we humans often cave. The next thing we know we are fat. The current crisis was fueled by the seemingly irresistible temptation to refinance the mortgage rather than to pay it off.

Not so very long ago, households would take out one of those old-fashioned mortgages and then set out to pay it off before retirement. Even if refinancing made sense, many people never got around to it, if only because it was such a nuisance.

Then came the helpful mortgage broker who made it all easy. By the turn of the century, the combination of declining interest rates, rising home prices, low initial 'teaser rates,' and aggressive mortgage brokers made refinancing (and second mortgages) seem like the apple in the Garden of Eden. But when home prices fell and interest rates increased, the party ended.

Social Influences

Why did so many people believe that real estate prices always go up? By historical standards, home prices jumped spectacularly from 1997 to 2004. In that period, many people thought, and said, that it is in the nature of home prices to increase over time, and people's behavior tracked their belief. But the belief was demonstrably false. From 1960 to 1997, home prices were relatively stable, until the unprecedented boom that began in 1997.

As Shiller has shown, the best explanation of the real estate bubble greatly overlaps with the best explanation of the stock market bubble of the late 1990s: in both cases, people were greatly influenced by a process of social contagion. This belief produced wildly unrealistic projections, with palpable consequences for home purchases and mortgage choices.

In 2005, Shiller and Karl Case conducted a survey among San Francisco home buyers. The median expected price increase, over the next decade, was 9 percent per year! In fact, one-third of those surveyed thought that the annual increase would be much higher than that. Their baseless optimism was based on two factors: salient price increases in the recent past and the apparent, and contagious, optimism of other people.

Of course the stock of public knowledge depends not merely on word of mouth and on visible sales, but on the media as well. In the late 1990s and early 2000s, it was widely reported that home prices were rapidly increasing (true) and that the prices would continue to increase over time (not true). If the apparent experts confirm 'what everyone knows,' then seemingly risky deals, of the sort that have led so many people to disaster, will seem hard to resist.

NUDGES

It would be foolish to suggest that the proper response to the economic crisis consists solely of nudges. Because of the costs that financial firms have imposed on the global economy, and because so many vulnerable workers and homeowners have been at risk, there will rightly be calls for increased scrutiny and also direct regulation. But for the future, nudge-like responses should also be an important part of the policy mix. In particular, regulators need to take steps to help people to manage complexity, to resist temptation, and to avoid being misled by social influences.

A potential response to complexity would be to require simplicity – as, for example, by allowing only the standard thirty-year fixed-rate mortgages. This would be a big mistake. To eliminate complexity is to stifle innovation. A better approach is to improve transparency and disclosure. Regulators can reduce the likelihood of a future meltdown by forcing all parties to make it easier to understand the true risks of their complicated products.

Recall our proposal for RECAP: for mortgages, current fine-print disclosure should be supplemented with machine-readable files, which would enable third-party Web sites to translate and digest the hidden details of the terms. Mandatory transparency in the investment banking and hedge fund world would also help. Even if the CEO did not understand the risks the firm was taking, investors would have a better chance of diagnosing the problem.

Both the government and the market should collaborate on ways of dealing with temptation. We hope that lenders will once again want families to have done some saving in order to qualify to buy a home. Conscientious lenders could use nudges to help people get off the refinancing merry-go-round, say by suggesting that the term of the loan be shortened when a loan is refinanced. More ambitiously, private and public institutions could try to reintroduce an old social norm, itself a nudge: try to pay off the mortgage sooner rather than later, and at the latest by the time you retire.

Improved information is also a good line of defense against the potentially destructive effects of social influences. Even if everyone you know says that the local restaurant is terrific, your own knowledge might protect you against a terrible meal. (And if everyone told you, in 2003, that you ought to be investing in real estate, you might have declined if you'd looked at some statistics.) Regulators should do a great deal more to help consumers to understand the risks associated with various investments. Law professor Elizabeth Warren has argued that the United States should create a Financial Product Safety Commission, one of whose goals might be to protect consumers by producing large statistical databases and by disseminating information about risks and trends on a timely basis.[2] It is not clear that the United States, or any other government, should create a new bureaucracy. But existing institutions should do a great deal more to mandate disclosure. As a possible model, consider regulations that require nutritional labeling on food in the supermarket. Most people do not read these labels, but some do, and the very existence of the labels is enough to make the market work better.

To combat bounded rationality, temptation, and social influences, it might even be worthwhile to consider the creation of simple default provisions, which would govern mortgages and other instruments unless consumers explicitly choose some alternative plan. The preferred approach would be private and voluntary – a private nudge. At least for most borrowers, a 'best practice' norm might develop, to the following effect: 'For people like you, this is the package that we essentially recommend.' Those who seek to deviate from the default, and to incur larger risks, might be given relevant information and asked to think seriously about their choice. A nudge-like regulatory intervention is worth considering as well, perhaps in the establishment of default terms and in provisions governing opt-out. Such an intervention would be far better than stronger mandates and bans.

Greed and corruption helped to create the crisis, but simple human frailty played key roles. We will not be able to protect against future crises if we rail against greed, corruption, and wrongdoing without looking in the mirror and understanding the potentially devastating effects of bounded rationality, self-control problems, and social influences.

Notes

Introduction

1. See http://www.coathanger.com.au/archive/dibblys/loo.htm. The example is also discussed by Vicente (2006).
2. Friedman and Friedman (1980).
3. For a similar definition, see Van De Veer (1986).

1. Biases and Blunders

For anyone interested in delving into the research discussed in this chapter we recommend two collections: Kahneman and Tversky (2000) and Gilovich, Griffin, and Kahneman (2002).

1. For a good survey of the research on dual process theories in psychology, see Chaiken and Trope (1999).
2. Lieberman et al. (2002); Ledoux (1998).
3. See Westen (2007).
4. One reason why adjustment is so often insufficient is that the Reflective System is easily waylaid – it requires significant cognitive resources, and thus when resources are scarce (you are distracted or tired, for example) it can't adjust the anchor. See Gilbert (2002).
5. Strack, Martin, and Schwarz (1988).
6. Slovic, Kunreuther, and White (1974).
7. For more than you ever wanted to know about this subject, including instructions on how to conduct your own test, go to the Hot Hand Web site: http://thehothand.blogspot.com/.
8. See http://www.cdc.gov/nceh/clusters/.
9. Paul Price, 'Are You as Good a Teacher as You Think?' (2006), available at http://www2.nea.org/he/heta06/images/2006pg7.pdf.

10. Mahar (2003).

11. Cooper, Woo, and Dunkelberg (1988).

12. For references for the central findings in this paragraph, see Sunstein (1998).

13. Kahneman, Knetsch, and Thaler (1991).

14. Tversky and Kahneman (1981).

2. Resisting Temptation

The Planner/Doer model is developed in Thaler and Shefrin (1981). For a review of recent research on self-control and intertemporal choice, see Frederick, Loewenstein, and O'Donoghue (2002). Modern behavioral economics treatments include Laibson (1997) and O'Donoghue and Rabin (1999).

1. See Camerer (2007), McClure et al. (2004).

2. See Wansink (2006) for a summary.

3. See Gruber (2002).

4. Thaler and Johnson (1990).

3. Following the Herd

We have drawn for part of this chapter on Sunstein (2003). There is a voluminous literature on social norms and their impact. Two especially good overviews are Ross and Nisbett (1991) and Cialdini (2000).

1. See Layton (1999) and Stephenson (2005).

2. See Akerlof, Yellen, and Katz (1996) (teenage pregnancy); Christakis and Fowler (2007) (obesity); Sacerdote (2001) (college roommate assignment); Sunstein et al. (2006) (judicial voting patterns).

3. See Berns et al. (2005). Conforming answers are associated with changes in the perceptual features of the brain rather than with changes in the prefrontal cortex, which is associated with conscious decision making. It turns out that people may not merely say that they see things as others do. If all others see things a certain way, we may actually see them that way.

4. Ross and Nisbett (1991), 29–30.

5. Jacobs and Campbell (1961).

6. Kuran (1998).

7. See Crutchfield (1955).

8. For a good account, see http://www.dontmesswithtexas.org/history.php.

9. Gilovich, Medvec, and Savitsky (2000).

10. An outline can be found at http://www.historylink.org/essays/output. cfm?file_id=5136.

11. Wansink (2006).

12. Coleman (1996).

13. See, e.g., Cialdini (1993).

14. See Cialdini, Reno, and Kallgren (2006).

15. See generally Perkins (2003), 7–8.

16. Wechsler et al. (2000).

17. See Perkins (2003), 8–9.

18. See Linkenbach (2003).

19. Linkenbach and Perkins (2003).

20. See Schultz et al. (2007).

21. See Sherman (1980).

22. See Greenwald et al. (1987).

23. See Morwitz and Johnson (1993).

24. See Levav and Fitzsimons (2006).

25. See Kay et al. (2004).

26. See Holland, Hendriks, and Aarts (2005).

27. See Bargh (1997).

5. Choice Architecture

1. Byrne and Bovair (1997).

2. Vicente (2006), 152.

3. See Zeliadt et al. (2006), 1869.

4. Sunstein (2007) explores this point in detail.

6. Save More Tomorrow

This chapter relies heavily on joint research with Shlomo Benartzi and especially Benartzi and Thaler (2007).

1. Beland (2005), 40–41.

2. Investment Company Institute (2006).

3. We thank David Blake and the U.K. Department of Work and Pensions for providing us with the data.

4. Choi, Laibson, and Madrian (2004). Duflo et al. (2005) find a similar

unexploited arbitrage opportunity in the context of tax filers eligible for the saver's tax credit.

5. Madrian and Shea (2001); Choi et al. (2004), (2002).

6. Choi et al. (2006).

7. Carroll et al. (2005).

8. Carroll et al. (2005).

9. Iyengar, Huberman, and Jiang (2004).

10. Benartzi and Thaler (1999).

11. Benartzi and Thaler (2007).

12. Choi et al. (2002).

13. Duflo and Saez (2002).

14. The Pension Protection Act says that if employers offer a 401(k) plan in which employees' contributions are matched by the employer, the matches are vested within two years, automatic enrollment is at a rate of at least 3 percent of income, and automatic increases are of at least 1 percent per year for three years or more, then the employer is presumed to satisfy something called the nondiscrimination rule. (More specifically, the employer has to match contributions at a 100 percent rate for the first 1 percent of pay that the employee saves, and then at least at a 50 percent rate up to a 6 percent savings rate, for a total match of 3.5 percent if the employee saves 6 percent.) Nondiscrimination rules limit the proportion of benefits that can be paid to the highest-paid workers in the firm. Since 401(k) plans already have dollar caps for each employee, it was assumed that this combination of plan features would attract enough enrollments from the lower-paid employees to pass the test. Although reasonable people can quibble with the specific provisions of the act (which represent the usual sort of political compromises), we think that it is an excellent example of nudging. Employers are not required to change their plans, but if they do, they get a free pass on an annoying form to fill out.

15. New Zealand Ministry of Economic Development (2008).

7. Naïve Investing

This chapter draws heavily on joint research with Shlomo Benartzi, especially Benartzi and Thaler (2007).

1. See Benartzi and Thaler (1999).

2. Quoted in Zweig (1998).

3. See Benartzi and Thaler (2001).

4. Read and Loewenstein (1995). See also Simonson (1990), who originated the idea.
5. Benartzi and Thaler (2001).
6. Benartzi and Thaler (2007).

8. Credit Markets

1. Thanks to Phil Maymin for suggesting this one.
2. Karlan and Zinman (2007).
3. Simon and Haggerty (2007).
4. Morton, Zettelmeyer, and Silva-Risso (2003).
5. Draut and Silva (2003).

9. Privatizing Social Security

This chapter draws heavily on Cronqvist and Thaler (2004). We thank Henrik Cronqvist for calculating some updated results for us.
1. For a discussion of required active choosing, see Carroll et al. (2005).
2. French and Poterba (1991).
3. See Samuelson and Zeckhauser (1988); Ameriks and Zeldes (2001).
4. See Kuran and Sunstein (1999).

10. Prescription Drugs

'D is for Daunting' was a headline from the *Pittsburgh Post-Gazette*'s special section on choosing plans in 2005. Huge thanks to Katie Merrill and Marion Wrobel for help guiding us through this morass.
1. White House (2006).
2. Medicare Prescription Drug Plan (n.d.).
3. McFadden (2007).
4. Quoted in Pear (2006).
5. Cubanski and Neuman (2007).
6. Henry J. Kaiser Family Foundation (2007).
7. Winter et al. (2006).
8. Henry J. Kaiser Family Foundation (2006).
9. Nemore (2005).

10. West et al. (2007).

11. Kling et al. (2007) report similarly low figures from their own survey of dual eligibles. They found that 6–7 percent of the Medicaid population queried actively chose a different plan in 2007 from the year before.

12. Hoadley et al. (2007).

13. Quoted in Lipman (2005).

14. The Kling et al. (2007) team conducted a small-scale audit of the 1–800-MEDICARE service. They found that the lowest-cost plan was identified in eight of the twelve calls they made.

15. Vaughan and Gunawardena (2006).

16. Depending on which state you live in, you'll have to be ready to deal with different plan sponsors: national and regional insurance companies and pharmacy benefit managers, with cosponsors that include drugstore chains, retailers, and AARP. Monthly premiums range from less than $20 to more than $100. Deductibles are set between zero and $265 (as of 2007). Some basic plans cover 75 percent of drug bills, while most plans have tier-leveled coverage. If you use any kind of coinsurance, or if you buy drugs in three-month supplies, as some seniors do, your cost-sharing arrangements will be different. Generic drug copayments range from zero to $10 per prescription; brand-name copayments range from $15 to more than $60. You'll need to keep track of all of these figures because monthly price changes can affect the overall bill. Plans cover between 73 and 96 percent of the two hundred most commonly used drugs, so you'll need to do your homework combing through plan formularies (the list of drugs covered by the plan). Coverage rates for less common drugs vary. A company generally cannot take drugs off its formulary in the middle of the year, but it can switch to generic drugs if those become available, and can drop them entirely at the end of the year. Every pharmacy network is different. There are different rules for getting an emergency prescription filled and for using an alternative pharmacy network. Coverage restrictions that apply to prior drug authorizations, step therapy, and quantity limits are disclosed in footnotes that require sharp eyes. And finally, each consumer must predict whether he will spend between $2,510 and $5,726 – the so-called doughnut hole, a gap where the government will not subsidize his costs – and figure out whether his plan is one of the few to provide some coverage in the gap. In addition to making no sense from an insurance perspective (it would be far better to give everyone a deductible that varied with income – possibly zero for the poor), the existence of the doughnut hole made the decision-making process even more complicated.

17. McFadden (2006).

18. Six other states use intelligent assignment for a small subset of people who are poor but not eligible for Medicaid.
19. Government Accountability Office (2007).
20. Medicare Rights Center (2006).
21. Kling et al. (2007).

11. How to Increase Organ Donations

1. We recommend the excellent report commissioned by the Institute of Medicine, Childress and Liverman (2006), for a comprehensive treatment of the topic.
2. Kurtz and Saks (1996), 802.
3. Childress and Liverman (2006), 241.
4. Childress and Liverman (2006), 253.
5. Childress and Liverman (2006), 217.

12. Saving the Planet

1. An alternative approach would involve government subsidies to those who engage in risk reduction. In many ways, the analysis of subsidies should be similar to the analysis of penalties.
2. See Nordhaus and Boyer (2000).
3. See Pew Center on Global Climate Change (undated), 2, 7.
4. Id. 7.
5. See Europa (2005).
6. See Ellerman, A. Denny and Barbara K. Buchner, 'The European Union Emissions Trading Scheme: Origins, Allocation, and Early Results', *Review of Environmental Economics and Policy* 1, (2007): 72 n.9.
7. See Europa (2007).
8. See generally Ellerman et al. (2000).
9. See Stewart and Wiener (2003). We do not mean to take a position on the choice between a greenhouse gas tax and a cap-and-trade program; Stewart and Wiener favor the latter, but reasonable people disagree.
10. 42 U.S.C. §§9601 et seq.
11. See Hamilton (2005).
12. See Fung and O'Rourke (2000).
13. See Hamilton (2005).
14. See Larrick and Soll (2008).

15. Quoted in Agence France-Presse (2008).
16. See Tierney (2008).
17. See Howarth, Haddad, and Paton (2000).
18. See EDN Europe (2007).

13. Privatizing Marriage

We have drawn for parts of this chapter on Sunstein (2005). A helpful discussion, from which we have learned a great deal, is Fineman (2004).

1. See Coleman (n.d.).
2. We draw here on Chambers (1996).
3. 29 U.S.C. 2601–54.
4. See Polikoff (1993).
5. See Nock (2003).
6. See Fineman (2004), 123: 'We should transfer the social and economic subsidies and privilege that marriage now receives to a new family core connection – that of the caretaker-dependent.'
7. See Fineman (2004) for a careful and detailed treatment.
8. Mahar (2003).
9. Smock, Manning, and Gupta (1999).
10. See Babcock and Lowenstein (1997).
11. See Baker and Emery (1993).

14. A Dozen Nudges

1. See Organization for Economic Co-Operation and Development (2008); Norwegian Tax Administration (2005); European eGovernment (2006).
2. See http://www.poverty-action.org/ourwork/projects_view.php?record ID = 33 for a similar plan.
3. Research is still ongoing, but see http://www.povertyactionlab.com/projects/project.php?pid=65.
4. Brown, Saunders, and Dick (1999).

15. Objections

1. A vigorous challenge, on which we draw here, is Glaeser (2006).
2. *Economist* (2006).

3. Some economists have actually made this point. See Becker (1983).

4. We thank Jesse Shapiro for posing this perceptive question.

5. Camerer et al. (2003).

6. 16 CFR §429.1(a) (2003).

7. See, for example, Cal Fam Code §2339(a) (requiring a six-month waiting period before a divorce decree becomes final); Conn Gen Stat Ann §46b–67(a) (requiring a ninety-day waiting period before the court may proceed on the divorce complaint). For a general discussion, see Scott (1990).

8. See Camerer et al. (2003), citing state statutes that 'force potential newlyweds to wait a short period of time after their license has been issued before they can tie the knot.'

9. An interesting defense of such laws can be found in Frank (1985).

Postscript

1. See Shiller, (2005).

2. See Shiller for a valuable discussion.

Bibliography

Abadie, Alberto, and Sebastien Gay. 'The Impact of Presumed Consent Legislation on Cadaveric Organ Donation: A Cross Country Study.' NBER Working Paper no. W10604, July 2004.http://ssrn.com/abstract =563048.

Ackerman, Bruce A., and William T. Hassler. *Clean Coal/Dirty Air: Or How the Clean Air Act Became a Multibillion-Dollar Bail-Out for High-Sulfur Coal Producers and What Should Be Done About It.* New Haven: Yale University Press, 1981.

Agence France-Presse. 'Japan to Label Goods' Carbon Footprints: Official.' August 19, 2008.

Akerlof, George A., Janet L. Yellen, and Michael L. Katz. 'An Analysis of Out-of-Wedlock Childbearing in the United States.' *Quarterly Journal of Economics* 111 (1996): 277–317.

Alkahami, Ali Siddig, and Paul Slovic. 'A Psychological Study of the Inverse Relationship Between Perceived Risk and Perceived Benefit.' *Risk Analysis* 14 (1994): 1085–96.

Allais, Maurice. 'Le comportement de l'homme rationnel devant le risque, critique des postulats et axioms de l'école Americaine.' *Econometrica* 21 (1953): 503–46.

Ameriks, John, and Stephen P. Zeldes. 'How do Household Portfolio Shares Vary with Age?' Working paper, Columbia University, 2001.

Asch, Solomon. 'Opinions and Social Pressure.' In *Readings About the Social Animal*, ed. Elliott Aronson, 13. New York: W. H. Freeman, 1995.

Ayres, Ian, and Robert Gertner. 'Filling Gaps in Incomplete Contracts: An Economic Theory of Default Rules.' *Yale Law Journal* 99 (1989): 87–130.

Ayres, Ian, and Barry Nalebuff. 'Skin in the Game.' *Forbes*, November 13, 2006.

Babcock, Linda, and George Loewenstein. 'Explaining Bargaining Impasse: The Role of Self-Serving Biases.' *Journal of Economic Perspectives* 11, no. 1 (1997): 109–26.

Badger, Gary J., Warren K. Bickel, Louis A. Giordano, Eric A. Jacobs, George Loewenstein, and Lisa Marsch. 2004. 'Altered States: The Impact of Immediate Craving on the Valuation of Current and Future Opioids.' *Journal of Health Economics* 26 (2007): 865–76.

Baker, Lynn A., and Robert E. Emery. 'When Every Relationship Is Above Average: Perceptions and Expectations of Divorce at the Time of Marriage.' *Law and Human Behavior* 17 (1993): 439–50.

Bargh, John. 'The Automaticity of Everyday Life.' In *Advances in Social Cognition*, vol. 10, *The Automaticity of Everyday Life*, ed. Robert Wyer, Jr., 1–61. Mahwah, N.J.: Lawrence Erlbaum 1997.

Baron, Robert, Joseph A. Vandello, and Bethany Brunsman. 'The Forgotten Variable in Conformity Research: Impact of Task Importance on Social Influence.' *Journal of Personality and Social Psychology* 71 (1996): 915–27.

Bateman, Ian J., and Kenneth G. Willis, eds. *Valuing Human Preferences*. Oxford: Oxford University Press, 1999.

Baumeister, Roy F., Ellen Bratslavsky, Catrin Finkenauer, and Kathleen Vohs. 'Bad Is Stronger Than Good.' *Review of General Psychology* 5 (2001): 323–70.

Beattie, Jane, Jonathan Baron, John C. Hershey, and Mark D. Spranca. 'Psychological Determinants of Decision Attitude.' *Journal of Behavioral Decision Making* 7 (1994): 129–44.

Becker, Gary S. 'A Theory of Competition Among Pressure Groups for Political Influence.' *Quarterly Journal of Economics* 98 (1983): 371–400.
——. *Accounting for Tastes*. Cambridge: Harvard University Press, 1996.

Becker, Gary S., and Julio Jorge Elias. 'Introducing Incentives in the Market for Live and Cadaveric Organ Donations.' *Journal of Economic Perspectives* 21, no. 3 (2007): 3–24.

Beland, Daniel. *Social Security: History and Politics from the New Deal to the Privatization Debate*. Lawrence: University Press of Kansas, 2005.

Benartzi, Shlomo. 'Excessive Extrapolation and the Allocation of 401(k) Accounts to Company Stock.' *Journal of Finance* 56 (2001): 1747–64.

Benartzi, Shlomo, and Richard H. Thaler. 'Risk Aversion or Myopia? Choices in Repeated Gambles and Retirement Investments.' *Management Science* 45 (1999): 364–81.
——. 'How Much Is Investor Autonomy Worth?' *Journal of Finance* 57 (2002): 1593–1616.

——. 'Heuristics and Biases in Retirement Savings Behavior.' *Journal of Economic Perspectives* 21, no. 3 (2007): 81–104.

Benjamin, Daniel, and Jesse Shapiro. 'Thin-Slice Forecasts of Gubernatorial Elections.' Working paper, University of Chicago, 2007.

Bentham, Jeremy. *An Introduction to the Principles of Morals and Legislation*. Oxford: Blackwell, 1789.

Berger, Jonah, Marc Meredith, and S. Christian Wheeler. 'Can Where People Vote Influence How They Vote? The Influence of Polling Location on Voting Behavior.' Stanford University Graduate School of Business Working Paper no. 1926, 2006. http://gsbapps.stanford.edu/research papers/library/RP1926.pdf.

Berns, Gregory S., Jonathan Chappelow, Caroline F. Zink, Giuseppe Pagnoni, Megan E. Martin-Skurski, and Jim Richards. 'Neurobiological Correlates of Social Conformity and Independence During Mental Rotation.' *Biological Psychiatry* 58 (2005): 245–53.

Bettinger, Eric, Bridget Long, and Phil Oreopoulos. 'Simplifying the FAFSA: The Effects on College Enrollment.' Research in progress.

Bikhchandani, Sushil, David Hirshleifer, and Ivo Welch. 'Learning from the Behavior of Others.' *Journal of Economic Perspectives* 12, no. 3 (1998): 151–70.

Boaz, David. *Libertarianism: A Primer*. New York: Free Press, 1997.

Bond, Rod, and Peter Smith. 'Culture and Conformity: A Meta-Analysis of Studies Using Asch's Line Judgment Task.' *Psychological Bulletin* 119 (1996): 111–37.

Boston Research Group. 'Enron Has Little Effect on 401(k) Participants' View of Company Stock.' 2002.

Breman, Anna. 'Give More Tomorrow: A Field Experiment on Intertemporal Choice in Charitable Giving.' Working paper, Stockholm University, November 7, 2006. http://www.hhs.se/NR/rdonlyres/A60 55D0E-49AE-4BBF-A9FC-ECC965E9DF84/0/GMT_jobmarket.pdf.

Brickman, Philip, Dan Coates, and Ronnie J. Janoff-Bulman. 'Lottery Winners and Accident Victims: Is Happiness Relative?' *Journal of Personality and Social Psychology* 36 (1978): 917–27.

Brodie, Mollyann, Erin Weltzien, Drew Altman, Robert J. Blendon, and John M. Benson. 'Experiences of Hurricane Katrina Evacuees in Houston Shelters: Implications for Future Planning.' *American Journal of Public Health* 96 (2006): 1402–8.

Brown, Lester R., Christopher Flavin, and Sandra Postrel. *Saving the Planet: How to Shape an Environmentally Sustainable Global Economy*. New York: Norton, 1991.

Buehler, Roger, Dale Griffin, and Michael Ross. 'Inside the Planning Fallacy: The Causes and Consequences of Optimistic Time Predictions.' In Gilovich, Griffin, and Kahneman (2002), 250–70.

Burke, Edmund. *Reflections on the Revolution in France*. Ed. L. G. Mitchell. Oxford: Oxford University Press, 1993.

Byrne, Michael D., and Susan Bovair. 'A Working Memory Model of a Common Procedural Error.' *Cognitive Science* 21 (1997): 31–61.

Calabresi, Guido, and A. Douglas Melamed. 'Property Rules, Liability Rules, and Inalienability: One View of the Cathedral.' *Harvard Law Review* 85 (1972): 1089–1128.

Calle, Eugenia E., Michael J. Thun, Jennifer M. Petrelli, Carmen Rodriguez, and Clark W. Heath. 'Body-Mass Index and Mortality in a Prospective Cohort of US Adults.' *New England Journal of Medicine* 341 (1999): 1097–1105.

Camerer, Colin F. 'Prospect Theory in the Wild: Evidence from the Field.' In Kahneman and Tversky (2000), 288–300.

——. *Behavioral Game Theory: Experiments in Strategic Interaction*. Princeton: Princeton University Press, 2003.

——. 'Neuroeconomics: Using Neuroscience to Make Economic Predictions.' *Economic Journal* 117 (2007): C26–42.

Camerer, Colin F., and Robin M. Hogarth. 'The Effects of Financial Incentives in Experiments: A Review and Capital-Labor-Production Framework.' *Journal of Risk and Uncertainty* 19 (1999): 7–42.

Camerer, Colin F., Samuel Issacharoff, George Loewenstein, Ted O'Donoghue, and Matthew Rabin. 'Regulation for Conservatives: Behavioral Economics and the Case for "Asymmetric Paternalism."' *University of Pennsylvania Law Review* 151 (2003): 1211–54.

Caplin, Andrew. 'Fear as a Policy Instrument.' In *Time and Decision: Economic and Psychological Perspectives on Intertemporal Choice*, ed. George Loewenstein, Daniel Read, and Roy Baumeister, 441–58. New York: Russell Sage, 2003.

Carroll, Gabriel D., James J. Choi, David Laibson, Brigitte Madrian, and Andrew Metrick. 'Optimal Defaults and Active Decisions.' NBER Working Paper no. 11074, 2005.http://www.nber.org/papers/w11074.pdf.

Chaiken, S., and Y. Trope. *Dual Process Theories in Social Psychology*. New York: Guilford, 1999.

Chambers, David L. 'What If? The Legal Consequences of Marriage and the Legal Needs of Lesbian and Gay Male Couples.' *Michigan Law Review* 95 (1996): 447–91.

Childress, James F., and Catharyn T. Liverman, eds. *Organ Donation: Opportunities for Action*. Washington, D.C.: National Academies Press, 2006.

Choi, James J., David Laibson, and Brigitte Madrian. '$100 Bills on the Sidewalk: Violation of No-Arbitrage in 401(k) Accounts.' Working paper, University of Pennsylvania, 2004.

Choi, James J., David Laibson, Brigitte Madrian, and Andrew Metrick. 'Defined Contribution Pensions: Plan Rules, Participant Decisions, and the Path of Least Resistance.' In *Tax Policy and the Economy*, vol. 16, ed. James Poterba, 67–113. Cambridge: MIT Press, 2002.

——. 'For Better or For Worse: Default Effects and 401(k) Savings Behavior.' In *Perspectives in the Economics of Aging*, ed. David Wise, 81–121. Chicago: University of Chicago Press, 2004.

——. 'Saving for Retirement on the Path of Least Resistance.' In *Behavioral Public Finance*, ed. Edward McCaffery and Joel Slemrod. New York: Russell Sage, 2006.

Christakis, Nicholas A., and James H. Fowler. 'The Spread of Obesity in a Large Social Network over 32 Years.' *New England Journal of Medicine* 357 (2007): 370–79.

Cialdini, Robert. *Influence: The Psychology of Persuasion*. New York: Quill, 1993.

——. *Influence: Science and Practice*. 4th ed. Needham Heights, Mass.: Allyn and Bacon, 2000.

——. 'Crafting Normative Messages to Protect the Environment.' *Current Directions in Psychological Science* 12 (2003): 105–9.

Cialdini, Robert B., Raymond R. Reno, and Carl A. Kallgren. 'A Focus Theory of Normative Conduct: Recycling the Concept of Norms to Reduce Littering in Public Places.' *Journal of Personality and Social Psychology* 58 (1990): 1015–26.

——. 'Activating and Aligning Social Norms for Persuasive Impact.' *Social Influence* 1 (2006), 3–15.

Clark, Andrew E., Ed Diener, Yannis Georgellis, and Richard E. Lucas. 'Lags and Leads in Life Satisfaction: A Test of the Baseline Hypothesis,' DELTA Working Paper 2003-14, 2003. http://www.delta.ens.fr/abstracts/wp200314.pdf.

Coleman, Stephen. 'The Minnesota Income Tax Compliance Experiment State Tax Results.' Minnesota Department of Revenue, 1996. http://www.state.mn.us/legal_policy/research_reports/content/complnce.pdf.

Coleman, Thomas F. 'The High Cost of Being Single in America; or, The Financial Consequences of Marital Status Discrimination.' Unmarried

America Web site, n.d. http://www.unmarriedamerica.org/cost-discrim
ination.htm.

Colin, Michael, Ted O'Donoghue, and Timothy Vogelsang. 'Projection
Bias in Catalogue Orders.' Working paper, Cornell University Economics
Department, 2004.

Cooper, Arnold C., Carolyn Y. Woo, and William C. Dunkelberg.
'Entrepreneurs' Perceived Chances for Success.' *Journal of Business
Venturing* 3, no. 2 (1988): 97–108.

Cronqvist, Henrik. 'Advertising and Portfolio Choice.' Working paper,
Ohio State University, 2007.

Cronqvist, Henrik, and Richard H. Thaler. 'Design Choices in Privatized
Social-Security Systems: Learning from the Swedish Experience,'
American Economic Review 94, no. 2 (2004): 425–28.

Cropper, Maureen L., Sema K. Aydede, and Paul R. Portney. 'Rates of
Time Preference for Saving Lives.' *American Economic Review* 82, no. 2
(1992): 469–72.

——. 'Preferences for Life Saving Programs: How the Public Discounts
Time and Age.' *Journal of Risk and Uncertainty* 8 (1994): 243–65.

Crutchfield, Richard S. 'Conformity and Character.' *American Psychologist*
10 (1955): 191–98.

Cubanski, Juliette, and Patricia Neuman, 'Status Report on Medicare
Part D Enrollment in 2006: Analysis of Plan-Specific Market Share and
Coverage.' *Health Affairs* 26 (2007): W1–12.

Daughety, Andrew, and Jennifer Reinganum. 'Stampede to Judgment.'
American Law and Economics Review 1 (1999): 158–89.

De Bondt, Werner F. M., and Richard H. Thaler. 'Do Security Analysts
Overreact?' *American Economic Review* 80, no. 2 (1990): 52–57.

Department of Health and Human Services. 'Medicare Drug Plans Strong
and Growing.' Press release, Washington D. C., June 30, 2007.

De Rothschild, David. *The Global Warming Survival Handbook*. Emmaus,
Pa.: Rodale, 2007.

Diamond, Peter A., and Jerry A. Hausman. 'Contingent Valuation: Is Some
Number Better Than No Number?' *Journal of Economic Perspectives* 8,
no. 4 (1994): 45–64.

Drabek, Thomas E. 'Social Processes in Disaster: Family Evacuation.' *Social
Problems* 16 (1969): 336–49.

Draut, Tamara, and Javier Silva. 'Borrowing to Make Ends Meet: The Rise
of Credit Card Debt in the '90s.' Demos Web site, 2003. http://www.
demos.org/pubs/borrowing_to_make_ends_meet.pdf.

Duflo, Esther, William Gale, Jeffrey Liebman, Peter Orszag, and Emmanuel

Saez. 'Saving Incentives for Low- and Middle-Income Families: Evidence from a Field Experiment with H&R Block,' NBER Working Paper no. 11680, 2005. http://www.nber.org/papers/w11680.pdf.

Duflo, Esther, and Emmanuel Saez. 'The Role of Information and Social Interactions in Retirement Plan Decisions: Evidence from a Randomized Experiment.' Massachusetts Institute of Technology Department of Economics Working Paper no. 0223, 2002. http://papers.ssrn.com/sol3/papers.cfm?abstract_id=315659.

Dworkin, Gerald. *The Theory and Practice of Autonomy.* Cambridge: Cambridge University Press, 1988.

Dynes, Russell R. 'The Importance of Social Capital in Disaster Response.' University of Delaware Disaster Research Center Preliminary Paper no. 327, 2002. http://www.udel.edu/DRC/Preliminary_Papers/PP327-THE%20IMPORTANCE%20OFpdf%20.pdf.

Economist, The. Editorial. 'The State Is Looking After You,' April 8, 2006.

Edgeworth, Francis Ysidro. *Mathematical Psychics.* London: C. K. Paul, 1881.

EDN Europe. 'Europe Switches to "Smart" Energy Meters.' August 28, 2007. http://www.edn-europe.com/europeswitchestosmartelectricity meters+article+1713+Europe.html (Accessed 27 September 2008).

Ellerman, A. Denny, Paul L. Joskow, Richard Schmalensee, Juan-Pablo Montero, and Elizabeth M. Bailey. *Markets for Clean Air.* Cambridge: Cambridge University Press, 2000.

Ellerman, A. Denny and Barbara K. Buchner. 'The European Union Emissions Trading Scheme: Origins, Allocation, and Early Results,' *Review of Environmental Economics and Policy* 1, 66, (2007): 72 n.9.

Ellickson, Robert C. *Order Without Law: How Neighbors Settle Disputes.* Cambridge: Harvard University Press, 1991.

Ellsberg, Daniel. 'Risk, Ambiguity, and the Savage Axioms.' *Quarterly Journal of Economics* 75 (1961): 643–69.

Elster, Jon. *Sour Grapes: Studies in the Subversion of Rationality.* Cambridge: Cambridge University Press, 1983.

Epley, Nicholas, and Thomas Gilovich. 'Just Going Along: Nonconscious Priming and Conformity to Social Pressure.' *Journal of Experimental Social Psychology* 35 (1999): 578–89.

Epstein, Richard A. 'In Defense of the Contract at Will.' *University of Chicago Law Review* 51 (1984): 947–82.

Europa. 'Questions & Answers on Emissions Trading and National Allocation Plans.' Europa, official Web site of the European Union. 2005. http://europa.eu/rapid/pressReleasesAction.do?reference=MEMO/

05/84&format=HTML&aged=1&language=EN&guiLanguage=en (Accessed 27 September 2008).

Europa. 'Emissions Trading: Strong Compliance in 2006, Emissions Decoupled From Economic Growth.' Europa, official Web site of the European Union. 2007. http://europa.eu/rapid/pressReleasesAction.do?reference=IP/07/776&format=HTML&aged=0&language=EN&guiLanguage=en (Accessed 27 September 2008).

European eGovernment News Roundup. 'FI: Awarding eGovernment innovation.' December 2006.

Fineman, Martha A. *The Autonomy Myth: A Theory of Dependency.* New York: New Press, 2004.

Frank, Richard G., and Joseph P. Newhouse. 'Mending the Medicare Prescription Drug Benefit: Improving Consumer Choices and Restructuring Purchasing.' Brookings Institution Web site, April 2007. http://www.brookings.edu/views/papers/200704frank_newhouse.htm.

Frank, Robert. *Choosing the Right Pond.* New York: Oxford University Press, 1985.

Frederick, Shane. 'Measuring Intergenerational Time Preference: Are Future Lives Valued Less?' *Journal of Risk and Uncertainty* 26 (2003): 39–53.

——. 'Cognitive Reflection and Decision Making.' *Journal of Economic Perspectives* 19, no. 4 (2005): 24–42.

Frederick, Shane, George Loewenstein, and Ted O'Donoghue. 'Time Discounting and Time Preference: A Critical Review.' *Journal of Economic Literature* 40 (2002): 351–401.

French, Kenneth R., and James M. Poterba. 'Investor Diversification and International Equity Markets.' *American Economic Review* 81, no. 2 (1991): 222–26.

Friedman, Milton, and Rose Friedman. *Free to Choose: A Personal Statement.* New York: Harcourt Brace Jovanovich, 1980.

Fung, Archon, and Dara O'Rourke. 'Reinventing Environmental Regulation from the Grassroots Up: Explaining and Expanding the Success of the Toxic Release Inventory.' *Environmental Management* 25 (2000): 115–27.

Gallagher, Maggie. 'Banned in Boston.' *Weekly Standard*, May 15, 2006.

Gerber, Alan S., and Todd Rogers. 'The Effect of Descriptive Social Norms on Voter Turnout: The Importance of Accentuating the Positive.' Working paper, 2007. http://www.iq.harvard.edu/NewsEvents/Seminars-WShops/PPBW/rogers.pdf.

Gilbert, Daniel T. 'Inferential Correction.' In Gilovich, Griffin, and Kahneman (2002), 167–84.

Gilbert, Daniel T., Erin Driver-Linn, and Timothy D. Wilson. 'The Trouble with Vronsky: Impact Bias in the Forecasting of Future Affective States.' In *The Wisdom in Feeling: Psychological Processes in Emotional Intelligence*, ed. L. F. Barrett and P. Salovey, 114–43. New York: Guilford, 2002.

Gilbert, Daniel T., M. Gill, and Timothy D. Wilson. 'How Do We Know What We Will Like? The Informational Basis of Affective Forecasting.' Manuscript, Harvard University, 1998.

Gilbert, Daniel T., Elizabeth C. Pinel, Timothy D. Wilson, Stephen J. Blumberg, and Thalia P. Wheatley. 'Immune Neglect: A Source of Durability Bias in Affective Forecasting.' *Journal of Personality and Social Psychology* 75 (1998): 617–38.

Gilbert, Daniel T., and Timothy D. Wilson. 'Miswanting: Some Problems in the Forecasting of Future Affective States.' In *Feeling and Thinking: The Role of Affect in Social Cognition*, ed. Joseph P. Forgas, 178–97. Cambridge: Cambridge University Press, 2000.

Gilovich, Thomas. *How We Know What Isn't So: The Fallibility of Human Reason in Everyday Life*. New York: Free Press, 1991.

Gilovich, Thomas, Dale Griffin, and Daniel Kahneman. *Heuristics and Biases: The Psychology of Intuitive Judgement*. Cambridge: Cambridge University Press, 2002.

Gilovich, Thomas, Victoria H. Medvec, and Kenneth Savitsky. 'The Spotlight Effect in Social Judgment: An Egocentric Bias in Estimates of the Salience of One's Own Actions and Appearance.' *Journal of Personality and Social Psychology* 78 (2000): 211–22.

Gilovich, Thomas, Robert Vallone, and Amos Tversky. 'The Hot Hand in Basketball: On the Misperception of Random Sequences.' *Cognitive Psychology* 17 (1985): 295–314.

Glaeser, Edward L. 'Paternalism and Psychology.' *University of Chicago Law Review* 73 (2006): 133–56.

Glaeser, Edward L., Bruce Sacerdote, and Jose Scheinkman. 'Crime and Social Interactions.' *Quarterly Journal of Economics* 111 (1996): 507–48.

Goldstein, Noah J., Robert B. Cialdini, and Vladas Griskevicius. 'A Room with a Viewpoint: The Role of Situational Similarity in Motivating Conformity to Social Norms.' Manuscript in preparation, 2007.

Goodin, Robert E. 'Permissible Paternalism: In Defense of the Nanny State.' *Responsive Community* 1 (1991): 42.

Goolsbee, Austan. 'The Simple Return: Reducing America's Tax Burden Through Return-Free Filing.' Brookings Institution Web site, July 2006. http://www.brookings.edu/papers/2006/07useconomics_goolsbee.aspx.

Gould, Stephen Jay. *Bully for Brontosaurus: Reflections in Natural History*. New York: Norton, 1991.

Government Accountability Office. 'Toxic Chemicals.' Report to the Congress, 1991.

——. 'Medicare Part D: Challenges in Enrolling New Dual-Eligible Beneficiaries.' June 2007. http://www.gao.gov/cgi-bin/getrpt?GAO-07–272.

Greenwald, Anthony G., Catherine G. Carnot, Rebecca Beach, and Barbara Young. 'Increasing Voting Behavior by Asking People if They Expect to Vote.' *Journal of Applied Psychology* 2 (1987): 315–18.

Grether, David M. 'Bayes Rule as a Descriptive Model: The Representativeness Heuristic.' *Quarterly Journal of Economics* 95 (1980): 537–57.

Gross, David B., and Nicholas S. Souleles. 'Do Liquidity Constraints and Interest Rates Matter for Consumer Behavior? Evidence from Credit Card Data.' *Quarterly Journal of Economics* 117 (2002): 149–85.

Gruber, Jonathan. 'Smoking's "Internalities."' *Regulation* 25, no. 4 (2002): 52–57.

Hamilton, James. *Regulation Through Revelation*. New York: Cambridge University Press, 2005.

Harrington, Brooke. *Pop Finance*. Princeton: Princeton University Press, 2008.

Heath, Chip, and Dan Heath. *Made to Stick: Why Some Ideas Survive and Others Die*. New York: Random House, 2007.

Heinrich, Joseph, Wulf Albers, Robert Boyd, Gerd Gigerenzer, Kevin A. McCabe, Axel Ockenfels, and H. Peyton Young. 'What Is the Role of Culture in Bounded Rationality?' In *Bounded Rationality: The Adaptive Toolbox*, ed. Gerd Gigerenzer and Reinhard Selten, 343–59. Cambridge: MIT Press, 2001.

Henry J. Kaiser Family Foundation. 'Seniors and the Medicare Prescription Drug Benefit.' December 2006. http://www.kff.org/kaiserpolls/pomr 121906pkg.cfm.

——. 'Low-Income Assistance Under the Medicare Drug Benefit.' July 2007. http://www.kff.org/medicare/7327.cfm.

Herzog, Don. *Happy Slaves: A Critique of the Consent Theory*. Chicago: University of Chicago Press, 1989.

Hirshleifer, David. 'The Blind Leading the Blind: Social Influence, Fads, and Informational Cascades.' In *The New Economics of Human Behavior*, ed. Mariano Tommasi and Kathryn Ierulli, 188. Cambridge: Cambridge University Press, 1995.

Hirshleifer, David, and Tyler Shumway. 'Good Day Sunshine: Stock Returns and the Weather.' March 2001. http://papers.ssrn.com/sol3/papers.cfm?abstract_id=265674.

Hoadley, Jack. Testimony to Government Reform Committee Briefing on the Medicare Drug Benefit. U.S. House Committee on Oversight and Government Reform. January 20, 2006. http://oversight.house.gov/documents/20060120130100-17757.pdf.

Hoadley, Jack, Laura Summer, Jennifer Thompson, Elizabeth Hargrave, and Katie Merrell. 'The Role of Beneficiary-Centered Assignment for Part D.' Georgetown University and the National Opinion Research Center at the University of Chicago for the Medicare Payment Advisory Commission. June 2007. http://www.medpac.gov/documents/June07_Bene_centered_assignment_contractor.pdf.

Holland, Rob W., Merel Hendriks, and Henk Aarts. 'Smells Like Clean Spirit.' Psychological Science 16 (2005): 689–93.

Howarth, Richard B., Brent M. Haddad, and Bruce Paton. 'The Economics of Energy Efficiency: Insights from Voluntary Participation Programs.' Energy Policy 28 (2000): 477–86.

Hsee, Christopher K. 'Attribute Evaluability and Its Implications for Joint-Separate Evaluation Reversals and Beyond.' In Kahneman and Tversky (2000), 543–63.

Huberman, Gur, and Wei Jiang. 'Offering vs. Choice in 401(k) Plans: Equity Exposure and Number of Funds.' Journal of Finance 61 (2006): 763–801.

Investment Company Institute. '401(k) Plans: A 25-Year Retrospective.' 2006: http://www.ici.org/pdf/per12-02.pdf.

Ivkovic, Zoran, and Scott Weisbrenner. 'Local Does as Local Is: Information Content of the Geography of Individual Investors' Common Stock Investments.' NBER Working Paper no. 9685, May 2003. http://www.nber.org/papers/w9685.pdf.

Iyengar, Sheena S., Gur Huberman, and Wei Jiang. 'How Much Choice Is Too Much? Contributions to 401(k) Retirement Plans.' In Pension Design and Structure: Lessons from Behavioral Finance, ed. Olivia S. Mitchell and Stephen P. Utkus, 83–95. Oxford: Oxford University Press, 2004.

Jacobs, R. C., and D. T. Campbell. 'Transmission of an Arbitrary Social Tradition.' Journal of Abnormal and Social Psychology 62 (1961): 649–58.

Jin, Ginger Zhe, and Phillip Leslie. 'The Effect of Information on Product Quality: Evidence from Restaurant Hygiene Grade Cards.' *Quarterly Journal of Economics* 118 (2003): 409–51.

Johnson, Branden B. 'Accounting for the Social Context of Risk Communication.' *Science and Technology Studies* 5 (1987): 103–11.

Johnson, Eric J., and Daniel Goldstein. 'Do Defaults Save Lives?' *Science* 302 (2003): 1338–39.

Johnson, Eric J., John Hershey, Jacqueline Meszaros, and Howard Kunreuther. 'Framing, Probability Distortions, and Insurance Decisions.' In Kahneman and Tversky (2000), 224–40.

Jolls, Christine, Cass R. Sunstein, and Richard Thaler. 'A Behavioral Approach to Law and Economics.' *Stanford Law Review* 50 (1998): 1471–550.

Jones-Lee, Michael, and Graham Loomes. 'Private Values and Public Policy.' In *Conflict and Tradeoffs in Decision Making*, ed. Elke U. Weber, Jonathan Baron, and Graham Loomes, 205–30. Cambridge: Cambridge University Press, 2001.

Kahneman, Daniel. 'New Challenges to the Rationality Assumption.' *Journal of Institutional and Theoretical Economics* 150 (1994): 18–36.

Kahneman, Daniel, and Shane Frederick. 'Representativeness Revisited: Attribute Substitution in Intuitive Judgement.' In Gilovich, Griffin, and Kahneman (2002), 49–81.

Kahneman, Daniel, Barbara L. Fredrickson, Charles A. Schreiber, and Donald A. Redelmeier. 'When More Pain Is Preferred to Less: Adding a Better End.' *Psychological Science* 4 (1993): 401–5.

Kahneman, Daniel, Jack L. Knetsch, and Richard H. Thaler. 'Experimental Tests of the Endowment Effect and the Coase Theorem.' *Journal of Political Economy* 98 (1990): 1325–48.

——. 'Anomalies: The Endowment Effect, Loss Aversion, and Status Quo Bias.' *Journal of Economic Perspectives* 5, no. 1 (1991): 193–206.

Kahneman, Daniel, and Richard H. Thaler. 'Anomalies: Utility Maximization and Experienced Utility.' *Journal of Economic Perspectives* 20, no. 1 (2006): 221–34.

Kahneman, Daniel, and Amos Tversky, eds. *Choices, Values, and Frames.* Cambridge: Cambridge University Press, 2000.

Kahneman, Daniel, Peter. P. Wakker, and Rakesh Sarin. 'Back to Bentham? Explorations of Experienced Welfare.' *Quarterly Journal of Economics* 112 (1997): 375–405.

Karlan, Dean S., and Jonathan Zinman. 'Expanding Credit Access: Using Randomized Supply Decisions to Estimate the Impacts.' 2007.

http://research.yale.edu/karlan/deankarlan/downloads/ExpandingCredit Access.pdf.

Kay, Aaron C., S. Christian Wheeler, John A. Bargh, and Lee Ross. 'Material Priming: The Influence of Mundane Physical Objects on Situational Construal and Competitive Behavioral Choice.' *Organizational Behavior and Human Decision Processes* 95 (2004): 83–96.

Kennedy, Robert. 'Strategy Fads and Strategic Positioning: An Empirical Test for Herd Behavior in Prime-Time Television Programming.' *Journal of Industrial Economics* 50 (2002): 57–84.

Klevmarken, N. Anders, 'Swedish Pension Reforms in the 1990s.' April 2002. http://www.nek.uu.se/Pdf/wp2002_6.pdf.

Kling, Jeffrey, Sendhil Mullainathan, Eldar Shafir, Lee Vermeulen, and Marian Wrobel. 'Choosing Well: The Case of Medicare Drug Plans.' Working paper, Harvard University, August 2007.

Koehler, Jay, and Caryn Conley. 'The "Hot Hand" Myth in Professional Basketball.' *Journal of Sport and Exercise Psychology* 25 (2003): 253–59.

Koppell, Jonathan G. S., and Jennifer A. Steen. 'The Effects of Ballot Position on Election Outcomes.' *Journal of Politics* 66 (2004): 267–81.

Korobkin, Russell. 'The Status Quo Bias and Contract Default Rules.' *Cornell Law Review* 83 (1998): 608–87.

Kraut, Robert E., and McConahay, John B. 'How Being Interviewed Affects Voting: An Experiment.' *Public Opinion Quarterly* 37 (1973): 398–406.

Krech, David, Richard S. Crutchfield, and Egerton S. Ballachey. *Individual in Society*. New York: McGraw-Hill, 1962.

Krueger, Alan B. *What Makes a Terrorist*. Princeton: Princeton University Press, 2007.

Kruse, Douglas L., and Joseph Blasi. 'Employee Ownership, Employee Attitudes, and Firm Performance.' NBER Working Paper no. 5277, September 1995. http://www .nber.org/papers/w5277.v5.pdf.

Kunreuther, Howard. 'Mitigating Disaster Losses Through Insurance.' *Journal of Risk and Uncertainty* 12 (1996): 171–87.

Kuran, Timur. *Private Truths, Public Lies: The Social Consequences of Preference Falsification*. Cambridge: Harvard University Press, 1998.

Kuran, Timur, and Cass R. Sunstein. 'Availability Cascades and Risk Regulation.' *Stanford Law Review* 51 (1999): 683–768.

Kurtz, Sheldon F. and Michael J. Saks. 'The Transplant Paradox: Overwhelming Public Support for Organ Donation vs. Under-Supply of

Organs: The Iowa Organ Procurement Study.' *Journal of Corporation Law* 21 (1996): 767–806.

Laibson, David. 'Golden Eggs and Hyperbolic Discounting.' *Quarterly Journal of Economics* 112 (1997): 443–77.

Larrick, Richard and Jack Soll. 'The MPG Illusion.' *Science* 320, no 5883 (2008): 1593–94.

Layton, Deborah. *Seductive Poison: A Jonestown Survivor's Story of Life and Death in the People's Temple*. New York: Anchor, 1999.

Leavitt, Michael. Remarks as Prepared to America's Health Insurance Plans (AHIP). U.S. Department of Health and Human Services. March 22, 2007. http://www.hhs.gov/news/speech/sp20070322a.html.

Ledoux, Joseph. *The Emotional Brain: The Mysterious Underpinnings of Emotional Life*. New York: Simon and Schuster, 1998.

Levav, Jonathan, and Gavan J. Fitzsimons. 'When Questions Change Behavior.' *Psychological Science* 17 (2006): 207–13.

Leventhal, Howard, Robert Singer, and Susan Jones. 'Effects of Fear and Specificity of Recommendation upon Attitudes and Behavior.' *Journal of Personality and Social Psychology* 2 (1965): 20–29.

Lichtenstein, Sarah, and Paul Slovic. 'Reversals of Preference Between Bids and Choices in Gambling Decisions.' *Journal of Experimental Psychology* 89 (1971): 46–55.

Lieberman, Matthew D., Ruth Gaunt, Daniel T. Gilbert, and Yaacov Trope. 'Reflection and Reflexion: A Social Cognitive Neuroscience Approach to Attributional Interference.' In *Advances in Experimental Social Psychology* 34, ed. Mark Zanna, 199–249. New York: Elsevier, 2002.

Linkenbach, Jeffrey W. 'The Montana Model: Development and Overview of a SevenStep Process for Implementing Macro-Level Social Norms Campaigns.' In Perkins (2003), 182–208.

Linkenbach, Jeffrey W., and H. Wesley Perkins. 'MOST of Us Are Tobacco Free: An Eight-Month Social Norms Campaign Reducing Youth Initiation of Smoking in Montana.' In Perkins (2003), 224–34.

Lipman, Larry. 'Medicare Offers Web Tools for Choosing a Drug Plan,' Cox NewsService. October 20, 2005. http://www.coxwashington.com/reporters/content/reporters/stories/2005/10/20/BC_MEDICARE18_COX.html.

Loewenstein, George. 'Out of Control: Visceral Influences on Behavior.' *Organizational Behavior and Human Decision Processes* 65 (1996): 272–92.

——. 'Costs and Benefits of Health- and Retirement-Related Choice.' In

Social Security and Medicare: Individual Versus Collective Risk and Responsibility, ed. Sheila Burke, Eric Kingson, and Uwe Reinhardt. Washington, D.C.: Brookings Institution Press, 2000.

Loewenstein, George, and Lisa Marsch. 'Altered States: The Impact of Immediate Craving on the Valuation of Current and Future Opioids.' Working paper, Carnegie-Mellon University, 2004.

Loewenstein, George, Ted O'Donoghue, and Matthew Rabin. 'Projection Bias in Predicting Future Welfare.' *Quarterly Journal of Economics* 118 (2003): 1209–48.

Loewenstein, George, and David Schkade. 'Wouldn't It Be Nice: Predicting Future Feelings.' In *Well-Being: The Foundations of Hedonic Psychology*, ed. Daniel Kahneman, Ed Diener, and Norbert Schwarz, 85–108. New York: Russell Sage, 1999.

Loewenstein, George, Elke U. Weber, Christopher K. Hsee, and Ned Welch. 'Risk as Feelings.' *Psychological Bulletin* 127 (2001): 267–86.

Madrian, Brigitte C., and Dennis F. Shea. 'The Power of Suggestion: Inertia in 401(k) Participation and Savings Behavior.' *Quarterly Journal of Economics* 116 (2001): 1149–1225.

Mahar, Heather. 'Why Are There So Few Prenuptial Agreements?' John M. Olin Center for Law, Economics, and Business, Harvard Law School, Discussion Paper no. 436. September 2003. http://www.law.harvard.edu/programs/olin_center/papers/pdf/436.pdf.

Malmendier, Ulrike, and Stefano DellaVigna. 'Paying Not to Go to the Gym.' *American Economic Review* 96, no. 3 (2006): 694–719.

McClure, Samuel M., David I. Laibson, George Loewenstein, and Jonathan D. Cohen. 'Separate Neural Systems Value Immediate and Delayed Monetary Rewards.' *Science* 306 (2004): 503–7

McFadden, Daniel. 'Free Markets and Fettered Consumers.' *American Economic Review* 96, no. 1 (2006): 5–29.

——. 'A Dog's Breakfast.' *Wall Street Journal*, February 16, 2007. Opinion section, Eastern ed.

McKay, Kim, and Jenny Bonnin. *True Green*. Washington, D.C.: National Geographic, 2007.

Medicare Prescription Drug Plan. 'Tips and Tools for People with Medicare and Those Who Care for Them.' U.S. Department of Health and Human Services. N.d. http://www.medicare.gov/medicarereform/drugbenefit.asp.

Medicare Rights Center. 'Part D 2007: Addressing Access Problems for Low Income People with Medicare.' November 2006. http://www.medicarerights.org/policy brief_autoreenrollment.pdf.

Meyer, Robert J. 'Why We Under-Prepare for Hazards.' In *On Risk and*

Disaster: Lessons from Hurricane Katrina, ed. Ronald J. Daniels, Donald F. Kettl, and Howard Kunreuther, 153–74. Philadelphia: University of Pennsylvania Press, 2006.

Milgram, Stanley. *Obedience to Authority*. New York: HarperCollins, 1974.

Mokdad, Ali H., Barbara A. Bowman, Earl S. Ford, Frank Vinicor, James S. Marks, and Jeffrey P. Koplan. 'The Continuing Epidemics of Obesity and Diabetes in the United States.' *Journal of the American Medical Association* 286 (2001): 1195–200.

Morrison, Edward R. 'Comment: Judicial Review of Discount Rates Used in Regulatory Cost-Benefit Analysis.' *University of Chicago Law Review* 65 (1998): 1333–70.

Morton, Fiona S., Florian Zettelmeyer, and Jorge Silva-Risso. 'Consumer Information and Discrimination: Does the Internet Affect the Pricing of New Cars to Women and Minorities?' *Quantitative Marketing and Economics* 1 (2003): 65–92.

Morwitz, Vicki G., and Eric Johnson. 'Does Measuring Intent Change Behavior?' *Journal of Consumer Research* 20 (1993): 46–61.

Moser, Christine, and Christopher Barrett. 'Labor, Liquidity, Learning, Conformity, and Smallholder Technology Adoption: The Case of SRI in Madagascar.' Manuscript, 2002. http://papers.ssrn.com/sol3/papers.cfm?abstract_id=328662.

Nemore, Patricia B. 'Medicare Part D: Issues for Dual-Eligibles on the Eve of Implementation.' Center for Medicare Advocacy for the Henry J. Kaiser Family Foundation. November 2005. http://www.kff.org/medicare/7431.cfm.

New Zealand Ministry of Economic Development. 'Inland Revenue, KiwiSaver Evaluation: Six Month Report 1, 1 July 2007–31 December, 2007.' Ministry of Economic Development, Housing New Zealand. February 2008.

Nisbett, Richard E., and David E. Kanouse. 'Obesity, Hunger, and Supermarket Shopping Behavior.' *Proceedings of the Seventh Annual Meeting of the American Psychological Association* 3 (1968): 683–84.

Nock, Steven L., Laura Sanchez, Julia C. Wilson, and James D. Wright. 'Covenant Marriage Turns Five Years Old.' *Michigan Journal of Gender and Law* 10 (2003): 169–88.

Nordhaus, William D. 'The Stern Review on the Economics of Climate Change.' *Journal of Economic Literature* 45 (2007): 686–702.

Nordhaus, William D., and Joseph Boyer. *Warming the World: Economic Models of Global Warming*. Cambridge: MIT Press, 2000.

Norman, Donald. *The Design of Everyday Things*. Sydney: Currency, 1990.

Normann, Goran, and Daniel J. Mitchell. 'Pension Reform in Sweden: Lessons for American Policymakers.' Heritage Foundation Backgrounder no. 1381, 2000. http://www.heritage.org/Research/SocialSecurity/bg1381.cfm.

Norwegian Tax Administration. Norwegian Tax Administration Annual Report. PowerPoint presentation. Slide 3, 2005.

O'Donoghue, Ted, and Matthew Rabin. 'Doing It Now or Later.' *American Economic Review* 89, no. 1 (1999): 103–24.

——. 'Studying Optimal Paternalism, Illustrated by a Model of Sin Taxes.' *American Economic Review* 93, no. 2 (2003): 186–91.

Okin, Susan Moller. *Justice, Gender, and the Family*. New York: Basic, 1989.

Organization for Economic Co-Operation and Development. 'Programs to Reduce the Administrative Burden of Tax Regulations in Selected Countries.' Centre for Tax Policy and Administration. January 22, 2008.

Payne, John W., James R. Bettman, and David A. Schkade. 'Measuring Constructed Preferences: Towards a Building Code.' *Journal of Risk and Uncertainty* 19 (1999): 243–70.

Peacock, Walter G., Betty Hearn Morrow, and Hugh Gladwin, eds. *Hurricane Andrew: Ethnicity, Gender, and the Sociology of Disasters*. New York: Routledge, 1997.

Pear, Robert. 'In Texas Town, Patients and Providers Find New Prescription Drug Plan Baffling.' *New York Times*, June 11, 2006, section 1, East Coast ed.

Perkins, H. Wesley, ed. *The Social Norms Approach to Preventing School and College Age Substance Abuse*. New York: Jossey-Bass, 2003.

Perry, Ronald W. *Comprehensive Emergency Management: Evacuating Threatened Populations*. Greenwich, Conn.: JAI Press, 1985.

Perry, Ronald W., and Michael K. Lindell. 'The Effects of Ethnicity on Evacuation Decision-Making.' *International Journal of Mass Emergencies and Disasters* 9 (1991): 47–68.

Perry, Ronald W., Michael K. Lindell, and Marjorie R. Greene. *Evacuation Planning in Emergency Management*. Lexington, Mass.: Lexington, 1981.

Pew Center on Global Climate Change. 'The European Union Emissions Trading Scheme (EU-ETS) Insights and Opportunities.' Arlington, Virginia. Undated. http://www.pewclimate.org/docUploads/EU-ETS%20White%20Paper.pdf (Accessed 27 September 2008).

Pittsburgh Post-Gazette. 'D Is for Daunting: The Medicare Drug Program.' November 6, 2005, Health section, Five-star ed.

Polikoff, Nancy D. 'We Will Get What We Ask For: Why Legalizing Gay and Lesbian Marriage Will Not "Dismantle the Legal Structure of Gender in Every Marriage."' *Virginia Law Review* 79 (1993): 1535–50.

Prelec, Drazen, and Duncan Simester. 'Always Leave Home Without It: A Further Investigation of the Credit-Card Effect on Willingness to Pay.' *Marketing Letters* 12 (2001): 5–12.

Prendergast, Canice. 'The Provision of Incentives in Firms.' *Journal of Economic Literature* 37 (1999): 7–63.

Rawls, John. *A Theory of Justice.* Oxford: Clarendon, 1971.

Read, Daniel, Gerrit Antonides, Laura Van Den Ouden, and Harry Trienekens 'Which Is Better: Simultaneous or Sequential Choice?' *Organizational Behavior and Human Decision Processes* 84 (2001): 54–70.

Read, Daniel, and George Loewenstein. 'Diversification Bias: Explaining the Discrepancy in Variety Seeking Between Combined and Separated Choices.' *Journal of Experimental Psychology: Applied* 1 (1995): 34–49.

Read, Daniel, George Loewenstein, and Shobana Kalyanarama. 'Mixing Virtue and Vice: Combining the Immediacy Effect and the Diversification Heuristic.' *Journal of Behavioral Decision Making* 12 (1999): 257–73.

Read, Daniel, and B. Van Leeuwen. 'Predicting Hunger: The Effects of Appetite and Delay on Choice.' *Organizational Behavior and Human Decision Processes* 76 (1998): 189–205.

Redelmeier, Donald A., Joel Katz, and Daniel Kahneman. 'Memories of Colonoscopy: A Randomized Trial.' *Pain* 104 (2003): 187–94.

Redelmeier, Donald A., Paul Rozin, and Daniel Kahneman. 'Understanding Patients' Decisions: Cognitive and Emotional Perspectives.' *Journal of the American Medical Association* 270 (1993): 72–76.

Revesz, Richard L. 'Environmental Regulation, Cost-Benefit Analysis, and the Discounting of Human Lives.' *Columbia Law Review* 99 (1999): 941–1017.

Ross, Lee, and Richard Nisbett. *The Person and the Situation.* New York: McGraw-Hill, 1991.

Rottenstreich, Yuval, and Christopher Hsee. 'Money, Kisses, and Electric Shocks: On the Affective Psychology of Risk.' *Psychological Science* 12 (2001): 185–90.

Rozin, Paul, and Edward B. Royzman. 'Negativity Bias, Negativity Dominance, and Contagion.' *Personality and Social Psychology Review* 5 (2001): 296–320.

Sacerdote, Bruce. 'Peer Effects with Random Assignment: Results for

Dartmouth Roommates.' *Quarterly Journal of Economics* 116 (2001): 681–704.

Sageman, Marc. *Understanding Terror Networks*. Philadelphia: University of Pennsylvania Press, 2003.

Salganik, Matthew J., Peter Sheridan Dodds, and Duncan J. Watts. 'Experimental Study of Inequality and Unpredictability in an Artificial Cultural Market.' *Science* 311 (2006): 854–56.

Samuelson, William, and Richard J. Zeckhauser. 'Status Quo Bias in Decision Making.' *Journal of Risk and Uncertainty* 1 (1988): 7–59.

Schkade, David A., and Daniel Kahneman. 'Does Living in California Make People Happy? A Focusing Illusion in Judgments of Life Satisfaction.' *Psychological Science* 9 (1998): 340–46.

Schkade, David, Cass R. Sunstein, and Daniel Kahneman. 'Deliberating About Dollars: The Severity Shift.' *Columbia Law Review* 100 (2000): 1139–76.

Schreiber, Charles A., and Daniel Kahneman. 'Determinants of the Remembered Welfare of Aversive Sounds.' *Journal of Experimental Psychology: General* 129 (2000): 27–42.

Schultz, P. Wesley, Jessica M. Nolan, Robert B. Cialdini, Noah J. Goldstein, and Vladas Griskevicius. 'The Constructive, Destructive, and Reconstructive Power of Social Norms.' *Psychological Science* 18 (2007): 429–34.

Schwarz, Norbert. *Cognition and Communication: Judgmental Biases, Research Methods, and the Logic of Conversation*. Mahwah, N.J.: Lawrence Erlbaum, 1996.

Scitovsky, Tibor. *The Joyless Economy*. Oxford: Oxford University Press, 1992.

Scott, Elizabeth. 'Rational Decisionmaking About Marriage and Divorce.' *Virginia Law Review* 76 (1990): 9–94.

Sen, Amartya. *Development as Freedom*. New York: Knopf, 1999.

Shapiro, Ian. 'Long Lines, Even Longer Odds, Looking for a Lucky Number? How About 1 in 76,275,360?' *Washington Post*, April 12, 2002.

Shepard, Roger. *Mind Sights: Original Visual Illusions, Ambiguities, and Other Anomalies, with a Commentary on the Play of Mind in Perception and Art*. New York: Freeman, 1990.

Sherif, Muzafer. 'An Experimental Approach to the Study of Attitudes.' *Sociometry* 1 (1937): 90–98.

Sherman, Steven J. 'On the Self-Erasing Nature of Errors of Prediction.' *Journal of Personality and Social Psychology* 39 (1980): 211–21.

Shiller, Robert J. *Irrational Exuberance*. Princeton: Princeton University Press, 2000.

Shiller, Robert. *The Subprime Solution*. Princeton: Princeton University Press, 2008.

Shu, Suzanne B. 'Choosing for the Long Run: Making Trade-offs in Multiperiod Borrowing.' Working paper, UCLA, 2007.

Silverstein, Shel. *Where the Sidewalk Ends*. New York: HarperCollins, 1974.

Simon, Ruth, and James Haggerty. 'Mortgage Mess Shines Light on Brokers' Role.' *Wall Street Journal*, July 5, 2007, front section, Eastern ed.

Simonson, Itamar. 'The Effect of Purchase Quantity and Timing on Variety-Seeking Behavior.' *Journal of Marketing Research* 28 (1990): 150–62.

Simonson, Itamar, and Russell S. Winer. 'The Influence of Purchase Quantity and Display Format on Consumer Preference for Variety.' *Journal of Consumer Research* 19 (1992): 133–38.

Slovic, Paul, Melissa L. Finucane, Ellen Peters, and Donald G. MacGregor. 'The Affect Heuristic.' In Gilovich, Griffin, and Kahneman (2002), 397–420.

Slovic, Paul, Howard Kunreuther, and Gilbert F. White. 'Decision Processes, Rationality, and Adjustment to Natural Hazards.' 1974. Rpt. in *The Perception of Risk*, ed. Paul Slovic, 1–31. London: Earthscan, 2000.

Smith, Vernon, Kathleen Gifford, Sandy Kramer, and Linda Elam. 'The Transition of Dual Eligibles to Medicare Part D Prescription Drug Coverage: State Actions During Implementation.' Henry J. Kaiser Family Foundation. February 2006. http://www.kff.org/medicaid/7467.cfm.

Smock, Pamela J., Wendy D. Manning, and Sanjiv Gupta. 'The Effect of Marriage and Divorce on Women's Economic Well-Being.' *American Sociological Review* 64 (1999): 794–812.

Stephenson, Denice, ed. *Dear People: Remembering Jonestown*. Berkeley, Calif.: Heyday, 2005.

Stewart, Richard B., and Jonathan B. Wiener. *Reconstructing Climate Policy: Beyond Kyoto*. Washington, D.C.: American Enterprise Institute Press, 2003.

Stone, Arthur A., Joan E. Broderick, Laura S. Porter, and Alan T. Kaell. 'The Experience of Rheumatoid Arthritis Pain and Fatigue: Examining Momentary Reports, and Correlates over One Week.' *Arthritis Care and Research* 10 (1997): 185–93.

Strack, Fritz, L. L. Martin, and Norbert Schwarz. 'Priming and

Communication: The Social Determinants of Information Use in Judgments of Life-Satisfaction.' *European Journal of Social Psychology* 18 (1988): 429–42.

Stroop, John R. 'Studies of Interference in Serial Verbal Reactions.' *Journal of Experimental Psychology* 12 (1935): 643–62.

Sunstein, Cass R. 'Endogenous Preferences, Environmental Law.' *Journal of Legal Studies* 22 (1993): 217–54.

——. 'Selective Fatalism.' *Journal of Legal Studies* 27 (1998): 799–823.

——. 'Human Behavior and the Law of Work.' *Virginia Law Review* 87 (2001): 205–76.

——. *Risk and Reason: Safety, Law, and the Environment.* Cambridge: Cambridge University Press, 2002.

——. 'Switching the Default Rule.' *New York University Law Review* 77 (2002): 106–34.

——. *Why Societies Need Dissent.* Cambridge: Harvard University Press, 2003.

——. 'Lives, Life-Years, and Willingness to Pay.' *Columbia Law Review* 104 (2004): 205–52.

——. 'The Right to Marry.' *Cardozo Law Review* 26 (2005): 2081–2120.

——. *Republic.com 2.0.* Princeton: Princeton University Press, 2007.

Sunstein, Cass R., Daniel Kahneman, David Schkade, and Ilana Ritov. 'Predictably Incoherent Judgments.' *Stanford Law Review* 54 (2002): 1153–1216.

Sunstein, Cass R., David Schkade, Lisa Ellman, and Andres Sawicki. *Are Judges Political?* Washington, D.C.: Brookings Institution Press, 2006.

Sunstein, Cass R., and Richard H. Thaler. 'Libertarian Paternalism Is Not an Oxymoron.' *University of Chicago Law Review* 70 (2003): 1159–1202.

Sunstein, Cass R., and Edna Ullman-Margalit. 'Second-Order Decisions.' *Ethics* 110 (1999): 5–31.

Thaler, Richard H. *Quasi-Rational Economics.* New York: Russell Sage, 1991.

——. *The Winner's Curse: Paradoxes and Anomalies of Economic Life.* New York: Free Press, 2002.

Thaler, Richard H., and Shlomo Benartzi. 'Save More Tomorrow: Using Behavioral Economics to Increase Employee Saving.' *Journal of Political Economy* 112 (2004): S164–87.

Thaler, Richard H., and Eric J. Johnson. 'Gambling with the House Money and Trying to Break Even: The Effects of Prior Outcomes on Risky Choice.' *Management Science* 36 (1990): 643–60.

Thaler, Richard H., and Hersh M. Shefrin. 'An Economic Theory of Self-Control.' *Journal of Political Economy* 89 (1981): 392–406.

Thaler, Richard H., and Cass R. Sunstein. 'Libertarian Paternalism.' *American Economic Review* 93, no. 2 (2003): 175–79.

Thompson, Dennis F. *Political Ethics and Public Office.* Cambridge: Harvard University Press, 1987.

Tierney, John. 'Magic Marker Strategy.' *New York Times*, September 6, 2005, Section A, Late ed.

——. 'Free and Easy Riders.' *New York Times*, June 17, 2006, Opinion section, Late ed.

——. 'Are We Ready to Track Carbon Footprints?' *New York Times*, March 25, 2008. Section D. Late ed.

Tierney, Kathleen J., Michael K. Lindell, and Ronald W. Perry. *Facing the Unexpected: Disaster Preparedness and Response in the USA.* Washington, D.C.: Joseph Henry, 2001.

Toderov, Alexander, Anesu N. Mandisodza, Amir Goren, and Crystal C. Hall. 'Inferences of Competence from Faces Predict Election Outcomes.' *Science* 308 (2005): 1623–26.

Tversky, Amos. 'Elimination by Aspects: A Theory of Choice.' *Psychological Review* 76 (1972): 31–48.

Tversky, Amos, and Daniel Kahneman. 'Availability: A Heuristic for Judging Frequency and Probability.' *Cognitive Psychology* 5 (1973): 207–32.

——. 'Judgment Under Uncertainty: Heuristics and Biases.' *Science* 185 (1974): 1124–31.

——. 'The Framing of Decisions and the Psychology of Choice.' *Science* 211 (1981): 453–58.

Van Boven, Leaf, David Dunning, and George Loewenstein. 'Egocentric Empathy Gaps Between Owners and Buyers: Misperceptions of the Endowment Effect.' *Journal of Personal and Social Psychology* 79 (2000): 66–76.

Van Boven, Leaf, and George Loewenstein. 'Social Projection of Transient Drive States.' *Personality and Social Psychology Bulletin* 29 (2003): 1159–68.

Van De Veer, Donald. *Paternalistic Intervention: The Moral Bounds on Benevolence.* Princeton: Princeton University Press, 1986.

Vaughan, William, and Delani Gunawardena. 'Letter to CMS Acting Administrator Leslie Norwalk.' Consumers Union. Washington, D.C., December 18, 2006.

Vicente, Kim J. *The Human Factor: Revolutionizing the Way People Live with Technology.* New York: Routledge, 2006.

Viscusi, W. Kip. 'Alarmist Decisions with Divergent Risk Information.' *Economic Journal* 107 (1997): 1657–70.

Vitality Program. 'Overview.' Destiny Health. 2007. http://www.destiny health.com.

Waldfogel, Joel. 'Does Consumer Irrationality Trump Consumer Sovereignty? Evidence from Gifts and Own Purchases.' April 2004. http://knowledge.wharton.upenn.edu/papers/1286.pdf.

Wansink, Brian. *Mindless Eating: Why We Eat More Than We Think*. New York: Bantam, 2006.

Watts, Duncan. 'The Kerry Cascade: How a '50s Psychology Experiment Can Explain the Democratic Primaries.' *Slate*, February 24, 2004. http://www.slate.com/id/2095993/.

Wechsler, Henry, Jae Eun Lee, Meichun Kuo, and Hang Lee. 'College Binge Drinking in the 1990s: A Continuing Problem. Results of the Harvard School of Public Health 1999 Alcohol Study.' *Journal of the American College of Health* 48 (2000) 199–210.

West, Joyce C., et al. 'Medication Access and Continuity: The Experiences of Dual Eligible Psychiatric Patients During the First Four Months of the Medicare Prescription Drug Benefit.' *American Journal of Psychiatry* 164 (2007): 789–96.

Westen, Drew. *The Political Brain: The Role of Emotion in Deciding the Fate of the Nation*. New York: PublicAffairs, 2007.

White House, The. 'President Bush Discusses Medicare Prescription Drug Benefit.' Press release, Washington, D.C., May 2006. http://www. whitehouse.gov/news/releases/2006/05/20060509–5.html.

Willis, Lauren. 'Decisionmaking and the Limits of Disclosure: The Problem of Predatory Lending: Price.' *Maryland Law Review* 65 (2006): 707–840.

Wilson, Timothy D., and Daniel T. Gilbert. 'Affective Forecasting.' *Advances in Experimental Social Psychology* 35 (2003): 345–411.

Winter, Joachim, Rowilma Balza, Frank Caro, Florian Heiss, Byung-hill Jun, Rosa Matzkin, and Daniel McFadden. 'Medicare Prescription Drug Coverage: Consumer Information and Preferences.' *Proceedings of the National Academy of Sciences* 103 (2006): 7929–34.

Woodward, Susan E. 'A Study of Closing Costs for FHA Mortgages.' Working paper, Sand Hill Econometrics, 2007.

Zeliadt, Steven B., Scott D. Ramsey, David F. Penson, Ingrid J. Hall, Donatus U. Ekwueme, Leonard Stroud, and Judith W. Lee. 'Why Do Men Choose One Treatment over Another?' *Cancer* 106 (2006): 1865–74.

Zelinsky, Edward A. 'Deregulating Marriage: The Pro-Marriage Case for Abolishing Civil Marriage.' *Cardozo Law Review* 27 (2006): 1161–220.

Zweig, Jason. 'Five Investing Lessons from America's Top Pension Fund.' *Money*, January 1998, 115–18.

Index

PENGUIN ECONOMICS

THE BLACK SWAN
THE IMPACT OF THE HIGHLY IMPROBABLE
NASSIM NICHOLAS TALEB

'Mindblowing ... a masterpiece' Chris Anderson, author of *The Long Tail*

What have the invention of the wheel, Pompeii, the Wall Street Crash, Harry Potter and the internet got in common?

Why should you never run for a train or read a newspaper?

What can Catherine the Great's lovers tell us about probability?

Why are almost all forecasters con-artists?

This book is all about Black Swans: the random events that underlie our lives, from bestsellers to world disasters. Their impact is huge; they're nearly impossible to predict; yet after they happen we always try to rationalize them. A rallying cry to ignore the 'experts', *The Black Swan* shows us how to stop trying to predict everything and take advantage of uncertainty.

'A deeply intelligent, provocative book' *Economist*

'An idiosyncratically brilliant new book' Niall Ferguson

'Great fun ... brash, stubborn, entertaining, opinionated, curious, cajoling' Stephen J. Dubner, author of *Freakonomics*

ECONOMICS

FREAKONOMICS

STEVEN D. LEVITT & STEPHEN J. DUBNER

'A sensation ... you'll be stimulated, provoked and entertained. Of how many books can that be said?' *Sunday Telegraph*

'The book is a delight; it educates, surprises and amuses ... dazzling' *Economist*

'Prepare to be dazzled' Malcolm Gladwell

What do estate agents and the Ku Klux Klan have in common?

Why do drug dealers live with their mothers?

How can your name affect how well you do in life?

The answer: Freakonomics. It's at the heart of everything we do and the things that affect us daily, from sex to crime, parenting to politics, fat to cheating, fear to traffic jams. And it's all about using information about the world around us to get to the heart of what's *really* happening under the surface of everyday life.

'If Indiana Jones were an economist he'd be Steven Levitt' *Wall Street Journal*

PENGUIN PSYCHOLOGY

BLINK
THE POWER OF THINKING WITHOUT THINKING
MALCOLM GLADWELL

'Astonishing ... *Blink* really does make you rethink the way you think' *Daily Mail*

'Trust my snap judgement, buy this book: you'll be delighted' *The New York Times*

An art expert sees a ten-million-dollar sculpture and instantly spots it's a fake. A marriage analyst knows within minutes whether a couple will stay together. A fire-fighter suddenly senses he has to get out of a blazing building. A speed dater clicks with the right person ...

This book is all about those moments when we 'know' something without knowing why. Here Malcolm Gladwell, one of the world's most original thinkers, explores the phenomenon of 'blink', showing how a snap judgement can be far more effective than a cautious decision. By trusting your instincts, he reveals, you'll never think about thinking in the same way again ...

'Compelling, fiendishly clever' *Evening Standard*

'Brilliant ... the implications for business, let alone love, are vast' *Observer*

'Superb ... this wonderful book should be compulsory reading' *New Statesman*

'*Blink* might just change your life' *Esquire*

'Should you buy this book? You already know the answer to that' *Independent on Sunday*